I0395263

The Saqīfa

Allāma Sayyid Murtaḍā Askarī

Translated by
Blake Archer Williams

LANTERN
PUBLICATIONS

Lantern Publications
info@lanternpublications.com
www.lanternpublications.com

Ordering Information:
Quantity sales. Special discounts are available on quantity purchases by corporations, associations, and others. For details, contact the distributor at the address below.

Shia Books Australia
www.shiabooks.com.au
info@shiabooks.com.au

NATIONAL LIBRARY OF AUSTRALIA

A catalogue record for this book is available from the National Library of Australia

ISBN - 978-1-922583-43-7

First Edition

We would like to especially acknowledge the generous gift from a lover of Ahlulbayt that make this work possible. Please recite a Surah al Fātiḥah for the souls of the deceased from their family.

بسم الله الرحمن الرحيم

In the Name of God ﷻ,
the Most Compassionate, the Most Merciful

A Note on Transliteration

The transliteration system used in this book is basically that of the ICAS Press method (which is based on the Library of Congress Romanization Tables), with the following changes: The *shamsi* and *qamari* consonants appear in the definitive article 'al' (in place of the 'l'). This is so that those who are not familiar with the pronunciation of the Arabic words can become familiar with the words as they should be pronounced (as opposed to how they are written), enabling them to pronounce the words properly. Persian words of Arabic origin are transliterated as they are pronounced in the Arabic language, rather than their Persian pronunciations. However, Persian words, proper names, and personal names are transliterated to reflect their proper Persian pronunciation. Thus, 'Bukhāri' is Bokhāri, Kulayni is Kolayni, etc. In such cases, the sound for the *kasra* is Romanized by 'e' rather than by 'i', the *Ḍamma* by 'o' rather than by 'a' or 'u'. Similarly, the ض, ذ, and ظ letters are all Romanized by the letter 'z' (for Persian words only). Thus, the *ezāfe* (*iḍāfa*) is Romanized *-e* after a consonant, and *-ah* or *-ye* after a vowel.

Acknowledgement

All translations of verses of the Quran are Muhammad Asad's, with the occasional minor change.

Prayers of God's Peace and Blessings

In keeping with the Islamic practice of showing respect for the name of God سبحانه وتعالى, and sending prayers of God's peace and blessings whenever the name of His blessed Prophet صلى الله عليه وآله وسلم, Lady Fātima, and the Twelve Imams is mentioned, as well as for asking God سبحانه وتعالى to hasten the reappearance of the Lord of the Age on the Earthly plane, one or more of the following Arabic symbols have been employed throughout the text. They are repeated for their great rewards.

سبحانه وتعالى	Used exclusively after the name of God, meaning "the Sublimely Exalted", or, as a prayer, "[May His name be] Sublimely Exalted".
صلى الله عليه وآله وسلم	Used exclusively after the name of the Prophet, meaning "May the peace and blessings of God be unto him and unto [the purified and inerrant members of] his family"
عليه السلام	Used for any of the Twelve Imams or past prophets of God, meaning "May God's peace be unto him".
عليهم السلام	Used for two or more of the Twelve Imams or past prophets of God, meaning "May God's peace be unto them".
عليها السلام	Used for Lady Fātima, meaning "May God's peace be unto her".
عليهم صلوات الله أجمعين	Used for a plurality of the Fourteen Immaculates, meaning "May God's peace be unto them all collectively".
عجل الله تعالى فرجه الشريف	Used for the Lord of the Age (the Twelfth Imam), meaning "May God hasten the advent of his noble person".

Table of Contents

A Note on Transliteration 4
Prayers of God's Peace and Blessings 5
Preface 13
Translators Preface 19

1 The Inception of the Saqīfa during the Lifetime of the Prophet ﷺ21
2 How the Saqīfa Plot was Implemented 32
3 The Judgment of the Companions about Allegiance to Abū Bakr 66
4 How the Caliphate dealt with the Opposition outside Medina 76
5 How the Caliphate dealt with the Opposition within Medina 81
6 Economic Warfare against the House of the Prophet ﷺ99
7 Lady Fātima's Illness 111
8 The Situation of the Islamic Lands and the Posture of the Imams 123
9 Abu Bakr's Will and Umar's Caliphate 125
10 Governance during Umar's Caliphate 127
11 Uthmān's Caliphate 143
12 The People's Uprising against 'Uthmān and Ali's Role in it 168
13 The *Shaqshaqīya* Sermon of Imām Ali ؑ 185

Detailed Table of Contents

1 The Inception of the Saqīfa during the Lifetime of the Prophet ﷺ 21

1. The Foreswearal (*Sūra at-Tahrīm*) 22
2. The Context of the Revelation (*sha'n an-nuzūl*) 23

2 How the Saqīfa Plot was Implemented 32

1. The Prophet's Illness and Death 32
2. What happened on the dawn of that day? 34
3. The ritual cleansing of the body of the Prophet ﷺ and its preparation [for burial] 35
4. The Prophet's testamentary instruction concerning Ali 38
5. Candidates for the succession (khilāfa) after the death of the Prophet ﷺ on the day of the Saqīfa 51
6. The Slogans of the Saqīfa 51
    - 6.1 The Slogans of the 'Helpers' (the Ansār) 51
    - 6.2 The Slogans of the 'Emigrants' (the Quraysh) 51
7. The Saqīfa coup d'etat and the pledge of allegiance given to Abū Bakr 52
8 The Saqīfa according to the Hadith Report in Sahīh Bukhari 53
9. The Saqīfa according to the Hadith Report in Tabari's History 54
10. The Role of the Aslam tribe in the Pledge of Allegiance to Abū Bakr 61
11. The pledge of allegiance on the part of the general public 63

3 The Judgment of the Companions of the Prophet ﷺ about the Pledge of Allegiance to Abū Bakr 66

1. Faḍl ibn 'Abbās 66
2. Utba[t] ibn Abī-Lahab 66
3. Salmān al-Fārsī 67
4. Abū-Dharr 67
5. Miqdād ibn 'Amr 68
6. Nu'mān ibn 'Ajlān 68
7. Umm Mistah ibn Uthātha 69
8. A Woman from the Banī-Najjār 70
9. Abū-Sufyān 70
10. Khālid ibn Sa'īd (of the Banī-Umayya) 73

10. Umar ibn al-Khattāb 73
11. Mu'āwiya 74
12. Sa'd ibn Ubāda 74

4 How the Caliphal Administration dealt with the Opposition outside Medina 76

1. The Murder of Mālik bin Nuwaira 76
2. Some Other Examples 79

5 How the Caliphal Administration dealt with the Opposition within Medina 81

1. The Murder of Sa'd ibn 'Abāda 81
2. The Attempted Enticement of 'Abbās 84
3. The Sit-in at Lady Fātima's $ House 87
4. The Attack on Lady Fātima's House 88
5. What Abu Bakr said on his Deathbed 91
6. What 'Umar ibn al-Khattāb said to His Eminence Alī ibn Abī-Tālib 92
7. How the Caliphate dealt with His Eminence Alī ibn Abī-Tālib 93
8. The Reaction of the House of the Prophet ﷺ after the Saqīfa 95
9. The Guidance the Prophet ﷺ 97

6 Economic Warfare against the House of the Prophet ﷺ 99

1. Sources of the Prophet's property and how they were acquired 99
2. The Context of Revelation of Verse 17:26 101
3. The Usurpation of Fadak by the Caliphs 102
4. The Usurpation of the Prophet's Inheritance 103
5. Lady Fātima's Speech in the Mosque 103
6. The Conversation of Lady Fātima with Imam Ali 109

7 Lady Fātima's Illness 111

1. The Passion of Lady Fātima in Hearing Bilal's Call to Prayer 112
2. The Womenfolk of the Emigrants and the Helpers pay Lady Fātima a Visit 112
3. Abu Bakr and Umar pay Lady Fātima a Visit 115
4. Lady Fātima's Will and her Burial by Night 116
5. The Situation of Medina after the Martyrdom of Lady Fātima, and the Fulfillment of her Prophecies 117

6. The Pledging of Allegiance of the Commander of the Faithful [Imam Ali to Abu Bakr] after the martyrdom of Lady Fātima, and the reason for it 120

8 The Situation of the Islamic Territories and the Behavior of the Imams 123

9 Abu Bakr's Will and Umar's Caliphate 125

10 Governance during Umar's Caliphate 127

Umar's conversation with Ibn Abbās 128
Mu'āwiya during Umar's reign 132
Umar's Confession, the Consultative Council, and the Pledge of Allegiance to Uthmān 133
The way Uthmān was elected to the Caliphate 138
The reason for Imam Ali's participation in Umar's six-man council 141

11 Uthmān's Caliphate 143

Abu Sufyan's Words 143
Walīd, 'Uthmān's Governor in Kūfa 144
The story of Walīd's drinking while he was the governor of Kufa 145
Walīd's Dismissal 148
The Situation in Kūfa during 'Uthmān's Reign. 149
The Story of Ibn Mas'ud 150
Walīd and the Christian poet Abu Zubayd 154
The story of Jundab al-Khair 155
The Story of Abdullah bin Sa'd bin Abi Sarh 156
The story of Hakam bin Abi al-Ās, the Caliph's Uncle 158
The Story of Sa'īd ibn Hakam ibn Abi al-Ās and Mālik Ashtar 159
Abdullah bin Āmir, the Governor of Basra 162
Mu'āwiya during 'Uthmān's Reign 163
'Uthmān's treatment of Ammār 164
Othman's performance with respect to the Public Treasury 164

12 The People's Uprising against 'Uthmān and Ali's Role in it 168

The Revolt of the Egyptians 168
Marwān's Sabotage 170

People Complaining to Ali and Ali's Refusal to be Involved any Further 171
Groups that Came from Different Cities 172
The Caliph's Ruse 174
'Āisha issues a Fatwa to kill 'Uthmān 175
The Words of Jahjāh al-Ghaffārī 177
The Siege of Osman's House 177
The Keys of the Treasury in Talha's Hands 179
Talha shuts off 'Uthmān's Water Supply, and Ali delivers Water to him 180
The Murder of 'Uthmān and Imam Ali's Reaction 182
The People's Pledge of Allegiance to Imam Ali, and 'Uthmān's Burial 183
The End of the Saqīfa 184

13 The Shaqshaqīya Sermon of Imām Ali ﷺ 185

Preface

by Professor Mehdi Dashti

Many books have been written about the Saqīfa throughout the history of Islam, either independently or as sponsored works, all of which vary, of course, in terms of their value and importance.

Most of these books have viewed the Saqīfa as an event that occurred in a single day. As such, they have striven to investigate the events that occurred during that day. Of course, at times, these authors have also examined some of the events that occurred during the one or two weeks before and after the event.

Few books can be found among classical works that have failed to make mention of the Saqīfa. A glance at thirty or so outstanding works [of history] from sources that date to the first Islamic millennium, in which the story of the Saqīfa is at times touched on briefly and at other times discussed in detail, reveals the fact that historians and scholars of the science of hadith have not been able to pass this story by without addressing it in some way.[1]

---

[1] In chronological order, these sources include:
Ibn Hishām, ʿAbd al-Malik, *al-Sīrah al-Nabawīyah* (213 AH);
Ibn Saʿd, Abu Abdallah Muhammad, *al-Tabaqāt al-Kubrā* (230 AH);
Ahmad b. Hanbal, *Musnad* (241 AH);
Dāramī, Abu Muhammad, *Musnad al-Dāramī* (255 AH);
Bukhārī, Muḥammad ibn Ismāʿīl, *Ṣaḥīḥ al-Bukhārī* (256 AH);
Zubayr ibn Bakkār, *al-Muwaffaqīāt* (256 AH);
Muslim ibn al-Ḥajjāj, *Ṣaḥīḥ Muslim* (261 AH);
Ibn Qutayba, Abd-Allāh ibn Muslim, *al-Imāma wa'l-Siyāsa* (270 or 276 AH);
Ibn Māja, Muhammad ibn Yazīd, *Sunan* (273 AH);
Balādhūrī, Ahmad ibn Yahyā ibn Jābir, *Ansāb al-Ashrāf* (279 AH);
Dīnwarī, Abū Ḥanīfah Aḥmad ibn Dāwūd, *Kitāb al-Akhbār al-Tiwāl* (282 AH);
Yaʿqūbī, Aḥmad ibn Isḥāq, *Tārīkh al-Yaʿqūbī* (292 AH);
Tabarī, Muhammad ibn Jarīr, *Tārīkh ar-Rusul wa'l-Mulūk* (210 AH);
Ibn ʿAbd Rabbih, *al-ʿIqd al-Farīd* (328 AH);

Among contemporary writers there have also been individuals who have made efforts in this regard and have and who have produced works that are noteworthy. This list includes scholars such as the late Muhammad Riḍā Muzaffar[2], Muhammad Bāqir Bihbūdī[3], Abd al-Fattāh Abd al-Maqsūd[4], and Wilferd Madelung[5].

In his book *Al-Saqīfa*, the late Muhammad Riḍā Muzaffar attempted to view the episode through the method of *kalām* or the rational creedal discourse of Islam, and to prove that what happened in the Saqīfa firstly, was not based on [a decision that was entered into] as a consequence of the informed consent and consensus of the community, and secondly, was inimical to the letter of the sacred law of Islam. This is not a new view, of course, and many Shī'a scholars have viewed the episode from this vantage, including the late Shaykh Mufīd

---

Mas'ūdī, Alī ibn al-Ḥusayn, *al-Tanbīh wa'l-Ishrāf* (346 AH);
Mas'ūdī, Alī ibn al-Ḥusayn, *Murawwij adh-Dhahab* (413 AH);
Isfahānī, Abī'l-Faraj, *al-Aghānī* (356 AH);
Mufīd, Shaykh Md. ibn Nu'mān, *al-Irshād fī Ma'rifat Hujaj Allāh 'al'al-'Ibād* (413 AH);
Mufīd, Shaykh Muhammad ibn Nu'mān, *Al-Amali* (413 AH);
Ibn Abd'al-Barr, Yusuf ibn Abdallah, *al-Istī'āb fī Ma'rifat al-Ashāb* (463 AH);
Ibn Jawzī, Abd al-Rahmān b. Ali, *Sifa*[t] *as-Safwah* (597 AH);
Ibn Athīr Jazarī, 'Alī, 1417 AH, *al-Kāmil fī al-Tārīkh* (630 AH);
Ibn Athīr, 'Alī ibn Muḥammad, *Usd al-Ghābah fī Ma'rifat al-Ṣaḥābah* (630 AH);
Ibn Abī'l-Hadīd, Abdul-Hamīd, *Sharh Nahj al-Balāgha* (655 or 656 AH);
Tabarī, Muhibbiddīn, *ar-Riyāḍ an-Naḍra* (694 AH);
Dhahabī, Shams al-Dīn Muhammad ibn Ahmad, *Tārīkh al-Islam* (748 AH);
Ibn Kathīr, Abu'al-Fiḍā Ismā'īl ibn Umar, *Tārīkh* (774 AH);
Suyūtī, Jalāladdīn, *Tarikh al-Khulafā* (911 AH);
Dayār Bakrī, Ḥusayn Ibn Md., *Tārīkh al-Khamīs fī Ahwāl Anfus Nafīs* (966 AH);
Muttaqī al-Hindī, *Kanz al-U'mmāl* (975 AH).

[2] The late Muzaffar was a scholar at the Najaf Seminary. His book *al-Saqīfa* was translated into Persian by Muḥammad Jawād Hujjatī under the title *Asrār al-Saqīfa*. Before that, the late Ghulām Riḍā Sa'īdī had translated this book into Persian under the title *Mājarā-ye Saqīfa*.

[3] The author of the book *Sīra 'Alawī*, who published it in 1989.

[4] 'Abd al-Fattāḥ 'Abd al-Maqṣūd is a Sunni Egyptian scholar and author. His book *al-Saqīfa wa'l-Khīlāfa* was translated into Persian by Sayyid Ḥasan Eftakhār-Zādah under the title *The Origin of the Caliphate*.

[5] Wilferd Madelung is a Western scholar of Islamic history who is originally from Germany, and who was a Professor of Arabic and Islamic Studies at the University of Oxford from 1978 to 1998. [A translation of] his book *The Succession to Muhammad: A Study of the Early Caliphate* was published in Iran under the title *Jānishīnī-ye Muhammad* by The Printing and Publishing Institution of Āstān-e Quds-e Razavī.

(d. 413 AH) in his *Amālī* and *Munāḍirāt*, and the late Sayyid Ibn Tāwūs (d. 664 AH) in his valuable book *Kashf al-Muhajja.*

In the book *Sīra-ye Alavī* (*The Ālid Way*), Mr. Muhammad Bāqir Bihbūdī examines the events from the time of the death of the Most Noble Prophet until the martyrdom of the Commander of the Faithful ﷺ, which includes a detailed and useful discussion of the events of the Saqīfa.

Bihbūdī considers the Saqīfa to be the product of a premeditated plan which presented the Muslim community with a *fait accompli.* But in doing so, he does not see the scope of this plan as going back to the time of 'Uthmān and Mu'awiyah. Thus, his treatment remains incomplete, notwithstanding the rigor of his scholarship.

Abd al-Fattāh Abd al-Maqsūd considers the Saqīfa to be the location where a pre-planned operation occurred in which neither was a consultative council (*shawrā*) involved, nor was the ruling of such a council enacted. In his view, the Saqīfa could be seen as the beginning of the reign of a party who wanted to keep and pass the reins of the steed of the state among themselves.[6] And while Abd al-Maqsūd also sees clear indications of prior planning[7], he ultimately considers as forgeries[8] the hadith reports that stipulate that 'Umar named certain people whom, if they were alive, he would have appointed to succeed him as leaders of the community. Ultimately, and contrary to what he states at the beginning of his book, Abd al-Maqsūd considers the collusion of these three friends (Abu Bakr, 'Umar, and Abu-Ūbayda al-Jarrāh) for the usurpation of the caliphate and keeping it between them to be weak and does not accept it.[9]

But the German orientalist Wilferd Madelung begins by mentioning Lammens' position with respect to the triangle of power) (Abu Bakr, 'Umar, and Abu-Ubayda al-Jarrāh)[10] who, citing [Leone] Caetani, asserts that 'Umar was the main inspiration in this triangle[11], and concludes that the Most Noble Prophet did not in any way consider Abu Bakr to be his natural successor, and did not assent to it.[12] He [Madelung rather than Lammens] states emphatically that the

---

[6] The Origin of the Caliphate, p. 241 onwards.
[7] Ibid, p.421 onwards.
[8] Ibid, p. 437.
[9] Ibid, pp. 438-9.
[10] The Succession to Muhammad, pp. 15-16.
[11] Ibid, p. 18.
[12] Ibid, p. 32.

privileged position of rulership over Islamic society which Abu Bakr had limited to belonging to the Quraysh had no Quranic basis[13].

Despite all this, Madelung does not believe that the Prophet ﷺ stipulated that the Commander of the Faithful Alī b. Abī-Tālib ؑ was to succeed him, and even has the following to say about the Sermon of Ghadīr Khumm:

Upon his return, just three months before the Prophet's death, Muhammad found it necessary to make a strong public statement in support of his cousin. It was evidently not a suitable occasion to appoint him successor. Muhammad might also have delayed a decision hoping to live long enough to be able to appoint one of his grandsons. His death was generally unexpected among his followers even during his mortal illness. He himself may also have been unaware of the approaching end until it was too late.[14]

Madelung ultimately concludes that the Prophet ﷺ passed away without appointing a successor[15]. In addition, Madelung discounts as unreliable[16] the hadith reports of Abdullah ibn Abbās in which 'Umar's explicit confession is reported with respect to preventing Ali ؑ from succeeding to the caliphate, without his bringing any acceptable reason to bear in this regard. ﷺ

In the final part of the book, Madelung goes even further, declaring the non-appointment of a successor to be a tradition of the Prophet ﷺ. He even goes as far as to state that perhaps, according to this same tradition, Ali ؑ was averse to choosing a successor during his caliphate, even though he ultimately bequeathed it to Hassan ؑ. [17] Madelung, of course, believes that Abu Bakr desired the caliphate, and that, undoubtedly, he had decided prior to the death of the Prophet ﷺ that he was to be the caliph, without having been appointed to the office by the Prophet ﷺ. Therefore, in order to achieve this aspiration, he decided to eliminate his powerful opponents, who were from the House of the Prophet ﷺ, and to wait for the right opportunity. This opportunity was given to him by the hasty mistake of the Helpers (*ansār*) in choosing the leader from among themselves.[18]

---

[13] Ibid, p. 84.
[14] Ibid, p. 34.
[15] Ibid, p. 35.
[16] Ibid, p. 40.
[17] Ibid, p. 427
[18] Ibid, pp. 62-63.

Thus, Madelung also affirms the existence of a premeditated plan to attain to the caliphate on the part of Abu Bakr, with the difference that he sees the manifestation and occurrence of this decision in the Saqīfa as incidental [to the overall plan or intention], and sees the cooperation of several other senior personalities of the Quraysh to be effective in accomplishing the task of saddling the majority of the Quraysh and the Helpers with Abu Bakr's succession. This was especially the case as Abu Bakr had bamboozled the Quraysh by saying that "the Quraysh have a collective right to rule as a tribe"; and the Quraysh, in their turn, were pleased not to have governance of the community to remain the exclusive province of the House of the Prophet ﷺ, as was the case with the institution of prophethood.[19]

It was necessary to provide a brief overview of what has been written about the Saqīfa in order properly to appreciate the importance of the work of the great scholar and historian, Allāma Sayyed Murtaḍā Askari, that is presented in the book that is before you. According to the findings of this book, the Saqīfa cannot be summarized as the events that occurred in a single day, or as the design of a single person for attaining to the caliphate. Rather, the Saqīfa is the beginning of the emergence and manifestation of the execution of a premeditated plan according to which specific people from the Quraysh [tribe] were to take the reins of power in hand one after another in succession in order to continually prevent the House of the Prophet ﷺ, (who, according to the Prophet's explicit stipulation (*nass*), were his rightful successors), and ultimately to vest the Umayyads with the office. This plan was carried out, but with the assassination of Uthmān and the investiture of the Commander of the Faithful ﵇ to the caliphate, it remained incomplete.

This analysis, which is based on primary sources from the 'School of the Caliphs' [= Sunni sources], is unique in its class. Allāma Askari corrects, codifies, and completes the scattered and incomplete (and in some cases inaccurate) material that has been written about the Saqīfa by ancient and contemporary scholars alike, and his analysis is

[19] Ibid, p. 63.

extremely elucidating for a better understanding of the history of Islam from the time of the passing of the Prophet ﷺ until the present.

Congress Publications seized the opportunity, and with the permission of the esteemed scholar and author, His Eminence Allāma Sayyid Murtaḍā Askari – long may his effulgence endure – brought this valuable work to fruition. In order to make the most [of the redaction of Allāma Askari's lecture series on the Saqīfa], the publisher[20] added the sources of the hadith reports, which appear in the book as footnotes using authentic sources. In certain instances, certain marginalia have also been added in order to explain certain issues.

It is hoped that this unworthy contribution might be looked upon with favor, God ﷻ grant, by the Master of the Monotheists and the Commander of the Faithful, His Eminence Ali b. Abī-Tālib ؑ. And let our final utterance be, 'Praise be unto Allāh, the Lord of Providence of all Worlds'.

Mahdī Dashtī
Tehran, the Winter of 1379 (2000-2001)

---

[20] The work of the editing of the redaction of the lecture series recordings, and the addition of the sources and footnotes was done by Professor Dashtī himself, of course.

Translator's Preface

I decided to write a short preface to this book because a word of caution is called for, as the book is intellectual dynamite. Its thesis is a dangerous one, and it is put forward by a most preeminent scholar whose qualifications are second to none when it comes to historical research and analytical insight. The book begins before the passing of the Prophet and continues until the death of Uthman. Chapter by chapter, Allāma Askari drives his thesis home with irresistible force. And he does so with an almost exclusive use of Sunni sources, which is a technique that he pioneered.

Allāma Askari is not very well known in the West as yet, but this book should change that. He was a scholar whose intellectual stature towered above all others in his own field. Allāma Askari was to Islamic historiography what Allāma Tabātabāī was to tafsīr and what Ayatollāh Khoeminī was to Shi'a political science, both theoretical and practical. These three were the giants in the Shia intellectual pantheon of the 20th century.

In this book Allāma Askari proves beyond a reasonable doubt that during the lifetime of the Prophet, six people conspired to take over the political leadership of the community after the Prophet's death against the Prophet's express wishes, who had designated Imam Ali as his heir, successor and legatee (wasī'). Three of those six people were the first three 'Rightly Guided' caliphs. That is why Allāma Askari's thesis is so dangerous. Combine that with some of the hadith reports that can be found in the Shia hadith report and zīārāt corpus concerning the imprecations of those who wrongfully usurped the leadership of the umma, and you get an explosive combination.

But it is only explosive if one is not aware of other reports that indicate how insistent all of the Imams were on the point of having good relations with the rest of the Muslim community; and only if the reader is not aware of the excellence and nobility of character with which the Imams dealt with our Sunni brothers – a term of endearment that they used for Muslims who were not their shī'a or followers. They maintained better than cordial or hasana relations with the Muslim community at large despite the usurpation of their rights by the leaders of that community; and that is the example that all of us have to follow.

Read this book and see how this coup d'état was hatched, and exactly how Islam was derailed from its divinely intended course, as it is now available for the first time in English thanks to the untiring efforts of the esteemed publisher. But do so knowing that the sunnah of the Imams, which is a continuation of the sunnah of the Prophet, demands that one must maintain cordial and even better than cordial relations with our brothers in the Sunni community despite the truths unearthed by Allāma Askari and contained in this book; just as one must, indeed, maintain better than cordial or ḥasana relations with non-Muslims as well.

Blake Williams
Tehran, February 2023

1 The Inception of the Saqīfa during the Lifetime of the Prophet

In order to examine the way in which [the events which occurred in] the Saqīfa [or portico of the Banī Sā'ida clan[21]] were conceived, it is necessary to examine the following Quranic verses (*āyāt*). God ﷻ, the Sublimely Exalted, states in the opening verses of the Sūra of The Foreswearal[22] (*Sūrat at-Tahrīm*):

[21] Translator note: The Quraysh tribe was in charge in Mecca prior to the commissioning of the Prophet to his prophethood and the coming of the Quranic revelation. The tribe consisted of several clans, the chieftains of which persecuted the Prophet and offered the staunchest resistance against God's message and the Prophet's efforts at establishing God's intended Order. The Saqīfa was a portico of the Banī Sā'ida clan where the Ansār (the clans of Yathrib/ Medina who had entered into Islam and were the "Helpers" of Islam) had gathered immediately upon the death of the Prophet in order to determine who was to succeed the Prophet in ruling their city. As will be demonstrated by Allāma Askarī in the following pages, the Saqīfa became the scene of the first manifestation of a carefully planned plot according to which six chieftains of the Quraysh were to succeed, one after another, in taking the reins of leadership of the community after the Prophet's passing, so that the *Ahl al-Bayt* (Household) of the Prophet ﷺ, headed by Imam Ali – who, according to the Prophet's own specific instructions, as well as that of God's, instructing him to deliver this message, were the rightful successors to this office – would be deprived of it, and so that it would revert back into the hands of the Banī-Umayya clan of the Quraysh tribe, the arch-enemies of the Prophet and of his House, the House of Hāshim.

[22] Translator note: This *sūra* is usually translated variously as "Banning", "Forbidding" or "Prohibition" (without the definite article), and while these give the general sense, it is clear by reading the *āyāt* of the *sūra* that a *specific form* of prohibition is referred to, namely, the Prophet's forswearal of the bedding of his bondswoman Māriya. The whole point of the surface meaning of the *sūra* is its urging the Prophet's *non*-forswearal of her. The subject of the opening section of the chapter is the explication of one of its major deeper meanings. My parenthetical additions to my translation of the *sūra* are based entirely on Allāma Askarī's exegesis; as such, they will be amply justified in the Allāma's exegetical passages which follow the *āyāt*.

1. The Foreswearal

بِسْمِ اللَّهِ الرَّحْمَٰنِ الرَّحِيمِ

أَيُّهَا النَّبِيُّ لِمَ تُحَرِّمُ مَا أَحَلَّ اللَّهُ لَكَ ۖ تَبْتَغِي مَرْضَاتَ أَزْوَاجِكَ ۚ وَاللَّهُ
غَفُورٌ رَّحِيمٌ ﴿١﴾ قَدْ فَرَضَ اللَّهُ لَكُمْ تَحِلَّةَ أَيْمَانِكُمْ ۚ وَاللَّهُ مَوْلَاكُمْ ۖ
وَهُوَ الْعَلِيمُ الْحَكِيمُ ﴿٢﴾ وَإِذْ أَسَرَّ النَّبِيُّ إِلَىٰ بَعْضِ أَزْوَاجِهِ حَدِيثًا فَلَمَّا
نَبَّأَتْ بِهِ وَأَظْهَرَهُ اللَّهُ عَلَيْهِ عَرَّفَ بَعْضَهُ وَأَعْرَضَ عَن بَعْضٍ ۖ فَلَمَّا
نَبَّأَهَا بِهِ قَالَتْ مَنْ أَنبَأَكَ هَٰذَا ۖ قَالَ نَبَّأَنِيَ الْعَلِيمُ الْخَبِيرُ ﴿٣﴾ إِن تَتُوبَا إِلَى
اللَّهِ فَقَدْ صَغَتْ قُلُوبُكُمَا ۖ وَإِن تَظَاهَرَا عَلَيْهِ فَإِنَّ اللَّهَ هُوَ مَوْلَاهُ
وَجِبْرِيلُ وَصَالِحُ الْمُؤْمِنِينَ ۖ وَالْمَلَائِكَةُ بَعْدَ ذَٰلِكَ ظَهِيرٌ ﴿٤﴾ عَسَىٰ رَبُّهُ إِن
طَلَّقَكُنَّ أَن يُبْدِلَهُ أَزْوَاجًا خَيْرًا مِّنكُنَّ مُسْلِمَاتٍ مُّؤْمِنَاتٍ قَانِتَاتٍ
تَائِبَاتٍ عَابِدَاتٍ سَائِحَاتٍ ثَيِّبَاتٍ وَأَبْكَارًا ﴿٥﴾

In the name of God ﷻ, Most Gracious, Most Merciful.

[66:1] Why dost thou, O Prophet ﷺ, foreswear that which God ﷻ hath made lawful unto thee, [in order] to please [two of] thy wives? Whereas [it is] God ﷻ, [rather, Who] is the Forgiver [of ultimate refuge] and the [limitless] Dispenser of Grace, [Whose pleasure it is, therefore, that you should be seeking].

[66:2] God ﷻ has already enjoined upon you, [O believers,] the breaking of [such of] your oaths [as might run counter to what is right and just, and shown you the means whereby such dissolutions are to be expiated, if necessary]: for God ﷻ is your Lord Patron (*mawlā*), and He [alone] knows all [there is to know about matters that concern you in this world], and is [your only positive source of] wisdom.

[66:3] And lo! [It so happened that] the Prophet ﷺ told something in confidence to one of his wives [about an intrigue hatched by 'Umar and Abu-Bakr and Uthmān and three others of their confederates to secure the succession after his passing]; and when she [Hafsa bt. 'Umar] thereupon divulged this [secret to ʻĀisha bt. Abu-Bakr] and God ﷻ made this [breach of confidence] known to him; he [the Prophet] acquainted her [Hafsa] with a part of it [the scheme] and did not reveal another part of it. And as soon as he let her know it [about it], she asked, "Who has told thee this?" – [to which] he replied, "The All-Knowing [and] All-Aware told [it] me."

[66:4] [Tell them, O Prophet:] "If the two of you [now] turn unto God ﷻ in repentance [it would be better for you], for the hearts of both of you have swerved [from what is right]! But if [instead] you collude with each other [and your parents] against the Prophet ﷺ, [know that it is] God ﷻ [Himself who] is the Prophet's guardian, as are Gabriel, the *sālih al-mu'minīn* [= Imām Ali[23]], and [all] the angles [besides, all of whom] shall come to his aid."

[66:5] Were the Prophet ﷺ to divorce you two [O Hafsa and ʻĀisha], it might [well turn out to] be [the case] that his Providential Lord will give him in your stead wives [who are] better than you – submissive unto their Lord, believing, devout, penitent, and inclined unto [worship] and fasting, [be they] widowed or virgin-maidens.

2. The Context of the Revelation (*sha'n an-nuzūl*)

In the above five *āyāt*, mention is made of three matters:

1. The self-prohibition by the Prophet ﷺ of that which God ﷻ had made licit for him in an effort to placate one of his wives and the fact that God ﷻ had already enjoined the expiation of oaths that run counter to what is right and just.
2. The disclosure of something said in confidence by the Prophet ﷺ to one of his wives, its divulgence by her to someone else, and the fact that God ﷻ made the betrayal of the Prophet's confidence known to him.
3. God's threatening of the two wives of the Prophet ﷺ.

What is *not* specified in these *āyāt* is (1) what lawful thing it was that the Prophet ﷺ foreswore to his wife in order to placate her, and (2) what the secret was which was told in the confidence that was

[23] Suyūṭī, Jalāl al-Dīn ʻAbd al-Raḥmān, *al-Durr al-Manthūr fī al-Tafsīr bi-al-Ma'thūr*, 6:244; as well as Shī'a sources too, of course.

subsequently betrayed, and what events followed which occasioned the use of such threatening language by our Lord.

In discussing these *āyāt*, it bears repeating that there are two types of revelation. In accordance with the following *āya* and other similar ones, *[16:44] And upon thee [too, O Muhammad] have We bestowed from on high this reminder, so that thou might* make clear *unto mankind all that has ever been thus bestowed upon them, and that they might reflect;* one of the Prophet's functions is to explain and *make clear* all that which is revealed in the Quran. The first is the Quranic text itself, which has been available to all from the time of the Prophet ﷺ to date; and the second type of revelation, which can be referred to as Explicatory Revelation, by means of which the Quran is explicated [and which is recorded in the form of *hadīth* reports and which forms the contents of the hadith report corpus].

By way of explication of the first *āya*, *hadīth* reports inform us that on the day of the week which was Hafsa's[24] turn [for the Prophet ﷺ to give preference to spending the night in her private quarters], the Prophet ﷺ bedded his bondswoman Māriya, and when Hafsa became aware of this [and raised a fuss], the Prophet ﷺ foreswore Māriya in order to placate Hafsa.[25] In the second *āya*, God ﷻ annuls this foreswearal, [or, to put it more precisely, informs the Prophet ﷺ that his self-imposed prohibition is invalid, and unnecessary besides]. In the third *āya* we are informed of the fact that *the Prophet* ﷺ *told something in confidence to one of his wives* – Hafsa – who divulges the secret, and that this betrayal of the confidence is revealed by God ﷻ to the Prophet ﷺ, who in turn lets Hafsa know that he is aware of her betrayal. Hafsa then asks the Prophet ﷺ "*Who has told thee this?*" to which the Prophet ﷺ replies, "*The All-Knowing [and] All-Aware told [it] me.*"[26] In the fourth *āya*, the tone changes, and, addressing the two women, [God] advises them to repent, *for the hearts of both of you have swerved [from what is right]!* and tells them that if they do not repent but instead continue to collude with each other [and their fathers, now that they too are "in" on their scheme] against the Prophet ﷺ, that they should

[24] 'Umar's daughter.
[25] Ṭabarī, Muḥammad ibn Jarīr, *Jāmi' al-Bayān fī Tafsīr al-Qur'ān*, 28:101; and a similar redaction also appears in Ibn Sa'd, Abu Abdallah Muhammad, *al-Tabaqāt al-Kubrā*, 8:135 of the European edition.
[26] Ṭabarī, Muḥammad ibn Jarīr, *Jāmi' al-Bayān fī Tafsīr al-Qur'ān*, 28:101.

know that God ﷻ Himself is the Prophet's guardian, as is Gabriel, the *sālih al-mu'minīn* (= Imām Ali)[27], and the [host of] angels.

What was it that took place in the Prophet's house which necessitated such a severe reaction, to the point that God ﷻ feels it is necessary to remind them that the Prophet ﷺ is not alone, and that God ﷻ and Gabriel and Imām Ali ﵇ and the angels have his back? What was it that prompted God ﷻ to threaten the Prophet's wives in the *āyāt* which follow? Let us return to the *sūra*:

يَا أَيُّهَا الَّذِينَ آمَنُوا قُوا أَنفُسَكُمْ وَأَهْلِيكُمْ نَارًا وَقُودُهَا النَّاسُ وَالْحِجَارَةُ
عَلَيْهَا مَلَائِكَةٌ غِلَاظٌ شِدَادٌ لَّا يَعْصُونَ اللَّهَ مَا أَمَرَهُمْ وَيَفْعَلُونَ مَا
يُؤْمَرُونَ ﴿٦﴾ يَا أَيُّهَا الَّذِينَ كَفَرُوا لَا تَعْتَذِرُوا الْيَوْمَ ۖ إِنَّمَا تُجْزَوْنَ مَا
كُنتُمْ تَعْمَلُونَ ﴿٧﴾ يَا أَيُّهَا الَّذِينَ آمَنُوا تُوبُوا إِلَى اللَّهِ تَوْبَةً نَّصُوحًا عَسَىٰ
رَبُّكُمْ أَن يُكَفِّرَ عَنكُمْ سَيِّئَاتِكُمْ وَيُدْخِلَكُمْ جَنَّاتٍ تَجْرِي مِن
تَحْتِهَا الْأَنْهَارُ يَوْمَ لَا يُخْزِي اللَّهُ النَّبِيَّ وَالَّذِينَ آمَنُوا مَعَهُ ۖ نُورُهُمْ يَسْعَىٰ
بَيْنَ أَيْدِيهِمْ وَبِأَيْمَانِهِمْ يَقُولُونَ رَبَّنَا أَتْمِمْ لَنَا نُورَنَا وَاغْفِرْ لَنَا ۖ إِنَّكَ عَلَىٰ
كُلِّ شَيْءٍ قَدِيرٌ ﴿٨﴾ يَا أَيُّهَا النَّبِيُّ جَاهِدِ الْكُفَّارَ وَالْمُنَافِقِينَ وَاغْلُظْ عَلَيْهِمْ ۚ
وَمَأْوَاهُمْ جَهَنَّمُ ۖ وَبِئْسَ الْمَصِيرُ ﴿٩﴾ ضَرَبَ اللَّهُ مَثَلًا لِّلَّذِينَ كَفَرُوا
امْرَأَتَ نُوحٍ وَامْرَأَتَ لُوطٍ ۖ كَانَتَا تَحْتَ عَبْدَيْنِ مِنْ عِبَادِنَا صَالِحَيْنِ
فَخَانَتَاهُمَا فَلَمْ يُغْنِيَا عَنْهُمَا مِنَ اللَّهِ شَيْئًا وَقِيلَ ادْخُلَا النَّارَ مَعَ
الدَّاخِلِينَ ﴿١٠﴾

[66:6] O ye who have attained to faith! Ward off from yourselves and your kin that fire [of the hereafter] whose fuel is men and stones [of sulfur], over which are [appointed] angels stern and awe-inspiring [in power], who flinch not [from executing] the Commands they receive from God ﷻ, but [always] do [precisely] what they are bidden.

[66:7] [On that day, it will be said to the Unbelievers,] "O you who are bent on denying the truth, make no [empty] excuses today! Ye are being but requited for all that ye did [in this world].

[27] Suyūṭī, Jalāl al-Dīn 'Abd al-Raḥmān, *al-Durr al-Manthūr fī al-Tafsīr bi-al-Ma'thūr*, 6:244.

[66:8] O you who have attained to faith! Turn unto God ﷻ in sincere repentance: it may well be that your Lord of Providence will [thereby] efface from you your bad deeds, and will admit you into gardens [under whose trees] running waters flow. On that Day, God ﷻ will not let down the Prophet ﷺ and those who share his faith: their light will spread rapidly before them, and on their right; [and] they will pray: "O our Lord of Providence! Perfect this light for us [causing it to shine for us forever], and forgive us our sins [with thy Grace]: for, verily, Thou hast power over all things!"

[66:9] Wage *jihād* against the Unbelievers and the Hypocrites, O Prophet ﷺ, and be severe with them! For [if they do not repent of their wickedness despite your efforts,] their abode shall be Hell – a vile destination [indeed]!

[66:10] God ﷻ sets forth, as an example for those who are bent on denying the truth, [the stories of] Noah's wife and Lot's wife: they were wedded to two of Our righteous servants, each of whom they betrayed; and neither of the two [husbands] will be of any avail to these two women before God ﷻ when they will be told [on Judgment Day], "Enter the fire [along] with all those [other sinners] who [shall] enter it!"

So again, exactly what took place? What intrigue was afoot about the person of the Prophet ﷺ, of which he was informed by way of revelation, a part of which he divulged to Hafsa and another part of which he did not reveal? What were these two wives of the Prophet ﷺ and their co-conspirators up to which required a warning in such threatening language which recalled the fate of the two wives of the prophets Noah and Lot, stipulating that both of these women engaged in treachery and betrayal which landed them in the fires of Hell? The answer that we find Sunni sources corroborating for us is the following: the Prophet ﷺ had told Hafsa that her father ('Umar) and 'Āisha's father (Abu Bakr) will rise in rebellion against him [and his expressed will]. This was the matter that was told in confidence to Hafsa; as a secret to be held between them. But Hafsa divulged her husband's secret to 'Āisha, who told her father, who in turn told 'Umar, who questioned his daughter Hafsa about it, instructing her to tell him so that they could be prepared; after which Hafsa told her father what the Prophet ﷺ had told her in confidence.

[We also know that] the Prophet ﷺ revealed a part of the story to Hafsa (i.e. the part about the two women betraying the Prophet's confidence), and demurred from disclosing the other part. What could this second undisclosed part have been? Could this secret be anything other than the readiness of the fathers of those two [women] for seizing the reins of power after the passing of the Prophet?

In order to extract the context of the revelation of these *āyāt* from 'Umar, Ibn-'Abbās cleverly posed the question to him in this way:

"It has been a year that I want to ask you a question, but I have held back out of concern for your reaction." 'Umar said, "What is the question?" Ibn-'Abbās said, "It concerns an *āya* of the Quran." 'Umar said, "Ibn-'Abbās, you believe that there is knowledge of the Quran that is with me and you do not ask me of it??"At this point, Ibn-'Abbās put forward his question: "Who was the *Sūra at-Tahrīm* revealed about?" 'Umar said, "About 'Āisha and Hafsa."[28]

Based on a *hadīth* report that makes its appearance in Suyutī's *ad-Durr al-Manthūr* (6:241), wherein we read, "And when the Prophet ﷺ told something in confidence to Hafsa bt. 'Umar that Abu Bakr would succeed him and that 'Umar would succeed Abu Bakr..."[29], we can see that there was a plot hatched between Abu Bakr and 'Umar to succeed the Prophet ﷺ in his capacity as the leader of the community,

---

[28] Ṭabarī, Muḥammad ibn Jarīr, *Jāmi' al-Bayān fī Tafsīr al-Qur'ān*, 28:104-105; Bokhārī, Muḥammad ibn Ismā'īl, *Ṣaḥīḥ al-Bokhārī*, 3:137-138 & 4:22; Muslim ibn al-Ḥajjāj, *Ṣaḥīḥ Muslim, Kitāb at-Talāq*, reports 31-34; Aḥmad ibn Ḥanbal, *Musnad Aḥmad ibn Ḥanbal*, 1:48; Tayālasī, *Musnad*, report #23.

[29] [It seems to me that, based on the style of the (run-on) sentences, this footnote was most probably added by professor Mahdī Dashti, the esteemed editor of the book – Tr.] In Sunnite sources, this prophecy of the Prophet concerning the succession of Abu Bakr and 'Umar to the caliphate is interpreted as the Prophet's giving good tidings concerning the caliphates of the two caliphs! This is false, because the text of the above-mentioned Quranic verses contains warnings and reproaches and threats, and speaks of the treachery of two of the wives of the Prophet ﷺ, who are compared to and equated with the wives of the prophets Noah and Lot; and the letter and spirit of the verses is at complete loggerheads with any "glad tidings". To the contrary, the are numerous examples of hadith reports in which the Prophet prophecies coming calamities and disasters and injustices that are to occur in the future.

a plot meant to be implemented during the lifetime of the Prophet ﷺ,[30] and a plot for what was to take place after his passing, the latter of which is what is pertinent to our present discussion, which plot is the foundation of [the events that occurred in] the Saqīfa.

The plot relating to the time immediately after the passing of the Prophet ﷺ involved six people: Abu Bakr, 'Umar, Abu-Ubayda, al-Jarrāh, Sālim the *mawlā* (patron/ master) of Abī-Khuzayfa, and Uthmān, all of whom conspired to cooperate in a *coup d'état* upon the passing of the Prophet ﷺ, as a consequence of which each of them would succeed to the leadership of the community (in the order listed, the sixth being 'Abd ur-Rahmān b. 'Awf). They wrote this agreement in a letter which they left with Abu-Ubayda al-Jarrāh [for safe-keeping].[31] It was for this reason that 'Umar would say "Abu-Ubayda is the trustee of the *ummah*."[32] And it is on account of this agreement that the second caliph repeatedly stated that "If Abu-Ubayda al-Jarrāh or Sālim the *mawlā* of Abī-Khuzayfa were alive, I would give [the office of] the caliphate to them."[33] In fact, the appointment of the second caliph to the caliphate was also predeterminate [per the confession of Uthmān] in the following report:

"When Abu-Bakr was passing the last hours of his life, he called for Uthmān. [When] the two were alone, Abu-Bakr said, "Write, *In the Name of God, the Compassionate, the Merciful,* this is that which Abu-

---

[30] The plot meant to be implemented during the lifetime of the Prophet could have been the one described in Ibn Hazm's valuable work *al-Muhallī* (Volume 11, page 224) in which the Andalusian Ibn Hazm (one of the greats among Sunnite scholars) quotes a *hadīth* report from Walīd b. Abdullāh b. Jamī' az-Zahrī wherein it is stated that Abū-Bakr, 'Umar, Uthmān, Talha, and Sa'd b. Abī-Waqqās *raḍi allāhu 'anhum* [!! – the prayer appears in the Ibn Hazm text.] wanted to kill the Prophet ﷺ by scaring his camel so that he would be thrown off its back and down a valley, which of course was averted thanks to the grace of God ﷻ. Of course, Ibn Hazm quickly goes on to dismiss this report as unsound on the basis that its narrator is unreliable. However, that which is "unsound" is Ibn Hazm's opinion concerning the reliability of the narrator, as Bokhārī and Muslim both consider Walīd b. Abdullāh b. Jamī' az-Zahrī to be *muaththaq* (reliable), which means that Bokhārī and Muslim have given their seal of approval to his reports, making them *sahīh* in the opinion of the two scholars of *hadith* that count most in the Sunni world.

[31] Majlisī, Allāma Muhammad Bāqir, *Bihār al-Anwār* 2:296:5 [– a Shī'a source, to be otherwise corroborated presently].

[32] Ibn Abd al-Rabbih, *al-'Iqd al-Farīd*, 4:274.

[33] Ibid.

Bakr wills to the Muslims..." After these words, Abu-Bakr lost consciousness, and Uthmān proceeded to continue writing: "To proceed, I appoint as my successor after me 'Umar b. al-Khattāb, and in doing so, have taken into consideration what is best for you." At this point, Abu-Bakr came to and told 'Uthmān to read what he had written so far. After 'Uthmān read the will, Abu-Bakr recited the *takbīr* (*allāhu akbar*; God is greater; God is greatest) and added, "I think you feared that if I died in my unconscious state that the people would be divided [as to who should succeed me]." 'Uthmān said, "Yes!" [And] Abu-Bakr said, "May God reward you [for what you have done] for Islam and its people," and signed the will that Uthmān had written."[34]

How did Uthmān know who Abu Bakr wanted to succeed him? He could not know this by any means other than that there was a plot to agree upon the succession that entailed a predetermined series [of appointments] which Uthmān was in on. And the series was what we presented above, namely, Abu Bakr, 'Umar, Abu-Ubayda al-Jarrāh, Sālim the *mawlā* of Abī-Khuzayfa, and 'Uthmān, a fact which is further corroborated by two other exhibits which are actions taken by 'Umar.

1. When 'Umar had been struck by the poisoned sword of Abu-Lu'lu' and was in his death throes, because Abu-Ubayda al-Jarrāh and Sālim had predeceased him[35], 'Umar arranged the *shawrā* (consultative assembly or council) in such a way as to ensure that Uthmān would be elected. [36]

---

[34] Tabarī, Muhammad ibn Jarīr, *Tārīkh ar-Rusul wa'l-Mulūk*, 1:2138 of the European edition, and 3:52.

[35] Ibn Abd al-Rabbih, *al-'Iqd al-Farīd*, 4:274. Sālim, the *mawlā* of Abī-Khuzayfa, was killed in a battle with Musaylama al-Kadhdhāb (the Liar) in the second year of Abu Bakr's caliphate, and Abu-Ubayda al-Jarrāh died of the Plague of Emmaus in the 18th year of the Islamic calendar, while he was the commander of the Muslim army in its war against Byzantium in the Levant, which at that time was referred to as the Eastern Roman Empire. [The Plague of Emmaus, also known as the Plague of Amwās, was an outbreak of plague, possibly bubonic plague, that occurred in 639 in the town of Emmaus (Amwās) in Palestine. The plague struck shortly after the conquest of Emmaus by the Muslims, who had set up a military encampment there.]

[36] Balādhurī, Aḥmad ibn Yaḥyā ibn Jabir, *Ansāb al-Ashrāf*, 5:15-19; Ibn Abd al-Rabbih, *al-'Iqd al-Farīd*, 3:73-74; Ibn Sa'd, Abu Abdallah Muhammad, *al-Tabaqāt al-Kubrā*, 3: Q 1:43; and Ya'qūbī, Aḥmad ibn Isḥāq, *Tārīkh al-Ya'qūbī*, 2:160. [See also Jafri, *Origins and Early Development of Shī'a Islam* and Madelung, *The Succession to Muhammad.*]

2. The episode that follows also makes it clear that the succession of the third caliph was determined during 'Umar's lifetime. We read in Ibn-Sa'd's *at-Tabaqāt al-Kubrā*, related by the 'Umayyad Sa'īd b. 'Ās, that he made a request of 'Umar for a plot of land adjacent to his own so that he could build an addition to his house, as 'Umar was known to grant such favors to certain people. The caliph told him to meet him on the following morning after the dawn prayer, and he would take care of his business for him. When they reached the desired plot on the morrow, the Caliph drew a line in the sand with his foot and said, "[Up to] this [line] here shall be yours." Sa'īd b. 'Ās continues: I said, "I have a family, O Commander of the Faithful, grant a portion more." 'Umar said, "For now, this much land suffices you. But I will tell you a secret; [be sure to] keep it to yourself. I shall be succeeded by one who is your kindred and will see to your needs." Sa'īd adds: I waited throughout the period of 'Umar's reign until Uthmān succeeded him upon his death, and just as 'Umar had said, he [Uthmān] acted to me like family and granted my request. [37]

The above hadith report makes it clear that the second caliph knew, based on the plan he had conceived for after his own demise, that his felicitous Umayyad kinsman, i.e. Uthmān, would succeed to the office of the caliphate.

Additionally, the details that follow will demonstrate that 'Umar intended for 'Abd ar-Rahmān b. 'Awf to succeed Uthmān. In the year of *'ām ar-ru'āf*, Uthmān was inflicted with a severe and life-threatening case of nose-bleeding. From his deathbed, he wrote a letter which he did not make a public proclamation about, appointing 'Abd ur-Rahmān b. 'Awf as his successor. When the latter got wind of this, he got very angry, saying, "I made him caliph publicly, but he appoints me covertly?!"[38] And this caused a rift between them, and they became sworn enemies, which was in part an answer to Imām Ali's

---

[37] Ibn Sa'd, Abu Abdallah Muhammad, *al-Tabaqāt al-Kubrā*, Brill (Leiden) edition, 5:20-22.

[38] Ibn Asākir, *at-Tārīkh al-Madīnat ad-Damishq* and Dhahabī, Shams ad-Dīn Muhammad ibn Ahmad, *Sīyar a'lām al-nubalā'*, under the heading 'Abd ar-Rahmān b. 'Awf.

imprecation of them both due to their collusion at the charade which came to be known as the *showrā*'.[39] Uthmān recovered from his illness and 'Abd or-Rahmān b. 'Awf died during the remainder of Uthmān's term as caliph. And this is also why on the day when 'Abd or-Rahmān cast his deciding vote in favor of Uthmān (as per the plan), Imām Ali ﷺ [who, of course, knew what shenanigans the two perpetrators of this fraud were up to], told him that he did not make Uthmān caliph but for the fact of their tacit reciprocation agreement [i.e. that there was a tacit understanding between the two that Uthmān would in turn appoint 'Abd ur-Rahmān b. 'Awf to succeed him as caliph].[40]

As far as 'Umar's desire to see Mu'āwiya succeed to the caliphate – this subject will be dealt with in the section having to do with Mu'āwiya during [our treatment of] the caliphate of 'Umar. Here it will suffice us to note that as a general principle, 'Umar wanted the caliphate to remain in the hands of the Quraysh but on condition that this be to the exclusion of the Banī-Hāshim; and that he and his allies did not want the Banī-Hāshim to attain to the position of the leadership of the community, not only in their own lifetimes, but also at any time thereafter.[41]

---

[39] Ibn Abī'l-Hadīd, Abdul-Hamīd, *Sharh Nahj al-Balāgha*, 1:188: *Khutba* 3 & 9:55: *Khutba* 139. For more on the enmity between the two, see Baladhurī, *Ansāb ul-Ashrāf* (Beirut, 1400 AH), 4:1:546-7.

[40] Tabarī, Muhammad ibn Jarīr, *Tārīkh ar-Rusul wa'l-Mulūk*, 3:297 (Year 23); Ibn Athīr, 'Alī ibn Muḥammad, *Usd al-Ghābah fī Ma'rifat al-Ṣaḥābah*, 3:37.

[41] A detailed discussion of this same topic is presented in this book in Chapter 10: Governance during Umar's Caliphate, and specifically under the heading 'Umar's conversation with Ibn Abbās'. Cf. Ahmad b. Hanbal, *Musnad*, 1:177; Ibn Abd'al-Birr, Yusuf ibn Abdallah, *al-Istī'āb fī Ma'rifat al-Ashāb*, 1:253; Ibn Abī'l-Hadīd, Abdul-Hamīd, *Sharh Nahj al-Balāgha*, 6:12-13; Ibn Hajar, Ahmad ibn Ali al-Asqalāni, *al-Iṣābah fī Tamyīz al-Ṣaḥābah*, 3:413; Ibn Kathīr, Abu'al-Fiḍā Ismā'īl ibn Umar, *Tārīkh*, 8:120; Mas'ūdī, Alī ibn al-Ḥusayn, *Murawwij adh-Dhahab*, 2:321-322; Tabarī, Muhammad ibn Jarīr, *Tārīkh ar-Rusul wa'l-Mulūk*, 5:2768 & 5:2770-2771 & 5:2787.

2 How the Saqīfa Plot was Implemented

1. The Prophet's Illness and Death

The Prophet ﷺ became ill in the last ten days of the month of Safar in the eleventh year of the Hijra. He appointed Usāma, the son of Zayd, who had become a freedman at the hands of the Prophet ﷺ, and who was eighteen years old at that time,[42] to the leadership of an army which was to go toward the Levant and fight the Christians of Byzantium. The Prophet ﷺ had ordered Abū Bakr, Umar, Abū Ubaydah al-Jarrāh, and Sa'd ibn Ubāda and the other leaders among the Companions (from both the Emigrants (*Muhājirūn*) and the Helpers (*Ansār*)) to participate in the battle. The Prophet ﷺ emphasized that none of these leaders should refrain from being a part of the muster call of that army.[43] The Prophet ﷺ added, "May God curse anyone who fails to join Usāma's muster call (and to go with him)."[44]

Having said this, the Prophet's ﷺ condition worsened. News of the Prophet's ﷺ imminent death reached Usāma's muster, which was encamped outside Medina. Those who were intent on interfering with the matter of the succession to the Prophet ﷺ returned to Medina and gathered around the Prophet ﷺ on the morning of that Monday. The

---

[42] Ibn Abd'al-Birr, Yusuf ibn Abdallah, *al-Istī'āb fi Ma'rifat al-Ashāb*, #12; Ibn Athīr, 'Alī ibn Muḥammad, *Usd al-Ghābah fī Ma'rifat al-Ṣaḥābah*, 1:65-66;

[43] Ibn Sa'd, Abū-Abdallah Muhammad, *al-Tabaqāt al-Kubrā*, 2:190-192 (Beirut edition); Ibn Sayyid an-Nās, Muhammad ibn Muhammad, *'Uyūn al-Athar*, 2:281. There are many sources which are explicit in stating that Abu Bakr and Umar were part of Usāma's Army: Muttaqī al-Hindī, *Kanz al-U'mmāl*, 5:312; *Muntakhab Kanz al-U'mmāl*, 4:180; Balādhūrī, Ahmad ibn Yahyā ibn Jābir, *Ansāb al-Ashrāf*, 1:474; [43] Ibn Sa'd, Abū-Abdallah Muhammad, *al-Tabaqāt al-Kubrā*, 4:44; Ibn 'Asākir, 'Alī, *Tahdhīb*, 2:391; Ya'qūbī, Aḥmad ibn Isḥāq, *Tārīkh al-Ya'qūbī*, 2:74 (Beirut edition); Ibn Athīr Jazarī, 'Alī, *al-Kāmil fī al-Tārīkh*, 2:123.

[44] Ibn Abī'l-Hadīd, Abdul-Hamīd, *Sharh Nahj al-Balāgha*, 6:52.

Prophet ﷺ said, "Bring me a scroll and a quill so that I can 'stipulate something' [*aktub lakum kitāban* = a final will and testament] for you by [adherence to] which you shall never go astray after my passing." Umar said, "The Prophet ﷺ is overcome by his illness". What Umar was hinting at is that the Prophet ﷺ had become delirious and did not know what he was talking about., and that we were in possession of God's Sacred Writ (*kitāb-e khodā*), and that God's Sacred Writ was sufficient for us (*hasbunā kitab-allāh*). [45] A group said that the Prophet's ﷺ order should be implemented. The group that wanted the Prophet's ﷺ order to be implemented ultimately gained the ascendancy.[46]

In another hadith report that appears in Ibn Sa'd's *at-Tabaqāt al-Kubrā*, it is stated that while the Prophet ﷺ was in that condition [i.e. in his death throes], someone among the crowd [that had gathered around the Prophet's deathbed] said, "Verily, the Apostle of God ﷺ is delirious,"[47]

The heavens shed tears of blood [at this effrontery]! [To think that it was possible for] a Companion [of the Prophet ﷺ] to make such an outrageous statement in the presence of God's Final Apostle! While it is true that [the transmitter of] the hadith report has not mentioned the name of the narrator, but nevertheless, given the report that appears in Bokhārī's *Sahīh* compendium (which we mentioned earlier), [the question can be posed as to] who other than Umar would have the temerity to make such a statement? And so yes, the speaker [in this hadith report] is none other than the person who said, "Sufficient unto us is God's Sacred Writ (*hasbunā kitab-allāh*)."[48]

---

[45] Bukhārī, Muḥammad ibn Ismā'īl, *Ṣaḥīḥ al-Bukhārī*, 1:22; Ahmad b. Hanbal, *Musnad*, hadith #2992; Ibn Sa'd, Abū-Abdallah Muhammad, *al-Tabaqāt al-Kubrā*; 2:244.

[46] Bukhārī, Muḥammad ibn Ismā'īl, *Ṣaḥīḥ al-Bukhārī*, 1:22; Ahmad b. Hanbal, *Musnad*, hadith #2676; Ibn Sa'd, Abū-Abdallah Muhammad, *al-Tabaqāt al-Kubrā*; 2:243-244.

[47] Ibn Sa'd, Abū-Abdallah Muhammad, *al-Tabaqāt al-Kubrā*; 2:242; Bukhārī, Muḥammad ibn Ismā'īl, *Ṣaḥīḥ al-Bukhārī*, 2:120 and 2:136, where the phrase appears as follows «فقالوا: هجر رسول الله صلّى الله عليه و سلّم»; Muslim ibn al-Ḥajjāj, *Ṣaḥīḥ Muslim*, 5:76; Tabarī, Muhammad ibn Jarīr, *Tārīkh ar-Rusul wa'l-Mulūk*, 3:193, where the phrase appears as follows: «انّ رسول الله صلّى الله عليه و سلّم يهجر».

[48] Umar admitted to this himself. According to Imam Abū'l-Faḍl Ahmad ibn Abī-Tāhir (in his *Tārikh al-Baghdād*) and Ibn Abī'l-Hadīd, Abdul-Hamīd, *Sharh Nahj al-Balāgha*, 3:97 (in a description of Umar), one day, in a lengthy

My God! Could there be a greater catastrophe than this?!

After this argument, those who were not involved in it asked that a scroll and a quill be brought, but the Prophet ﷺ said, "What, [you mean to do so] after this [= after the argument that just took place]?"[49] If a scroll and a quill were to be brought [to the Prophet ﷺ] after what had been said, and if the Prophet ﷺ had indeed written his last will and testament and mentioned Ali's ؑ name [as the Prophet's ﷺ successor], those who were against this could easily gather up a few people to give false testimony that the Prophet ﷺ made his last will and testament while in a state of delirium.

Because a quarrel had broken out [among those present], the Prophet ﷺ said, "Get up and leave [me alone]!"[50]

What happened on the dawn of that day?

2. What happened on the dawn of that day?

Whenever Bilāl finished making the call to the ritual devotions, he would come to the house of the Prophet ﷺ and say, "[It is time for] the ritual devotions, O Prophet!" At the dawn of that Monday morning, Bilāl came up to the Prophet's ﷺ house at the time of the call to the ritual devotions, and repeated his usual words. The Prophet ﷺ was in 'Āisha's quarters and was unconscious, his head resting on Ali's knee. 'Āisha went over to the door and told Bilāl, "Tell my father [Abū Bakr] to come and lead the congregational devotions." Abū Bakr came and stood in the position of the leader of the devotions. The Prophet ﷺ then regained his consciousness and realized that the congregational devotions were being performed in the mosque while Ali was sitting at his bedside.

The Prophet ﷺ got up despite the state he was in and managed to make his ablutions, and allowed Faḍl ibn 'Abbās and His Eminence Alī ibn Abī-Tālib ؑ to support him, who walked the Prophet ﷺ to the mosque while he was in such a poor state of health that his feet dragged along on the floor. Abū Bakr was leading the congregational

---

discussion that took place between Ibn Abbās and Umar, Umar said, "The Prophet intended to stipulate [the succession] in his [Ali ibn Abī-Tālib's] name when he was ill, but I did not let him. Also cf. Allāma Sharīf ad-Dīn's *al-Murāji'āt*, pp. 442-443 of the Persian translation by Muhammad Ja'far Imāmī.

[49] Ibn Sa'd, Abū-Abdallah Muhammad, *al-Tabaqāt al-Kubrā*, 2:242.

[50] Abū al-Fidā, Ismā'īl ibn Ali, *Tarikh al-Mukhtasar fi Akhbar al-Bashar*, 1:151; Bukhārī, Muḥammad ibn Ismā'īl, *Ṣaḥīḥ al-Bukhārī*, 1:22, where the phrase appears as follows: «قال (ص): قوموا عنّى و لا ينبغى عندى التّنازع»

devotions. The Prophet ﷺ came to Abū Bakr, stood in front of him, and voided his devotions, and [led] the congregational devotions in a sitting position. The Companions deferred to the Prophet ﷺ, and the morning congregational devotions were thus completed in this way.[51] The rest of the events occurred on the same Monday, and the Prophet ﷺ passed on the same fateful day as well.

3. The ritual cleansing of the body of the Prophet ﷺ and its preparation [for burial]

The people who performed the ritual cleansing of the pure and sacred body of the Prophet ﷺ and who participated in the burial of the Prophet ﷺ and in its wake consisted of the following: His Eminence Alī ibn Abī-Tālib ؑ, 'Abbās, the Prophet's uncle, Faḍl ibn 'Abbās, and Sālih (a freedman freed by the Prophet). Thus, the Companions of the Prophet ﷺ left his body among the members of the Prophet's ﷺ family, such that it was only this handful of people who took on the responsibility of the ritual cleansing of the body of the Prophet ﷺ and its preparation for burial.[52]

According to another hadith report, the people who took on the responsibility of the ritual cleansing of the body of the Prophet ﷺ and its preparation for burial were His Eminence Alī ibn Abī-Tālib ؑ, Faḍl ibn 'Abbās, and Quth'thām ibn 'Abbās, and Shuqrān (another freedman freed by the Prophet; and according to yet another hadith report,

[51] Ibn Abī'l-Hadīd, Abdul-Hamīd, *Sharh Nahj al-Balāgha*, 9:197 (Sermon 156); Mufīd, Shaykh Muhammad ibn Muhammad, *al-Irshād fī ma'rifat Hujaj Allah 'al'al-'Ibād*, pp. 86-87; For a more in-depth familiarization with this subject, cf. Bukhārī, Muḥammad ibn Ismā'īl, *Ṣaḥīḥ al-Bukhārī*, 1:92, and Muslim ibn al-Ḥajjāj, *Ṣaḥīḥ Muslim*, 2:32, and Ibn Māja, Muhammad ibn Yazīd, *Sunan*,
باب ما جاء في صلاة رسول الله (ص): فكان ابو بكر يأتمّ بالنّبي و النّاس يأتمّون به .
Wording close to this appears in the following sources: Ibn Sa'd, Abū-Abdallah Muhammad, *al-Tabaqāt al-Kubrā*, 3:179; Ahmad b. Hanbal, *Musnad*, 6:120 & 6:224; and Balādhūrī, Ahmad ibn Yahyā ibn Jābir, *Ansāb al-Ashrāf*, 1:557.

[52] Ibn Sa'd, Abū-Abdallah Muhammad, *al-Tabaqāt al-Kubrā*, 2:70; Muttaqī al-Hindī, *Kanz al-U'mmāl*, 4:54 & 4:60. Another hadith report states that Aws ibn Hawlī al-Ansārī was also with these four people. See Askarī, Allāma Murtaḍā, *Abdullāh ibn Sabā*, 1:110.

Usāma ibn Zayd); [53] and neither Abū Bakr nor Umar participated in this ritual.[54]

While these rituals were taking place, 'Abbās said to His Eminence Alī ibn Abī-Tālib ﷺ, "O son of my brother. Come forward so that I can pledge allegiance to you, so that after this, no one will go against you."[55] His Eminence Alī ibn Abī-Tālib ﷺ replied, "Presently, our duty is to prepare the Prophet's ﷺ body for burial."[56]

At that same moment, the 'Helpers' (*ansār*) had gathered in the portico (*saqīfa*) of the Banī Sā'ida [tribe] in order to elect a leader.[57] As soon as the news of this gathering reached Abū Bakr, Umar, Abū

---

[53] Ibn 'Abd Rabbih, *al-'Iqd al-Farīd*, 3:61. See also, Dhahabī, Shams al-Dīn Muhammad ibn Ahmad, *Tārīkh al-Islām wa-Wafayāt al-Mashāhīr wa-al-A'lām*, 1:321, 324, & 326, where a phrase similar to that of *al-'Iqd al-Farīd* appears.

[54] Muttaqī al-Hindī, *Kanz al-U'mmāl*, 3:140. 'Āisha was also absent from this ceremony, and was unaware of the burial of the Messenger of God, until, as she put it, she heard the sound of the spades at the midnight of Wednesday: « ما علمنا بدفن الرّسول حتّى سمعنا صوت المساحى من جوف اللّيل ليلة الأربعاء» Ibn Hishām, 'Abd al-Malik, *al-Sīrah al-Nabawīyah*, 4:344; Tabarī, Muhammad ibn Jarīr, *Tārīkh ar-Rusul wa'l-Mulūk*, 2:452 & 2:455 (of the European edition); Ibn Athīr, 'Alī ibn Muḥammad, *Usd al-Ghābah fī Ma'rifat al-Ṣaḥābah*, 1:34; and Ahmad b. Hanbal, *Musnad*, 6:62, 242, & 274.

[55] Mas'ūdī, Ali ibn al-Husayn, *Murawwij adh-Dhahab*, 2:200; Dhahabī, Shams al-Dīn Muhammad ibn Ahmad, *Tārīkh al-Islam*, 1:329; Amīn, Ahmad, *Ḍuhay al-Islām*, 3:291. The sentence appears in Ibn Qutayba, Abū Muhammad Abd-Allāh ibn Muslim, *al-Imāma wa'l-Siyāsa* as follows: «ابسط يدك ابايعك فيقال عمّ رسول الله بايع ابن عمّ رسول الله و يبايعك اهل بيتك. فانّ هذا الأمر اذا كان لم يقل». And in Ibn Sa'd, Abu Abdallah Muhammad, *al-Tabaqāt al-Kubrā*, 2:2nd C:38 as follows: « انّ العبّاس قال لعليّ: امدد يدك ابايعك يبايعك النّاس».

[56] Ibn Abī'l-Hadīd, Abdul-Hamīd, *Sharh Nahj al-Balāgha*, 1:131 in the first Egyptian edition, quoting Abī-Bakr al-Jawharī's *Saqīfa*.

[57] Aḥmad b. Hanbal, *Musnad*, 1:260, Ibn Kathīr, Abu'al-Fiḍā Ismā'īl ibn Umar, *Tārīkh*, 5:260; Ibn Jawzī, Abd al-Rahmān b. Ali, *Siffa^t as-Safwah*, 1:85; Dīyār-Bakri, Husain ibn Muhammad, *Tārīkh al-Khamīs fī Ahwāl an-Nafs an-Nafīs*, 1:189; Tabarī, Muhammad ibn Jarīr, *Tārīkh ar-Rusul wa'l-Mulūk*, 2:451, and 1:1830-1831 of the European edition; Abū al-Fidā, Ismā'īl ibn Ali, *Tarikh al-Mukhtasar fī Akhbar al-Bashar*, 1:152; Ibn Athīr, 'Alī ibn Muḥammad, *Usd al-Ghābah fī Ma'rifat al-Ṣaḥābah*, 1:34 & 5:188; Ibn 'Abd Rabbih, *al-'Iqd al-Farīd*, 3:61; Dhahabī, Shams al-Dīn Muhammad ibn Ahmad, *Tārīkh al-Islam*, 1:321; Ibn Sa'd, Abu Abdallah Muhammad, *al-Tabaqāt al-Kubrā*, 2:2nd C:70; Ya'qūbī, Aḥmad ibn Isḥāq, *Tārīkh al-Ya'qūbī*, 2:94; Abū-Nasr ibn Mutahhar ibn Tāhir, *al-Baladu wa'l-Tārīkh*, 5:68; Ibn Abd'al-Birr, Yusuf ibn Abdallah, *al-Istī'āb fī Ma'rifat al-Ashāb*, 4:65.

Ubaydah al-Jarrāh, and their associates, they rushed over to the *Saqīfa*.[58]

Thus, excepting the Prophet's ﷺ immediate family, no one stayed behind to see to the burial of the Prophet's ﷺ body. The Prophet's ﷺ immediate family consisted of His Eminence Alī ibn Abī-Tālib ﷺ, 'Abbās ibn 'Abd al-Muttalib (the Prophet's ﷺ uncle), Faḍl ibn 'Abbās (the Prophet's ﷺ nephew), Quth'thām ibn 'Abbās, (another nephew of the Prophet's ﷺ), Usāma ibn Zayd (a freedman freed by the Prophet ﷺ), Sālih (another freedman freed by the Prophet ﷺ), and Aws ibn Khawlā (one of the 'Helpers'); and it was only these people who took on the responsibility of burying the Prophet's ﷺ body.[59]

The performance of the ritual devotions for the Prophet's ﷺ corpse was an act that was religiously incumbent on each and every individual (*wājib-e 'aynī*).[60] The performance of the ritual devotions for

---

[58] Bukhārī, Muḥammad ibn Ismā'īl, *Ṣaḥīḥ al-Bukhārī*, 4:120; Ibn Hishām, 'Abd al-Malik, *al-Sīrah al-Nabawīyah*, 4:336; Tabarī, Muhibbiddīn, *ar-Riyāḍ an-Naḍra*, 1:63; Dayār-Bakrī, Ḥusayn Ibn Md., *Tārīkh al-Khamīs fī Ahwāl Anfus Nafīs*, 1:186; Abī-Bakr al-Jawharī's *Saqīfa* quoted in Ibn Abī'l-Hadīd, Abdul-Hamīd, *Sharh Nahj al-Balāgha*, 2:2; Tabarī, Muhammad ibn Jarīr, *Tārīkh ar-Rusul wa'l-Mulūk*, 1:1839 of the European edition; Abū-Nasr ibn Mutahhar ibn Tāhir, *al-Baladu wa'l-Tārīkh*, 5:65.

[59] Ahmad b. Hanbal, *Musnad*, 1:260; Ibn Kathīr, Abu'al-Fiḍā Ismā'īl ibn Umar, *Tārīkh*, 5:260; Ibn Jawzī, Abd al-Rahmān b. Ali, *Siffa^t as-Safwa*, 1:85; Dayār-Bakrī, Ḥusayn Ibn Md., *Tārīkh al-Khamīs fī Ahwāl Anfus Nafīs*, 1:189; Tabarī, Muhammad ibn Jarīr, *Tārīkh ar-Rusul wa'l-Mulūk*, 2:451 & 1:1830-1831 in the European edition; Ibn Shahna, Md ibn Md, *Bihāmish (?) al-Kāmil*, p. 100; Abū al-Fidā, Ismā'īl ibn Ali, *Tarikh al-Mukhtasar fī Akhbar al-Bashar*, 1:252; Ibn Athīr, 'Alī ibn Muḥammad, *Usd al-Ghābah fī Ma'rifat al-Ṣaḥābah*; 1:34; Ibn 'Abd Rabbih, *al-'Iqd al-Farīd*, 3:61; Dhahabī, Shams al-Dīn Muhammad ibn Ahmad, *Tārīkh al-Islam*, 1:321; Ibn Sa'd, Abu Abdallah Muhammad, *al-Tabaqāt al-Kubrā*, 2:2nd C:70; Ya'qūbī, Aḥmad ibn Isḥāq, *Tārīkh al-Ya'qūbī*, 2:94; Abū-Nasr ibn Mutahhar ibn Tāhir, *al-Baladu wa'l-Tārīkh*, 5:68; Mas'ūdī, Alī ibn al-Ḥusayn, *al-Tanbīh wa'l-Ishrāf*, p. 244.

[60] Translator's note: [*Wājib kifāī* is a "representatively" incumbent obligation which can be fulfilled by one or more members of the community on behalf of everyone else. *Wājib 'aynī* is a "personally and individually" incumbent obligation which must be fulfilled by every legally competent obligor, irrespective of whether or not other members of the community also happen to fulfill the obligation.] Author's footnote: This is my own inference [concerning this issue, i.e. the incumbency of prayer for the Prophet on each and every Muslim], which is based on the fact that the burial of the Prophet's ﷺ body took two days and two nights, despite the fact that delaying the burial of the dead is a highly reprehensible act in Islam, so that all of the people of Medina, male and female, and young and old, could offer their prayers for His Eminence the Prophet #.

the Prophet ﷺ is not the same as doing so for anyone else, as it requires an *imām* (leader) to lead the ceremony. As His Eminence Alī ibn Abī-Tālib ﵇ has stated, the Prophet ﷺ was everyone's *imām.* Thus, people would come in groups of five or six, and Imam Ali ﵇ would recite the words of the devotional ritual aloud, and they would repeat it after him. The males took their turns first to recite the words of the devotional ritual, and then the womenfolk, who were followed by children who had not yet reached the age of majority. This rite was performed starting on Monday morning, and it continued until Tuesday evening.[61] The body of the Prophet ﷺ was buried on Wednesday evening in the presence of a handful of people in the same room in which he passed away.[62]

Other than the Prophet's ﷺ immediate family, no one participated in his burial. And the Banī Ghanam tribe heard the sound of the shovels when they were resting in their homes.[63] 'Āisha says, "We were unaware of the Prophet's burial ceremony until the middle of the night of the Wednesday, when we heard the sounds of the shovels."[64]

4. The Prophet's testamentary instruction concerning Ali

In order to attain a greater understanding of the Prophet's testamentary instruction concerning Ali ﵇, it behooves us to present some information by way of a preamble. In verse 3:144 of the Quran, God ﷻ has stated:

وَمَا مُحَمَّدٌ إِلَّا رَسُولٌ قَدْ خَلَتْ مِن قَبْلِهِ الرُّسُلُ ۚ أَفَإِن مَّاتَ أَوْ قُتِلَ انقَلَبْتُمْ عَلَىٰ أَعْقَابِكُمْ ۚ وَمَن يَنقَلِبْ عَلَىٰ عَقِبَيْهِ فَلَن يَضُرَّ اللَّهَ شَيْئًا ۗ وَسَيَجْزِي اللَّهُ الشَّاكِرِينَ ﴿١٤٤﴾

---

61 Tabresī, Abu-Ali Faḍl ibn Hasan, *I'lām al-Warī bi I'lām al-Hudā*, p. 144; Ibn Sa'd, Abu Abdallah Muhammad, *al-Tabaqāt al-Kubrā*, 2:256-257; Majlisī, Allāma Muhammad Bāqir, *Bihār al-Anwār*, 22:525 & 22:539.

62 Ibn Sa'd, Abu Abdallah Muhammad, *al-Tabaqāt al-Kubrā*, 2:292-294; Ibn Hishām, 'Abd al-Malik, *al-Sīrah al-Nabawīyah*, 4:343.

63 Ibn Sa'd, Abu Abdallah Muhammad, *al-Tabaqāt al-Kubrā*, 2:2nd C:78

64 Ibn Sa'd, Abu Abdallah Muhammad, *al-Tabaqāt al-Kubrā*, 2:205; Ibn Hishām, 'Abd al-Malik, *al-Sīrah al-Nabawīyah*, 4:344; Ahmad b. Hanbal, *Musnad*, 6:62, 242 & 247; Tabarī, Muhammad ibn Jarīr, *Tārīkh ar-Rusul wa'l-Mulūk*, 3:313.

[3:144] And Muhammad is only an apostle; all the [other] apostles have passed away before him: if, then, he dies or is slain, will you turn about on your heels? But he that turns about on his heels can in no wise harm God - whereas God will requite all who are grateful [to Him].

As stated earlier, the sacred law or dispensation was revealed unto the Prophet ﷺ with two different kinds of revelation: Quranic Revelation and Explicatory Revelation [see Figure 1, below].

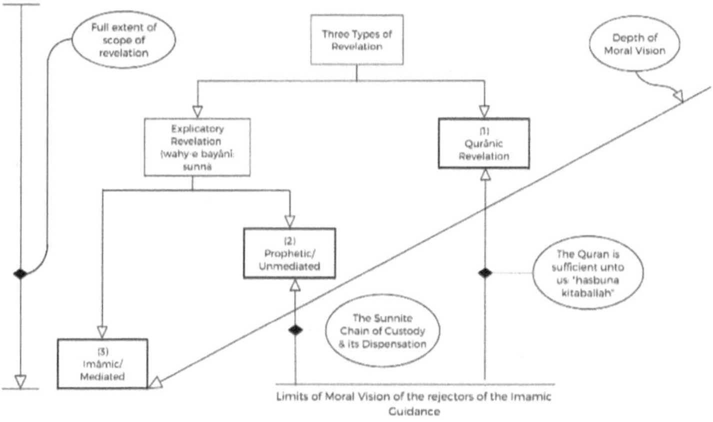

Figure 1: The Scope of Islamic Revelation

Taken from Blake Archer Williams's *Creedal Foundations of Walīyic Islam*
(but based on Allāma Askari's own work)

1. Quranic Revelation, which consists of the text of the Quran which has reached us unchanged from the time of the Prophet ﷺ, and all of whose words are from God ﷻ, which inform us about the principles of the sacred law (*sharīa*), namely, the oneness of creatorship, and the exclusivity of providential lordship (of the Lawgiver), about the Return [to our Maker], about the Gathering [on the Day of Resurrection], and [Judgment] and the Reckoning concerning right and wrong, and the commissioning of prophets to prophethood, and the obligation to obey them, from Adam, [the first prophet, to [Muhammad ﷺ] the last [prophet]; and all of the ordinances of Islam and its codes of conduct such as the five daily ritual devotions, the major pilgrimage (*hajj*), struggling in God's cause (*jihād*), fasting, paying the purifying

alms (*zakat*), and the fifth share (*khums*);[65] and ordinances having to do with the moral stewardship of the community (*ahkām-e nizāratī*) such as *al-amr bi'l-ma'rūf wa an-nahy anil-munkar* which is a pillar of the religion and which refers to the imperative to enjoin the doing of that which is right and to forbid the doing of that which is wrong.

2. Explicatory Revelation, which is a [type of] revelation that was revealed together with its Quranic counterpart, and which had an explicatory function concerning the Quranic Revelations that it was revealed with. For example, on the day that the Sermon of Ghadir Khumm was delivered, when the following verse was revealed,

۞ يَا أَيُّهَا الرَّسُولُ بَلِّغْ مَا أُنزِلَ إِلَيْكَ مِن رَّبِّكَ ۖ وَإِن لَّمْ تَفْعَلْ فَمَا بَلَّغْتَ رِسَالَتَهُ ۚ وَاللَّهُ يَعْصِمُكَ مِنَ النَّاسِ ۗ إِنَّ اللَّهَ لَا يَهْدِي الْقَوْمَ الْكَافِرِينَ ﴿٦٧﴾

[5:67] O Apostle! Announce all that has been bestowed from on high upon thee by thy Sustainer: for unless thou doest it fully, thou wilt not have delivered His message [at all].

An explicatory revelation was revealed along with the above verse

يَا أَيُّهَا الرَّسُولُ بَلِّغْ مَا أُنزِلَ إِلَيْكَ في علي... ﴿٦٧﴾

O Apostle! Announce all that has been bestowed from on high upon thee by thy Lord and Sustainer *concerning Ali.*[66]

Thus, the words "concerning Ali" are an explicatory revelation which the Prophet ﷺ explicated in his own words and which have reached us via the hadith report corpus. As such, the words

[65] *Khums* is the Arabic word for 'one-fifth'. In Shī'a law, one-fifth of certain items which a person acquires as wealth must be paid as a tax on a yearly basis to the Imam, or, in his absence, to a religious authority of one's choosing.
[66] Majlisī, Allāma Muhammad Bāqir, *Bihār al-Anwār,* 37:155 & 37:189; Hākim al-Haskānī al-Neyshāpūrī, *al-Mustadrak 'Alā's-Sahīhayn,* 1:189 & 1:190; Ibn Asākir, *at-Tārīkh al-Madīna*[t] *ad-Damishq,* hadith #451; Wāḥidī, 'Alī ibn Aḥmad, *Asbāb al-Nuzūl,* p. 135; Suyūṭī, Jalāl al-Dīn 'Abd al-Raḥmān, *al-Durr al-Manthūr fī al-Tafsīr bi-al-Ma'thūr,* 2:298; Shawkānī, Muḥammad, *Fatḥ al-Qadīr,* 2:57; Neyshāpūrī, Nizām'ad-dīn Hasan, *Gharā'ib al-Qur'ān wa Raghā'ib al-Furqān* (*Tafsīr al- Neyshāpūrī*), 6:194.

"concerning Ali" are revelations from God ﷻ. The Prophet ﷺ never spoke 'out of his own desire', just as Almighty God ﷻ has stated concerning this matter:

وَمَا يَنطِقُ عَنِ الْهَوَىٰ ﴿٣﴾ إِنْ هُوَ إِلَّا وَحْيٌ يُوحَىٰ ﴿٤﴾

[53:3] and neither does he speak out of his own desire: [53:4] that [which he conveys to you] is but [a divine] inspiration with which he is being inspired –

And Almighty God ﷻ states the matter more definitively here:

تَنزِيلٌ مِّن رَّبِّ الْعَالَمِينَ ﴿٤٣﴾ وَلَوْ تَقَوَّلَ عَلَيْنَا بَعْضَ الْأَقَاوِيلِ ﴿٤٤﴾ لَأَخَذْنَا
مِنْهُ بِالْيَمِينِ ﴿٤٥﴾ ثُمَّ لَقَطَعْنَا مِنْهُ الْوَتِينَ ﴿٤٦﴾ فَمَا مِنكُم مِّنْ أَحَدٍ عَنْهُ
حَاجِزِينَ ﴿٤٧﴾

[69:43] [it is] a revelation from the Sustainer of all the worlds. [69:44] Now if he [whom We have entrusted with it] had dared to attribute some [of his own] sayings unto Us, [69:45] We would indeed have seized him by his right hand, [69:46] and would indeed have cut his life-vein. [69:47] and none of you could have saved him!

Thus, Quranic Revelation consists of the revelations that constitute the Quranic text, all of whose words come [unmediatedly] from God ﷻ, and which no one can produce a *surah* of it, even if be a *surah* that is as small as Surah al-Kawthar.[67] As such, it is the living miracle of the Prophet ﷺ for whose preservation God ﷻ Himself has taken responsibility:

إِنَّا نَحْنُ نَزَّلْنَا الذِّكْرَ وَإِنَّا لَهُ لَحَافِظُونَ ﴿٩﴾

[15:9] Behold, it is We Ourselves who have bestowed from on high, step by step, this reminder? and, behold, it is We who shall truly guard it [from all corruption].

---

[67] See Sura al-Baqara 23-24 (2:23-24).

But Explicatory Revelation differs from Quranic revelation in that the content and meaning of the revelation is from God ﷻ, but their words are that of the Prophet's ﷺ ; and it is not conditioned on a challenge as to its miraculous nature, and its function is to explicate the Quranic verses in the words of the Prophet ﷺ, just as Almighty God ﷻ has stated:

بِالْبَيِّنَاتِ وَالزُّبُرِ ۗ وَأَنزَلْنَا إِلَيْكَ الذِّكْرَ لِتُبَيِّنَ لِلنَّاسِ مَا نُزِّلَ إِلَيْهِمْ وَلَعَلَّهُمْ يَتَفَكَّرُونَ ﴿٤٤﴾

[16:44] [and they will tell you that their prophets, too, were but mortal men whom We had endowed] with all evidence of the truth and with books of divine wisdom. And upon thee [too] have We bestowed from on high this reminder, *so that thou might make clear* unto mankind all that has ever been thus bestowed upon them, and that they might take thought.

The Prophet ﷺ recited every verse of the Quran, which he received by way of revelation, to whomsoever he explicated the verses of the revelation. He would also explicate the words that had been revealed unto him by God ﷻ to whoever it was that he explicated the Quranic Revelation to, thus completing that which was revealed to him by God ﷻ.

Abdullah ibn Mas'ūd, the great companion of the Prophet ﷺ, says: "I learned seventy surahs from the mouth of the Prophet ﷺ". For example, when a verse was revealed to the effect that: [17:60] ... *and so We have ordained that the vision which We have shown thee - as also the tree [of hell,] cursed in this Quran* (وَالشَّجَرَةَ الْمَلْعُونَةَ فِي الْقُرْآنِ ﴿٦٠﴾), the Prophet ﷺ would tell Abdullah ibn Mas'ūd that the reference of *shajara mal'ūna* is the Umayyad clan.[68]

It has been reported in the *Musnad* of Ahmad ibn Hanbal, in a report narrated by one of the companions of the Prophet ﷺ, that the companions of the Prophet ﷺ used to memorize the Quran in groups of ten verses, and that they would not start on the next group of ten verses unless they had learned the tenets and ordinances of the

[68] Suyūṭī, Jalāl al-Dīn 'Abd al-Raḥmān, *al-Durr al-Manthūr fī al-Tafsīr bi-al-Ma'thūr*, 4:191.

previous ten verses.[69] For example, if mention had been made of the prophets of the past, His Eminence the Prophet ﷺ would tell them the tales of the prophets. Or if a verse pertained to the Resurrection, the Prophet ﷺ would tell them what the Day of Judgment would be like. And if the revelation had something to do with the practical ordinances of Islam, such as ablution, the ritual devotions, and *tayammum*,[70] then the Prophet ﷺ would teach them the exact manner of how to perform these duties. As such, the Prophet ﷺ did not promulgate any Quranic verse without also providing the Explicatory Revelation that went along with the verse in order to explain its meaning to the community of the faithful.

For example, in teaching the following verse,

إِنَّمَا يُرِيدُ اللَّهُ لِيُذْهِبَ عَنكُمُ الرِّجْسَ أَهْلَ الْبَيْتِ وَيُطَهِّرَكُمْ تَطْهِيرًا ﴿٣٣﴾

[33:33] for God only wants to remove from you all that might be loathsome, O you Members of the [Prophet's] House, and to purify you to utmost purity.

The Prophet ﷺ would say "The People of my House are Ali ؑ, Fātima ؑ, Hasan ؑ, and Husain ؑ.[71] Similarly, with respect to the promulgation of the following verse,

إِن تَتُوبَا إِلَى اللَّهِ فَقَدْ صَغَتْ قُلُوبُكُمَا ۖ وَإِن تَظَاهَرَا عَلَيْهِ فَإِنَّ اللَّهَ هُوَ مَوْلَاهُ وَجِبْرِيلُ وَصَالِحُ الْمُؤْمِنِينَ ۖ وَالْمَلَائِكَةُ بَعْدَ ذَٰلِكَ ظَهِيرٌ ﴿٤﴾

---

[69] Ahmad b. Hanbal, *Musnad*, 5:410; Qurṭubī, Muḥammad ibn Aḥmad, *al-Jāmi' li-Aḥkām al-Qur'ān*, 1:39; Dhahabī, Shams al-Dīn Muhammad ibn Ahmad, *Ma'rifa al-Qurrā' al-Kubar*, p. 48; Haythamī, Ahmad Ibn-Hajar, *Majma' az-Zawāid wa Manba' al-Fawā'id*, 1:165; Ṭabarī, Muḥammad ibn Jarīr, *Jāmi' al-Bayān fī Tafsīr al-Qur'ān*, 1:27; Muttaqī al-Hindī, *Kanz al-U'mmāl*, hadiths 4213 & 4215.

[70] [*Tayammum*: ritual purification with sand when water is not available.]

[71] Hākim al-Haskānī an-Neyshāpūrī, *al-Mustadrak 'Alā's-Sahīhayn*, 3:147; Muslim ibn al-Ḥajjāj, *Ṣaḥīḥ Muslim*, 7:130; Bayhaqī, Ahmad ibn Husayn, *Sunan al-Kubrā*, 2:149; Suyūṭī, Jalāl al-Dīn 'Abd al-Raḥmān, *al-Durr al-Manthūr fī al-Tafsīr bi-al-Ma'thūr*, and Ṭabarī, Muḥammad ibn Jarīr, *Jāmi' al-Bayān fī Tafsīr al-Qur'ān*, under verse 133 of Surah al-Ahzāb, and Zamakhshari, Ab'al-Qāsim Mahmūd ibn Umar, *al-Kashshāf* under the Ayat al-Mubāhila; and Ibn Athīr, 'Alī ibn Muḥammad, *Usd al-Ghābah fī Ma'rifat al-Ṣaḥābah*, 2:20.

[66:4] [Say, O Prophet:] "Would that you two turn unto God in repentance, for the hearts of both of you have swerved [from what is right]! And if you uphold each other against him [who is God's message-bearer, know that] God Himself is his Protector, and [that,] therefore, Gabriel, and all the righteous among the believers and all the [other] angels will come to his aid."

The Prophet ﷺ would say that the pair referred to in the revelation are the wives of the Prophet ﷺ, the Mother of the Faithful 'Āisha, and the Mother of the Faithful Hafsa.[72] In teaching these kinds of revelation, the Prophet ﷺ would teach their meanings [or referents], and the teaching of practical matters was such that when, for example, a revelation was revealed that had a practical application such as the following verse,

أَقِمِ الصَّلَاةَ لِدُلُوكِ الشَّمْسِ إِلَىٰ غَسَقِ اللَّيْلِ وَقُرْآنَ الْفَجْرِ ۖ إِنَّ قُرْآنَ
الْفَجْرِ كَانَ مَشْهُودًا ﴿٧٨﴾

[17:78] Be constant in [thy] prayer from the time when the sun has passed its zenith till the darkness of night, and [be ever mindful of its] recitation at dawn: for, behold, the recitation [of prayer] at dawn is indeed witnessed [by all that is holy].

The Prophet ﷺ would teach the believers how the five turns of the ritual devotions were to be performed and what utterances should be mentioned at what point of the rite. And in the verse that states,

يَا أَيُّهَا الَّذِينَ آمَنُوا إِذَا قُمْتُمْ إِلَى الصَّلَاةِ فَاغْسِلُوا وُجُوهَكُمْ وَأَيْدِيَكُمْ
إِلَى الْمَرَافِقِ وَامْسَحُوا بِرُءُوسِكُمْ وَأَرْجُلَكُمْ إِلَى الْكَعْبَيْنِ ۚ ... ﴿٦﴾

[5:6] O you who have attained to faith! When you are about to pray, wash your face, and your hands and arms up to the elbows, and pass your [wet] hands lightly over your head and your feet up to the ankles...

---

[72] Bukhārī, Muḥammad ibn Ismā'īl, *Ṣaḥīḥ al-Bukhārī*, 3:137-138; Muslim ibn al-Ḥajjāj, *Ṣaḥīḥ Muslim*, 2:1108 & 2:1111.

The Prophet ﷺ would demonstrate what was meant by the revelation and how the ritual ablution was to be performed, and the kind of water that was to be used.

In all these instances, everything that the Prophet ﷺ taught the Companions with respect to the meaning of the verses and their interpretations was redacted by any of the Companions who could write and who had heard the Prophet ﷺ explain the meaning of the verses. Therefore, all of the Companions who could write had redacted the entirety of the Quran, together with the interpretation of all of the verses that they had personally heard the Prophet ﷺ explain. Needless to say, the interpretation of each and every verse was not written in the Quran codices of each Companion [who could write]; but the Quran that was kept in the Prophet's house did indeed contain *all* of the explicatory revelation as well. In other words, this Quran consisted of the complete Quranic revelations, as well as the complete explicatory revelations.

To be sure: every time a unit of revelation (*āya*) was revealed, the Prophet ﷺ would have each of the companions who were close to the Prophet ﷺ and knew how to write, redact the revelation together with the explanations of the verses that had been revealed to the Prophet ﷺ on whatever was at hand – be it a piece of parchment, a piece of wood, or the shoulder blade of sheep or a camel, or whatever else was available to them at the time. These redactions were kept by the Prophet ﷺ in his own house.

At the time of his death, the Prophet ﷺ stipulated to Ali ؑ as follows: "After preparing my body for burial, refrain from donning a cloak and going outside the house until you have finished [the task of] collecting and collating this Quran.[73] Ali ؑ pierced holes in the material (parchment, a piece of wood, or the shoulder blade of sheep or a camel) that the verses of the Quran were written on, and ran threads through them, and thus collected the verses of every surah together with their [prophetic] interpretations and explications. This work started on a Wednesday (the day after the Prophet's burial) and was completed by Friday.

[73] Majlisī, Allāma Muhammad Bāqir, *Bihār al-Anwār*, 92:48 & 92:51-52, quoting Qomī, 'Alī ibn Ibrāhīm *Tafsīr al-Qomī*, p. 745; 'Ayni, Badr'ad-dīn, *'Umdat al-Qārī*, 20:16; Ibn Hajar, Ahmad ibn Ali al-Asqalāni, *Fath al-Bārī fī Sharh Sahīh al-Bukhārī*, 10:386;
Suyūṭī, Jalāl al-Dīn 'Abd al-Raḥmān, *al-Itqān fī 'Ulūm al-Qur'ān*, 1:59.

His Eminence Alī ibn Abī-Tālib ﷺ took that Quran to the mosque on Friday, with the help of his freedman Qanbar, where the faithful had gathered for the Friday congregational prayers at the Prophet's Mosque. The Imam said to them, "This is the Quran that was in the house of the Prophet that I have brought for you." They responded by saying, "We have no need for this Quran; we have our own Quran! His Eminence Alī ibn Abī-Tālib ﷺ said, "[In that case,] you will no longer see this Quran."[74]

That Quran, which contained the explicatory commentary and interpretation of all of the verses, was then passed on from hand to hand by the hands of Alī ibn Abī-Tālib's ﷺ eleven progeny and is currently in the hands of His Eminence the Mahdi ﷺ, who shall reveal it when he reappears.[75] The Quran that we now possess is the same Quran that existed at the time of the Prophet ﷺ, with the difference that it does not contain the explicatory revelation and commentary

---

[74] Shahrastānī, Muhammad ibn Abdul-Karīm, *Mafātīh al-Asrār wa Masābīh al-Abrār fī Tafsīr al-Qur'ān*, page 15 of the introduction. The text of the hadith report is as follows:

لمّا فرغ من جمعه اخرجه هو (ع) و غلامه قنبر الى النّاس و هم فى المسجد يحملانه و لا يقلانه. و قيل انّه كان حمل بعير. و قال لهم هذا كتاب الله كما انزل الله على محمّد (ص) جمعته بين اللّوحين. فقالوا: ارفع مصحفك لا حاجة بنا اليه. فقال (ع): و لله لا ترونه بعد هذا ابدا، انّما كان علىّ ان اخبركم به حين جمعته فرجع الى بيته.

The story is described in greater detail and explicitness on pages 18-19 of *The Book of Sulaym ibn Qays al-Hilāli.* A portion of the report is as follows:

فجمعه فى ثوب واحد و ختمه ثمّ خرج الى النّاس و هم يجتمعون مع ابى بكر فى مسجد رسول الله (ص) فنادى علىّ (ع) باعلى صوته: ايّها النّاس انّى لم ازل منذ قبض رسول الله (ص) مشغولا بغسله ثمّ بالقرآن حتّى جمعته كلّه فى هذا الثّوب الواحد، فلم ينزل الله على رسول الله آية الّا و قد جمعتها و ليست منه آية الّا و قد اقرأنيها رسول الله (ص) و علّمنى تأويلها. ثمّ قال لهم علىّ (ع) لئلّا تقولوا غدا انّا كنّا عن هذا غافلين. ثمّ قال لهم علىّ (ع): لا تقولوا يوم القيامة انّى لم ادعكم الى نصرتى و لم اذكّركم حقّى و لم ادعكم الى كتاب الله من فاتحته الى خاتمته. فقال له عمر: ما اغنانا بما معنا من القرآن ممّا تدعونا اليه. ثمّ دخل علىّ (ع) بيته.

(To get acquainted with the degree of the credibility of *The Book of Sulaym ibn Qays al-Hilāli* and other hadith reports that are included in the books of the School of the Caliphs [the Sunni corpus] on this subject, see the author's *Mu'ālim al-Madrisatayn*, 2: 396-408.)

[75] Kolaynī, Shaykh Muhammad b. Ya'qūb, *'Usūl al-Kāfī*, 2:633, hadith #23. (For hadith reports wherein the [Shi'a] Imams attribute their knowledge to the Commander of the Faithful [Ali ibn Abī-Tālib], and through him, to the Prophet ﷺ, cf. the author's *Mu'ālim al-Madrisatayn*, 2:312-320.)

[that was provided by the Prophet ﷺ]. In other words, it consists only of the Quranic revelation and is devoid of any explicatory revelation.[76]

But why did they not accept the Quran which the Commander of the Faithful ﷺ had compiled, which, in addition to the Quranic verses, included the interpretation and explication of the meaning of the verses as revealed to the Prophet ﷺ? The reason is that the explicatory revelations that were revealed to the Prophet ﷺ and which consisted of his words and were considered to be hadith reports that explicated the verses of the Quran, there were certain matters that went against the policy of the incumbent statesmen and which precluded the continuation of their reign. For example, as mentioned earlier, it was revealed to the Prophet ﷺ that the following verse [17:60] ... *as also the tree [of hell,] cursed in this Quran* (وَالشَّجَرَةَ الْمَلْعُونَةَ فِي الْقُرْآنِ), was a reference to the Umayyads; and this [revealed explication] had been recorded on the scrolls and papyri (*masāhif*). Given such a hadith report, Uthmān, Mu'āwiya, Yazīd, Walīd and their ilk could no longer justify their reigns. Another example consists of verses of Surah at-Tahrīr in which

[76] Abu Bakr ordered that a Quran be redacted that does not contain any commentary. The work on this started during the reign of Abu Bakr and was completed during Umar's caliphate. Umar left this Quran with Hafsa. During Uthmān's reign, because the Companions came to oppose him and recited verses to him in which the Umayyads were the subject of reproach and which had been recorded in their [personal] scrolls (*mushaf*; pl. *masāhif*) on which they relied, 'Uthmān took the commentary-free Qur'an from Hafsa and ordered seven copies to be made of it. He sent a copy each to Mecca, Yemen, Damascus, Homs, Kufa and Basra, and kept one copy in Medina. Then he ordered the Companions to burn the *masāhif*, which contained the text of the Qur'an along with the interpretation of the verses that they had heard the Prophet make, which is why he was called the Burner of the Scrolls (*harrāq al-masāhīf*). Abdullah ibn Mas'ūd was the only companion who refused to give up his *mushaf*, so, acting at the behest of the Umayyads, the narrators of hadith reports [dutifully] fabricated and narrated false hadith reports about him. The Quran that is presently in the possession of Muslims today is the same Quran that was reproduced during 'Uthmān's reign, and the text is the same as that which was revealed to the Final Prophet ﷺ, and does not have any words added or subtracted, or relocated. The only thing that they did was to eliminate the 'Explicatory Revelation' (*wahy-e bayānī*, see figure 1, above). For a detailed discussion of this issue, cf. Askari, Allāma Murtaḍā, *al-Qurān al-Karīm wa Riwāyāt al-Madrisatayn*, 1:264-277 & 2:71-86. [Until this valuable work is translated, those who are interested can refer to Section 4.4.4 (Explicatory Revelation: the Jāmi'a) in my *Creedal Foundations of Walīyic Islam*, which is based on Allāma Askari's work and research. There is also the booklet *Imamic Revelation*, which is taken from my *Creedal Foundations* – Tr.]

the two women are 'Āisha and Hafsa, below the verse [ياأيها الذّين آمنوا لاترفعوا أصْوَاتَكم فوق صَوْتِ الٰ نبی ...] (Al-Hujrat: 2) It has come to be revealed in the honor of Abū Bakr and Umar. The first ten verses at the beginning of the chapter called The Foreswearal (*Sūra*ᵗ *at-Tahrīm*) are another case in point. These verses have a very threatening tone whose referents are 'Āisha and Hafsa.[77] Or the following verse that was revealed about Abū Bakr and Umar:[78]

يَا أَيُّهَا الَّذِينَ آمَنُوا لَا تَرْفَعُوا أَصْوَاتَكُمْ فَوْقَ صَوْتِ النَّبِيِّ وَلَا تَجْهَرُوا لَهُ بِالْقَوْلِ كَجَهْرِ بَعْضِكُمْ لِبَعْضٍ أَن تَحْبَطَ أَعْمَالُكُمْ وَأَنتُمْ لَا تَشْعُرُونَ ﴿٢﴾

[[49:2] O you who have attained to faith! Do not raise your voices above the voice of the Prophet, and neither speak loudly to him, as you would speak loudly to one another, lest all your [good] deeds come to naught without your perceiving it.

Or there are the first ten verses at the beginning of the chapter named The Foreswearal (*Sūra*ᵗ *at-Tahrīm*). When these verses were revealed, the Prophet ﷺ entrusted the verses to Abū Bakr and Umar to take to Mecca, and to promulgate them amongst the polytheists during the Major Pilgrimage (*Hajj*). At that point, a non-Quranic revelation was revealed instructing the Prophet ﷺ that either he should explicate these verses himself, or have one who is "of you" [= of his House]. Therefore, the Prophet ﷺ sent Ali ibn Abi Talib ﵇ to take those verses from Abū Bakr and Umar, and that Ali ﵇ himself should take the verses to Mecca and promulgate them amongst the polytheists during the *Hajj* Pilgrimage.[79] Or there are verses that were revealed that pertain to the Prophet ﷺ and his [purified and immaculate] House, such as The Āya of Purification (*Āya*ᵗ *ut-Tat'hīr*),[80] The Āya of Mutual Imprecation (the

---

77 ['Āisha and Hafsa are the daughters of Abū Bakr and Umar, respectively.]

78 Bukhārī, Muḥammad ibn Ismā'īl, *Ṣaḥīḥ al-Bukhārī*, Commentary on Surah al-Hujarāt, 3:190-191.

79 Cf. Askari, Allāma Murtaḍā, *al-Qurān al-Karīm wa Riwāyāt al-Madrisatayn*, 1:226-227 for a detailed bibliography of the sources on this subject.

80 [33:33] *God wishes to remove all filth and impurity from you, O People of House [of the Prophet], and to render you utterly free of all pollution.*

Mubāhila),[81] the verse that called for the Prophet ﷺ to deliver the Sermon of Ghadir Khumm,[82] and after the sermon having been delivered,[83] the Āya of Guardianship,[84] the Āya of Najwā,[85] and numerous other verses.[86]

In other words, not only did they not accept the Commander of the Faithful's Quran, but they also strove to collate the Quran absent its explicatory revelations supplement.[87] By so doing, they prevented the explication and propagation of hadith reports of the Prophet ﷺ, and acted to hide and falsify and distort these revelations.[88]

What is meant here by *khilāfa* (caliph) is the successor to the Messenger of God ﷺ (*khilāfa ar-rasūl*), that is, the one who succeeds the Prophet ﷺ in taking to the helm of the ship of state and is the ostensible ruler. The meaning of the term is not rooted in the etymological sense of the word, nor does it have any Islamic signification, but is something that has been made up by the leaders of the School of the Caliphs after the Prophet ﷺ because the word *khilāfa*

---

81 [3:61] *And if anyone should argue with thee about this [truth] after all the knowledge that has come unto thee, say: "Come! Let us summon our sons and your sons, and our women and your women, and ourselves and yourselves.*

82 [5:67] *O Apostle! Announce all that has been bestowed from on high upon thee by thy Sustainer: for unless thou doest it fully, thou wilt not have delivered His message [at all]. And God will protect thee from [unbelieving] men: behold, God does not guide people who refuse to acknowledge the truth.*

83 [5:3] *Today have I perfected your religious law for you, and have bestowed upon you the full measure of My blessings, and willed that self-surrender unto Me shall be your religion. As for him, however, who is driven [to what is forbidden] by dire necessity and not by an inclination to sinning -behold, God is much-forgiving, a dispenser of grace.*

84 [5:55] *Behold, your only helper is God, His Apostle, and those who have attained to faith - those that are constant in prayer, and render the purifying dues while bowing down [before God].*

85 [58:12] *O you who have attained to faith! Whenever you [intend to] consult the Apostle, offer up something in charity on the occasion of your consultation: this will be for your own good, and more conducive to your [inner] purity. Yet if you are unable to do so, [know that,] verily, God is much-forgiving, a dispenser of grace.*

86 Cf. Askari, Allāma Murtaḍā, *al-Qurān al-Karīm wa Riwāyāt al-Madrisatayn*, 1:218-248 for a detailed bibliography of the sources on this subject.

87 Op. cit. 1:264-274 and 2:413-417.

88 Op. cit. 2:417-431, 2:510-515, 2:572-582; Askari, Allāma Murtaḍā, *Mu'ālim al-Madrisatayn*, 1:329-392, 1:402-483; Askari, Allāma Murtaḍā, *Ahādith Umm al-Mu'minīn 'Āisha'*, volume 2 *passim*; and Askari, Allāma Murtaḍā, *Naqsh-e A'imma dar ihyā'-e dīn*, 2:5 and hadith #9.

(caliph) means successor to a person; that is, the one who continues that person's work in his absence.

According to the Holy Qur'an's text, the Holy Prophet's main work and all the divine prophets is to propagate the religion of God ﷻ to the people: The Messenger is not the informant [Nahl: 35] and not the government. Therefore, most prophets did not have an apparent government, such as Jesus, John, Zechariah and Noah (peace be upon them).

Also, this is not the meaning of the *shar'ī* term, and in the hadith of the Prophet ﷺ, the caliph of the Messenger refers to a person who narrates the hadith and the Sunnah of the Prophet ﷺ. (Meanings of *Al-Akhbar as-Saduq* pp. 374-375; from not attending the jurisprudent 4/420; *Al-Fatah Al-Kabir,* Suyuti 4/233; the honor of the companions of the hadith Khatib Baghdadi, p. 30) Because the Caliph of God ﷻ is said to be a person whom God ﷻ has appointed to reveal the religion of God through revelation (if he is the Prophet ﷺ) or through the Prophet ﷺ (if he is the guardian of the Prophet ﷺ like the Imams ﷷ), to take and inform the people. Of course, governance is also one of the affairs of this divine caliphate, and the Caliph of God ﷻ himself has no duty to take it unless the people gather around him and ask him to rule and help him in this matter, like the Prophet ﷺ. The Most Noble Prophet ﷺ was able to form a government in Medina thanks to the allegiance and help of the people, but did not do so in Mecca (because the people there did not want him and did not help him). The Prophet ﷺ was thus satisfied with his main duty, which was to preach the religion of God ﷻ. The situation was the same with Amir al-Mu'minin Ali ibn Abi Talib ﷷ. His main duty and that of all the Imams ﷷ, like the Prophet ﷺ, was to preserve the religion of God ﷻ and communicate it to the people, and of course, if the people wanted and helped him, he would rise up to the government. And this was obligatory for them, but the people did not want to and did not come except for three people (*Tarikh Ya'qubi* 2/105; *Sharh Nahj al-Balaghah Ibn Abi Al-Hadid* 2/4) or four or five people (*Sharh Nahj al-Balaghah Ibn Abi Al-Hadid,* Tahiqiq Muhammad Abu 47/2 الفضل ابراهيم); As the Imam himself said: But after 25 years, that is, after 'Uthmān was killed, because the people came to the house of the Imam and asked him to take over the government, he revolted (*Sharh Nahj al-Balaghah Ibn Abi Al-Hadid* 2/50; Ibn Jawzi, Chapter 6). This act of Hazrat Amir ﷷ was exactly what the Prophet ﷺ had asked of him: If the people's attack you, let them know what is behind them ... "(*Usd Al-Ghaba* 4/31).

Now, if the name of Amir al-Mu'minin ☪ is mentioned here as one of the candidates for the caliphate, it does not mean that he himself wanted this matter and the insurgent to take it, but it expresses the opinion of a few people in the society of that day. It is Medina, which was due to the fact that Imam Ali ☪ was considered the guardian of the Messenger of God ☪ and the government was considered as being one of his affairs and rights (such as Salman, Abu Dharr, Miqdad and Ammar) or due to prejudices. The family (such as Abbas, the uncle of the Prophet ☪) or tribal prejudices (such as Abu Sufyan) demanded the apparent rule of Amir al-Mu'minin ☪.

5. Candidates for the succession (*khilāfa*) [89] after the death of the Prophet ☪ on the day of the *Saqīfa*

5.1 His Eminence Alī ibn Abī-Tālib ☪, who had been appointed by God ☪ to be the leader of the community of the faithful (*umma*ʰ), and the Prophet ☪ had stated this fact.

5.2 Sa'd ibn Ubāda, who was the leader of most but not all of the 'Helpers' (the *ansār*)

5.3 Abū Bakr, who was the candidate of a throng of the Emigrants of the Quraysh, but not all of them.

6. The Slogans of the Saqīfa
6.1 The Slogans of the 'Helpers' (the Ansār)
1. The 'Helpers' helped Islam.[90]
2. The 'Helpers' drew out their swords in order to establish the Way of the Prophet ☪.[91]
3. The city of Medina is the city of the 'Helpers'.[92]

6.2 The Slogans of the 'Emigrants' (the Quraysh)[93]
1. The Prophet ☪ is from the tribe of the 'Emigrants.'
2. The Arabs would not accept a leader other than the tribe of the Quraysh; therefore, the leader has to be from the Quraysh.

---

[89] 36
[90] Askari, Allāma Murtaḍā, *Abdullāh ibn Sabā*, 1:113.
[91] Askari, Allāma Murtaḍā, *Abdullāh ibn Sabā*, 1:113.
[92] Askari, Allāma Murtaḍā, *Abdullāh ibn Sabā*, 1:115.
[93] Askari, Allāma Murtaḍā, *Abdullāh ibn Sabā*, 1:115-116.

7. The Saqīfa coup d'etat and the pledge of allegiance given to Abū Bakr

After the passing of the Messenger of God ﷺ, the Ansār gathered at the Banī Sā'ida's portico (*saqīfa*). The Khazraj tribe[94] wanted Sa'd ibn 'Abāda to succeed the Prophet ﷺ.[95] It is not as if the Khazraj was not aware that the Prophet ﷺ had appointed a successor, and acted in ignorance. Not at all! They knew full well that the Prophet ﷺ had appointed a legatee and successor (*wasī*),[96] and acted in the best interest of their tribe [rather than in the interest of the community of believers].

Meanwhile, a group of the 'Emigrants' who had heard the news joined them.[97] All of them left the body of the Prophet ﷺ among a handful of the members of the Prophet's family, preferring to go over to the portico and join the fight over who was to succeed the Prophet ﷺ. The Aws tribe[98] were against Sa'd ibn 'Abāda succeeding the Prophet ﷺ. Among the Khazraj tribe, Bashīr ibn Sa'd, who was one of the elders of their tribe, envied Sa'd ibn 'Abāda and was not in favor of his succeeding to the office vacated by the Prophet's ﷺ passing.[99]

---

[94] The name of one of the two major clans in Medina

[95] Askari, Allāma Murtaḍā, *Abdullāh ibn Sabā*, 1:113.

[96] *Wasīy*; plural, *awsīā*: In his definition of this technical tern, A. A. A. Feyzee tell us that "the word *wasī* is untranslatable in English, except in a legal context, where executor is an exact rendering. "Plenipotentiary" or "vicegerent" may also be used in certain cases." It has in Shi'a works the following chief attributes: (1) *wasī* is a person who is, by command of Allah, specially instructed and authorized by the *nabī* (prophet) to perform certain acts. These are considered to be the commands of the *nabī* and the duties of the *wasī*. (2) During the lifetime of the *nabī*, the *wasī* holds a position next after him as vicegerent; and for particular religious and political functions, he acts as his plenipotentiary. (3) After the death of the *nabī*, the *wasī* is his *khalīfa* (successor), his executor and the leader of the community, being the most excellent of men after the Prophet. The distinction between him and the Imam is that the latter has not had the advantage of personal intimacy and direct instruction from the *nabī*; although in the absence of the *nabī*, the *wasī* and the Imam have similar powers. Thus, *wasī* is superior to Imam, Ali ؑ being superior to all Imams.

[97] People such as Abu Bakr, Umar, Abū-'Ubayda ibn al-Jarrāh, Mughayra ibn Sha'ba, and Abd'ar-Rahmān ibn 'Awf. Askari, Allāma Murtaḍā, *Abdullāh ibn Sabā*, 1:113-115.

[98] The name of one of the two major clans in Medina

[99] Ibn Abī'l-Hadīd, Abdul-Hamīd, *Sharh Nahj al-Balāgha*, 2:2, quoting Jawharī's *Saqīfa*.

8 The Saqīfa, according to the Hadith Report in *Sahīh Bukhari*

According to a Hadith Report in *Sahīh Bukhari*, 'Umar has described the story in the following way:

When the Prophet ﷺ passed away, one of the news reports that we received was that the 'Helpers' (the Ansār) had gathered at the portico (*saqīfa*) of the Banī Sā'ida. I suggested to Abū Bakr that we too should join our Ansār brothers. Abū Bakr agreed, and the two of us made out way to the Saqīfa. Ali and Zubayr and their companions were not with us. When we reached *saqīfa*, we discovered that the Ansar tribe had brought a man with them who was feverish and wrapped in a kilim. We were told that he was Sa'd ibn 'Abāda. We sat next to him, and their speaker stood up and, after praising and thanking God ﷻ, he said: "We are the Helpers of God ﷻ. We are the concentrated fighting force of Islam; and you, the group of immigrants, are a paltry number of people..." and so on.

I (Umar) wanted to say something in response to them, but Abū Bakr pulled my sleeve back and told me to hold back. Then he got up and spoke, and upon my oath before God ﷻ, he did not omit any of the points I wanted to make. He either said what I wanted to say or said something better. He said,

"O you people of the Ansār, there can be no doubt that you are indeed worthy of what you mentioned as your virtues and merits. But the matter of succession and the leadership of the community is something that can only belong to the tribe of Quraysh because the Quraysh are distinguished in terms of their honor and lineage among the Arab tribes. This is why I propose to you that it is in your own best interests to select one of these two people to the caliphate and to pledge allegiance to him."

Having said this, he took my hand and that of Abū Ubaydah's and offered us [as candidates for leadership] to them. It was only these last words of his that I did not like. At that point, one of the Ansār stood up and said: "I am like the stick with which camels scratch their own backs, and the tree under whose shade they take refuge.[100] [But be that as it

[100] The allegory refers to something that people take refuge to in times of hardship and difficulty. What the speaker is saying is that the people of his

may, I believe that] you Emigrants [should] choose a ruler for yourselves, and that we [should] choose a ruler for ourselves."

Following this oration, a clamor arose from the gathering, betraying the depth of division and factiousness that was present. I took advantage of this situation and asked Abū Bakr to extend his hand so that I could pledge allegiance to him. Abū Bakr extended his hand, and I pledged allegiance to him. After having done so, we rushed onto Sa'd ibn 'Abāda...

If someone pledges allegiance [to someone else] on the matter of the caliphate without consulting the other Muslims [of the community], do not follow him or the person to whom allegiance has been pledged, as both of them deserve to be killed.[101]

9. The Saqīfa, according to the Hadith Report in Tabari's *History*

Tabari writes in his *Tārikh* regarding the events of the *saqīfa* and the pledging of allegiance to Abū Bakr, as follows:

The Ansār tribe left the body of the Messenger of God ﷺ to his family so that his family could prepare the body for burial and see to its burial [on their own], and gathered in the *saqīfa* of the Bani Sā'ida [tribe] designated Sa'd ibn 'Abāda as their leader after the passing of the Prophet ﷺ. They had taken Sa'd ibn 'Abāda, who was ill, to the portico...

Sa'd ibn 'Abāda praised God ﷻ, mentioned the precedence of the Ansār in attaining to faith in Islam and [therefore] their superior rank in Islam, and recalled the help they gave to the Prophet ﷺ and his companions, and the wars they fought against the enemies of Islam, and emphasized the fact that the Prophet of God ﷺ passed away while he was well satisfied with the Ansār. Sa'd ibn 'Abāda closed by advising that the Ansār should take the helm of leadership and not to let anyone else do so.

---

tribe 'take refuge in' [= defer to] his vote, and that [as their leader] he is like a tree of life, whose protective shade is a refuge for the feeble and weary [in the desert sun]. – Tr.

[101] Bukhārī, Muḥammad ibn Ismā'īl, *Ṣaḥīḥ al-Bukhārī*, 4:119-120; Ibn Hishām, 'Abd al-Malik, *al-Sīrah al-Nabawīyah*, 4:336-338; Muttaqī al-Hindī, *Kanz al-U'mmāl*, 3:193, hadith #2326.

In response to Sa'd ibn 'Abāda's oration, all of the Ansār cried out: "Your opinion and thoughts are absolutely right, and your words are true and firmly grounded. We shall never do anything against your will, and will elect you to be our ruler."

After this definitive agreement, another issue was discussed, after which the hypothetical situation was discussed as to what they should say if the Quraysh Emigrants did not accept their decision, and declare that they were the first companions of the Prophet ﷺ, and state that they are of the same tribe as he is, and countermand the rightfulness of the Ansār's position. A group of the Ansār said that in that case, we will choose a leader for ourselves and you can choose a leader for yourselves. Sa'd ibn 'Abāda said: "And this would in itself be the first defeat and retreat."[102]

When the news of this gathering reached Abū Bakr and Umar's ears, they rushed to the Saqīfa together with Abū-Ubayda al-Jarrāh. Usayd ibn Huḍayr,[103] Ūwaym ibn Sā'ida,[104] and 'A'awl ibn 'Adī,[105] from the Banī Ajlān joined them to make sure that Sa'd ibn 'Abāda did not become vested in the office of the caliph. Mughīra ibn Shu'ba and Abd al-Rahman ibn Awf also joined their ranks there.

After having prevented Umar from speaking, Abū Bakr stood up, praised and thanked God ﷻ, and then mentioned the fact that the Emigrants had precedent over the Ansār because they were the first to enter into Islam compared with all of their other Arab compatriots, and in recognizing [the veracity of] the Prophet's mission and ministry. After making these points, he said,

"The emigrants were the first people on earth to worship God and to believe in the mission of the Prophet." Abū Bakr continued, "The Emigrants are close friends and relatives of the Prophet, which is why they are more deserving of taking over the governance [of the community of the faithful] after the passing of His Eminence the Prophet." Abū Bakr then said that only knaves and oppressors would disagree with his statements and position, and rise up in rebellion against Qurayshite rule. After having made these statements, Abū Bakr spoke of the virtues of the Ansār, and continued in this same vein: "Of

---

[102] Tabarī, Muhammad ibn Jarīr, *Tārīkh ar-Rusul wa'l-Mulūk*, events of the year 11 AH, hadith #838.
[103] 46
[104] 47
[105] 48

course, after the emigrants and those who have overtaken [other Muslims] in their Islam, no one has the high rank and status of the Ansār to our minds. Thus, let the business of government belong to the Quraysh, and let the Helpers have the high position and status within the ministry of the Prophet."

At this juncture, Hubāb ibn Munzir stood up and, addressing the Ansar said:

O assembly of Helpers (*ansār*), take charge of the affairs of state as these Emigrants live in your city and can only survive under the protective shade that you provide! And there is no one among them that will have the temerity to contravene your command. Therefore, avoid division and dissension among your own ranks, as this will lead to the destruction and corruption of your work, and it will lead you to failure, and leadership and governance will be taken from your clutches. If they do not submit and do not say anything other than what you have already heard them say, then we will choose a ruler from among ourselves, and let them choose a leader for themselves.

Here Umar stood up and said:

"This will never happen, just as two swords can never be placed in a single scabbard. Upon my word of honor with God, the Arab nation will never suffer taking on the yoke of your governance, given the fact that their prophet is other than from the Ansār. But the Arabs will not be against or act to intervene [in the affairs of state] when they are governed by one who is from the House of Prophethood. We have a decisive argument against anyone who acts against us, and that is, Who will [have the temerity to] take the governance [of the community of believers] out of our clutches and fight with us over it, when it is we who are the kith and kin of the Prophet, and are of his House? Only one who has lost his way, has been tainted with sin, or has [irredeemably] fallen into the whirlpool of perdition."[106]

---

[106] When the Commander of the Faithful [Ali ibn Abī-Tālib] heard about this need of the emigrants, he said, احتجّوا بالشّجرة و اضاعوا الثّمرة, which means, 'they resorted to the tree in their reasoning, but forgot about its fruit', referring to the fact that the Emigrants (the *muhājirūn*) reasoned with the Helpers (the *ansār*) that they have a greater right to the succession (because they are of the Quraysh and the Prophet was of the Quraysh also). The Commander of the

Hubāb ibn Munzir rose again and said:

"O assembly of Helpers (*ansār*), remain united and do not listen to the words of this man and his companions, for if you do not remain united, you will lose your right to rule [over yourselves]. If they do not accept your wishes, expel them from your lands and execute your words [by force of arms] and take charge of the affairs of state, for, by God, you are more deserving than them for the office of the caliphate. Recall that it was to the strikes of your swords that the unbelievers bowed down and deferred to and submitted and came to believe in this religion.

"I am like the stick with which camels scratch their own backs."[107] The reference is to someone whose opinion people take refuge in at times of hardship and difficulty, and who is like a tree under whose shade they take refuge. "I swear upon my oath before God if this is what you want, we will resume war and bloodshed again."[108]

Umar said: "If that were to happen, God would kill you."[109]
Hubāb ibn Munzir said: "God would kill *you*."

Seeing this state of affairs, Abū Ubaydah said to the Ansār: "O assembly of the Ansār, you were the first to rise up [in righteous insurrection against the old order] and come to the aid of the Messenger of God and defend Islam. [Therefore,] do not be the first to change the religion, which is the basis of the unity of the community of Muslims."

After the cunning words of Abū Ubaydah were delivered, Bashir ibn Sa'd al-Khazrajī[110] stood up and said:

Faithful is saying that based on that line of reasoning, he has a greater right to the succession, as he is of the House of the Prophet himself, and he is the fruit of that tree; but that the Emigrants chose to forget that, thereby violating his right.

[107] This is an Arab expression for someone who has gained experience through conflict.

[108] The exact text is the following: اما و الله لو شئتم لنعيدنّها جذعة.

[109] Umar was threatening murder.

[110] Bashir ibn Sa'd al-Khazrajī was the father of Nu'man ibn Bashīr, and was one of the elders of the Khazraj tribe. There was a history of envy between him and Sa'd ibn 'Ubāda - Ibn Abī'l-Hadīd, Abdul-Hamīd, *Sharh Nahj al-Balāgha*, 2:2-5.

O assembly of the Ansār, I swear upon my oath before God that we have attained a lofty [spiritual] station in fighting the idolaters and being pioneers in entering into Islam. Nor have we sought anything in doing so but the good pleasure of God and obeying the Prophet, longanimity, and working towards the purification of our souls. Therefore, it would not be appropriate for us, as a nation that has all these virtues over other peoples, to be arrogant and mean, and to use this [moral] capital as a means of earning worldly gains. God is our patron and provider of assistance (*walī*), and it is He who graces us. O people, know that Muhammad is from the Quraysh [tribe], and know that the members of his tribe are closer to him and more deserving than anyone else in taking over the leadership and reign [of his ministry and nation]. And I pray to God for Him never to see me engaged in a dispute with them [the tribe of Quraysh] in matters concerning governance. My advice to you, therefore, is for you to fear God too, and not oppose them, and do not quarrel with them in the matter of governance, and do not let there be any hostility between you."

When Bashir had finished his speech, Abū Bakr stood up and said: Here is Umar, and here is Abū Ubaydah; choose whichever one you want and pledge [your allegiance to him]; with [the presence of a leader as preeminent as] you [in our midst], we would never have the temerity to preempt you and to take on such a burden of responsibility.[111]

Abd al-Rahmān ibn 'Awf also stood up and, among other things, said, "O assembly of the Ansār, while it is true that you have a lofty [spiritual] station, one cannot find among your ranks someone such as Abū Bakr or Umar."

Munidhr ibn al-Larqam also stood up and faced Abd al-Rahmān ibn 'Awf and said, "We do not deny the preeminence of those whom you have named, especially since there is a man among them who, if he were to take the initiative to take over the affairs of governance, he would not be opposed by anyone. {The referent is Alī ibn Abī-Tālib ﷺ, according to Ya'qūbī's *Tārīkh* 2:103}.[112]

---

[111] و الله ما كنّا لنتقدمك و أنت صاحب رسول الله و ثاني اثنين

[112] That which appears in the brackets are Ya'qūbī's words; Ya'qūbī, Aḥmad ibn Isḥāq, *Tārīkh al-Ya'qūbī*, 2:123.

At this point, some of the Ansār raised their voices, stating that they would only swear allegiance to Ali. ʻUmar himself says:

The sound and commotion of the audience arose every quarter, and words that were indistinct could be heard from every corner to the point that I was afraid that it would lead to dissension and become an obstacle to the progress of our business. That is why I said to Abū Bakr, "Extend your hand so that I can pledge allegiance to you."[113]

But before Umar could shake Abū Bakr's hand, he was preempted by Bashīr ibn Saʻd, who was the first person to shake Abū Bakr's hand and pledge allegiance to him.[114]

Munidhr ibn al-Larqam, who had seen the pledge taking place, shouted at Bashir: "O Bashir! O cursed of your family! Did you cut off your ties to your kin? And were you envious of your cousin coming to power?" To this Bashir said: "No, I swear upon my oath before God; but I did not want to transgress the rights of those for whom God has allowed [this]."

When the ʻAws tribe saw what Bashīr ibn Saʻd did and what the intentions of the Quraysh were, and when they also realized what the Khazraj tribe intended by bringing Saʻd ibn ʻAbāda to power, they addressed some of the other members of their tribe, (including Ūsayd ibn Khuḍayr, who was one of the elders of the ʻAws tribe) and said: "By

---

[113] After Umar was able to dissuade the Ansār from pledging allegiance to Saʻd ibn ʻUbāda, they turned their attention to Ali, so much so, in fact, that they said that they would only pledge allegiance to Ali. Umar was afraid of this attraction of the Ansār to Ali, and feared that if this session were to come to a close without reaching a conclusion, the Ansār would meet up with the Banī Hāshim, who would no longer be preoccupied with attending to the burial ceremonies for the burial of the Prophet ﷺ, at which point this handful of people (Abu Bakr, Umar, ʻUthmān, Abū Úbayda al-Jarrāh, and Sālim the freedman of Abī-Hudhayfa) would no longer be able to accede to the caliphate. He thus quickly urged them to pledge allegiance to Abu Bakr and brought the matter to a conclusion.

[114] The caliphs used to grant riches and positions of authority to three people of the Ansār on account of the help that they gave the in the Saqīfa. One of these was Bashīr ibn Saʻd al-Khazrajī, who was the first person to pledge allegiance to Abu Bakr. The second was Zaid ibn Thābit, who used to be appointed by Umar as his successor whenever he travelled [outside of Medina]. The third person was Hassān ibn Thābit, the renowned poet, who refrained from pledging allegiance to the Commander of the Faithful when he [Ali ibn Abī-Tālib] acceded to the caliphate – Mufīd, Shaykh Md. ibn Nuʻmān, *al-Irshād fī Maʻrifat Hujaj Allāh ʻal'al-ʻIbād*, 1:237.

God, if the Khazraj tribe takes over the caliphate, this honor will be theirs forever, and they will gloat over it and will never include you [= your interests] in their reign. So, get up and pledge allegiance to Abū Bakr."

Then they all stood up and pledged allegiance to Abū Bakr, and by doing so, thwarted the action of Sa'd ibn 'Abāda and the members of the Khazraj tribe who were attempting to take on the leadership of the community. The people gathered there rushed from all sides to pledge allegiance to Abū Bakr, and almost trampled Sa'd ibn 'Abāda (who was ailing) to death, such that one of his relatives shouted, "Be careful not to trample on Sa'd."

In response, Umar cried out, "Kill him! For [would that] God would kill him!" He then pushed the throng aside and reached Sa'd ibn 'Abāda

Then he pushed the people back and stood above Sa'd and said: "I wanted to kick you so much that there wouldn't be an unbroken bone in your body! Qais ibn Sa'd, who was standing over his father, grabbed Umar's beard and said: "By God, if you so much as remove a single hair from his head, you not a single healthy tooth will remain in your mouth!"

Abū Bakr also said to Umar: "Be calm, Umar. Moderation and flexibility are what is needed in such situations, not ferocity and vehemence." Upon hearing Abū Bakr's words, Umar turned his back on Qais and walked away from him. But Sa'd said to Umar: "I swear upon my oath before God, if I was not ill and I was able to get up, you would hear my [roar] so loud in the streets and alleys of Medina that you and your companions would hide in the thickets out of fear. And at the same time, I swear upon my oath before God, I would send you to those who, just until yesterday, were your underlings, not people over whom you reigned." Sa'd ibn 'Abāda then turned to his own people and said, "Take me back to my house." And his companions complied with his request.

Abū Bakr al-Jawhari has stated the following in his book *The Saqīfa*: On the day that the events occurred in the portico (*saqīfa*) of the Bani Sa'ida, i.e., on the same day that Umar pledged allegiance to Abū Bakr, Umar was wearing his sash and ran in front of Abū Bakr, shouting: "Attention! Attention! The people have pledged allegiance to Abū Bakr."[115]

In this way, the throng that accompanied Abū Bakr from the portico of the Bani Sa'ida would force anyone they came in contact with to pledge his allegiance.

Tabari' *History* continues the narrative as follows: The people of the Aslam tribe had all come to Medina to buy food and supplies on the day the events occurred in the portico of the Bani Sa'ida. Their presence in Medina had crowded the streets so much that it was difficult to cross the streets. Umar has made the following statement about the Aslam tribe: "I was not certain about whether we would be victorious [in our coup] until I saw that the Aslam tribe had come and filled the streets of Medina.[116]

10. The Role of the Aslam tribe in the Pledge of Allegiance to Abū Bakr

This story is narrated by Sheikh Mufid in his book *al-Jamal*. At that time, the whole of a given tribe from among the Arab nomads would come to the city as a whole to buy groceries and supplies. This was because the desert was unsafe, and if a small number of them came, [bandits] would take their supplies and kill them. So the tribesmen bought food and supplies all together at the same time. The men of the Aslam tribe had come to Medina from the desert to purchase food and supplies. By the time they entered Medina, allegiance to Abū Bakr had already taken place in the portico (*saqīfa*) of the Bani Sa'ida. Umar and some other people said to them, "Come and help us obtain pledges of allegiance to the successor (*khalīfa*; caliph) of the Prophet ﷺ, then we will give you free food and supplies. The men of the Aslam tribe were happy to hear this. They first pledged allegiance themselves, and then became a part of Abū Bakr's entourage.; They wrapped their Arab gowns around their waists and proceeded to fill the streets of Medina. Everywhere they went, (in the bazaar, on the street, etc.), they saw different people, every one of which they brought before Abū Bakr, in order for them to pledge allegiance to him. Thus, Abū Bakr became the caliph with the help of the Aslam tribe.[117]

---

[115] Quoted in Ibn Abī'l-Hadīd, Abdul-Hamīd, *Sharh Nahj al-Balāgha*, 1:133.
[116] Tabarī, Muhammad ibn Jarīr, *Tārīkh ar-Rusul wa'l-Mulūk*, 1:1843.
[117] Mufīd, Shaykh Muhammad ibn Nu'mān, *al-Jamal*, p. 43. Zubayr ibn Bakkār has also cited the hadith report that appears in Ibn Abī'l-Hadīd, Abdul-Hamīd,

11. The Reasons for the Selection of Abū Bakr to the Caliphate

Abū Bakr's companions have stated the reason that he was the Helpers' (*ansār*) choice for the Ansar to be the following. Since the Prophet ﷺ is from the tribe of Quraysh, his successor must also be from the Quraysh (this is according to the law of the Arabs).[118] The other reason was that Abū Bakr was a companion of the Prophet ﷺ who was one of the first people to enter into Islam.[119] His Eminence Alī ibn Abī-Tālib ؑ has something to say about this: "They based their justification of [the pledge of allegiance to Abū Bakr] by referring to the 'tree of prophethood' (which is from the Quraysh), but ignored its fruit (which was the cousin and son-in-law of the Prophet)."[120] They reasoned that they were from the lineage of the Prophet ﷺ, but they ignored the fruit of this lineage, which is the Bani Hāshim. The value of a date tree or a grape vine does not lie in its branches or foliage; rather, it lies in its fruit.

His Eminence Alī ibn Abī-Tālib ؑ also has something to say concerning Abū Bakr being the Prophet's ﷺ companion. This is what he said about [people] saying that Abū Bakr is the companion of the Prophet: "These people say that Abū Bakr should be the successor of the Prophet ﷺ because he was a companion of the Prophet ﷺ. But if that is the case, how is it, then, that they don't select one who was both a companion of the Prophet ﷺ as well as being his next of kin??" The reference is to himself, who was the cousin and son-in-law of the Prophet ﷺ as well as being a companion. We all know that His Eminence Alī ibn Abī-Tālib ؑ was a young child when the Prophet ﷺ took him from his father Abū Talib [who could not afford his upkeep], and raised him as his own son. We all know that Imam Ali was brought home by the Prophet ﷺ as a young child. Here he describes his upbringing at the hands of the Prophet ﷺ (in the sermon known as al-Qāsi'a):[121]

Sharh Nahj al-Balāgha, 6:287 in his *Muwaffaqīyāt*, 2:40: فقوى بهم– بني اسلم– ابو بكر و لم يعيّنا متى جاءت اسلم. See also, Tabarī, Muhammad ibn Jarīr, *Tārīkh ar-Rusul wa'l-Mulūk*, 1:1843.

[118] Bukhārī, Muḥammad ibn Ismā'īl, *Ṣaḥīḥ al-Bukhārī*, 4:120; Ibn Hishām, 'Abd al-Malik, *al-Sīrah al-Nabawīyah*, 4:339.

[119] Askari, Allāma Murtaḍā, *Abdullāh ibn Sabā*, p. 121, quoting Tabari.

[120] Ibn Abī'l-Hadīd, Abdul-Hamīd, *Sharh Nahj al-Balāgha*, 2:2.

[121] *Nahj al-Balāgha*, pp. 300-301 (The Qāsi'a Sermon – Sermon 192). See also Abduh's commentary on the *Nahj al-Balāgha*, 1:182.

And [all of] you are well aware of the intimacy of my familial relationship with the Prophet of God, and the special rank I enjoyed in his sight... When I was a child, he supervised my upbringing in his own house. He used to hug me and hold me close to his chest and place me beside him in his bed, bringing his body close to mine, and affording me [the unique opportunity] to take in the sweet fragrance [of his body] and to feel its warmth. [Sometimes] he would [even] feed me with food which he chewed [for me]... Every year he would go into seclusion [in a cave] in the mountain of Hirā, where none but I witnessed his presence. In those days, no household was ordered on [the basis of the teachings of] Islam except that of the Prophet of God's and [his wife Lady] Khadīja, and I, who was the third of this threesome.[122]

Until the passing of His Eminence the Prophet ﷺ, Alī ibn Abī-Tālib ؑ was always at his side. The Prophet's ﷺ blessed head was [resting] on the shoulders of Alī ibn Abī-Tālib ؑ when he passed away. Imam Ali was both the boon companion of the Prophet ﷺ as well as being his next of kin.[123] He followed the Prophet ﷺ like a shadow everywhere he went.

11. The pledge of allegiance on the part of the general public

After swearing allegiance to Abū Bakr in the portico (*saqīfa*) of the Bani Sā'ida, those who had pledged allegiance gleefully took him to the Prophet's mosque, as if he was a groom being taken to the bridal chamber. When Abū Bakr and his followers entered the mosque, the work of the succession was instituted.[124]

The mosque of the Prophet ﷺ was the seat of government. It was the place where the army's ensign was posted, where the troops were dispatched, where the official meetings of the Prophet ﷺ were held, and the disputes between Muslims were settled. In short, all of the public affairs of the Muslim community of that day were transacted in

---

[122] The Sermon known as "*al-Khutba al-Qasi'a*" (variously numbered 190, 191 and 192 – and others); in any event, it is the longest sermon in the *Nahj al-Balāgha* and the passage appears at its end.

[123] Ibn Sa'd, Abu Abdallah Muhammad, *al-Tabaqāt al-Kubrā*, 2:263; Muttaqī al-Hindī, *Kanz al-U'mmāl*, 2:262-263, 7:178-179; Nasr ibn Muzāhim, *Waq'at Siffīn*, p. 224.

[124] Dayār-Bakrī, Ḥusayn Ibn Md., *Tārīkh al-Khamīs fī Ahwāl Anfus Nafīs*, 1:188; Tabarī, Muhibbiddīn, *ar-Riyāḍ an-Naḍra*, 1:164.

the mosque of the Prophet ﷺ. The pulpit in that mosque acted as what the contemporary equivalent of radio and television would be.

At the beginning of the transformation of any social order, the first thing the *coup d'etat* plotters attempt to do is to seize the radio and television center, and the central government building(s). If they succeed in seizing these three institutions, they will have succeeded in controlling the governmental apparatus.

On Tuesday, which was the day after the pledges of allegiance were given to Abū Bakr in the portico of the Bani Sā'ida, the coup plotters brought Abū Bakr to the pulpit (*minbar*)[125] of the Prophet ﷺ, and had him sit down on it. Before Abū Bakr spoke, Umar stood up and, after praising God ﷻ, said that his denial yesterday of the demise of the Messenger of God ﷺ was based neither on the Sacred Writ of God ﷻ, nor on a [standing] order from the Prophet ﷺ. Rather, it was because he believed that the Prophet ﷺ would personally see to the affairs of the community, and that His Eminence would be the last person to pass from this world [to the next]![126] In closing, Umar said that God ﷻ has placed His sacred writ, which was a source of guidance for His Prophet as well, with the community. If you clutch onto it, Almighty God ﷻ will guide you to the same place where He guided His Prophet ﷺ. Now God ﷻ has blessed you with the best ruler; with someone who was the Prophet's companion in the cave [when they fled by night from Mecca to Medina to escape the posse of the idolaters]. So rise up and pledge allegiance to him![127]

Thus, the general public pledged allegiance to Abū Bakr, just as some people had done so the day before in the portico of the Bani Sā'ida.

It has been written in *Sahih Bukhāri* that after a group of people pledged allegiance to Abū Bakr in the portico of the Bani Sa'ida, the general public pledged allegiance to him while he was sitting on the pulpit.[128]

Anas ibn Mālik reports: I heard with my own ears on that day that Umar repeatedly told Abū Bakr to go up and sit at the top of the

---

[125] [Islamic pulpits consist of a series of steps that end in a seat on which the speaker sits.]
[126] Askari, Allāma Murtaḍā, *Abdullāh ibn Sabā*, 1:121, quoting Tabari as well as many other sources.
[127] Ibid.
[128] Bukhārī, Muḥammad ibn Ismā'īl, *Ṣaḥīḥ al-Bukhārī*, 4:165.

pulpit; and he continued saying this until Abū Bakr finally sat on the pulpit and everyone present pledged allegiance to him. Then Abū Bakr recited a sermon and said:

O people, I am not better than you, but have taken the helm of leadership over you. So, if you find my actions to be good and my work to be praiseworthy, then help me; and if I do something that is bad and erroneous, then bring me back to the right path... Now arise and offer your ritual devotions,[129] and God might have mercy on you.[130]

After that, the people offered their ritual devotions in congregation with Abū Bark leading the prayers, after which they returned to their homes. (The people of Medina were ignorant of the burial rites of their Prophet from Monday to Tuesday evening!) During this time, they were first occupied with the orations that took place in the portico of the Bani Sa'ida, then they were occupied with the pledging of allegiance to Abū Bakr in the streets and alleys of Medina, then they were busy pledging allegiance to him in the Mosque of the Prophet ﷺ, and finally, they were busy listening to the speeches of Umar and Abū Bakr, after which Abū Bakr stood to lead the public in the ritual devotions.

---

[129] It seems that this was the *ẓuhr* or noontide devotions.
[130] Ibn Abī'l-Hadīd, Abdul-Hamīd, *Sharh Nahj al-Balāgha*, 1:134; Ibn Jawzī, Abd al-Rahmān b. Ali, *Siffa^t as-Safwa*, 1:98.

3 The Judgment of the Companions of the Prophet about the Pledge of Allegiance to Abū Bakr

1. Faḍl ibn ʻAbbās

The Bani-Hāshim [clan] was preoccupied with the preparation of the Prophet's ﷺ body for burial when news about the pledge of allegiance to Abū Bakr reached them. Faḍl ibn 'Abbās exited his house and said, "O people of the Quraysh, the caliphate will not become yours by delusional thinking and covering up [the harsh realities]. It is we who deserve the caliphate, not you; we and our Lord and Master Ali ؑ. He deserves the caliphate more than you do."

2. Utbat ibn Abī-Lahab

Utbat ibn Abī-Lahab composed the following verses upon hearing the news about the pledge of allegiance to Abū Bakr.

ما كُنْتُ أَحْسَبُ هذا الأمرَ مُنْصَرِفاً   عَنْ هاشِمٍ ثُمَّ مِنها عَن أبي الحَسَنِ

عَن أوّلِ النّاسِ إيماناً و سابِقَةً   وَ أعْلَمِ النّاسِ بِالقُرآنِ وَ السُّنَنِ

وَ آخِرِ النّاسِ عَهداً بِالنّبي وَ مَنْ   جِبريلُ عَونٌ لَهُ في الغَسلِ وَالكَفَنِ

مَنْ فيهِ ما فيهِم لا يَمْتَرُونَ بِهِ   وَ لَيْسَ في القَومِ ما فيهِ مِنَ الحَسَنِ

فَلَوْلا اتّقاءُ اللّهِ لَمْ تَذْهَبُوا بِها   وَلكِنَّ هذا الخَيْرَ أَجْمَعُ لِلصَّبْرِ

I never thought that the matter of the caliphate would ever be taken away from the Banī-Hāshim, and especially from Ab'al-Hasan [Imam Ali], because Ab'al-Hasan is the one who attained to faith [in Islam] before anyone else, such that no one has as good a precedent in Islam than he has. Furthermore, he is more knowledgeable than anyone in the Quranic sciences, as well as in the Way of the Prophet ﷺ. And he is the only person who was at the service of the Prophet ﷺ until his final moments, and prepared his body for burial with the help of Gabriel. Ali alone is endowed with the praiseworthy attributes and spiritual virtues of everyone else, but others are bereft of his spiritual perfections and moral virtues.[131]

3. Salmān al-Fārsī

Abū Bakr al-Jawharī reports:

Salmān and Zubayr and the Ansār were inclined to pledge allegiance to Ali. And because allegiance had been pledged to Abū Bakr, Salmān al-Fārsī said, "You attained only a little benefit when you acquired the caliphate, but you lost the mine of goodness [by so doing]. You selected the aged man but abandoned the House of your own Prophet. If you had let the caliphate remain in the House of the Prophet, there would not be any divisions [in the community,] even to the point of two people disagreeing with each other on any matter; and would thus have benefited all the more from the fruits of its tree.[132]

Another thing that Salmān is reported to have said is, "You did, and you didn't". In other words, it would have been better had you not done what you did, and what you did was not right. And that if the Muslims had pledged allegiance to Ali, God's mercy and grace would reach them from all directions, and they would have attained to felicity and preeminence.[133]

4. Abū-Dharr

When the Apostle of God ﷺ passed away, Abū Dharr was not in Medina. When news of the fact that Abū Bakr had acceded to the caliphate, he responded as follows:

---

[131] Ya'qūbī, Aḥmad ibn Isḥāq, *Tārīkh al-Ya'qūbī*, 2:103; Ibn Abī'l-Hadīd, Abdul-Hamīd, *Sharh Nahj al-Balāgha*, 1:287; Zubayr ibn Bakkār, *al-Muwaffaqīāt*, pp. 580-607. It is interesting to note that the Commander of the Faithful sent an agent to Faḍl ibn Abbās, telling his to cease his eulogizing, saying انّ سلامة الدّين احبّ الينا من غيره (Ibn Abī'l-Hadīd, Abdul-Hamīd, *Sharh Nahj al-Balāgha*, 2:8). Ibn Hajar, Ahmad ibn Ali al-Asqalāni, *al-Iṣābah fī Tamyīz al-Ṣaḥābah*, 2:263, and Abū al-Fidā, Ismā'īl ibn Ali, *Tarikh al-Mukhtasar fi Akhbar al-Bashar*, 1:164, both attribute these verses to Faḍl ibn Abbās ibn Abī-Tālib al-Hāshimī – an attribution which we do not believe to be correct.

[132] Ibn Abī'l-Hadīd, Abdul-Hamīd, *Sharh Nahj al-Balāgha*, 2:131-2 and 6:17, quoting Abū Bakr Jawharī's *Saqīfa*.

[133] Balādhūrī, Ahmad ibn Yahyā ibn Jābir, *Ansāb al-Ashrāf*, 1:591; as well as Jāhiẓ in his *Uthmānīa*. Here is the original:

كرداذ و ناكرداذ. (اى عملتم) لو بايعوا عليّا لا كلوا من فوقهم و من تحت ارجلهم.

You reached [for] a paltry thing, and are content with it, and lost the House of the Prophet. If you had left the functions of this office (*kār*) to the House of your Prophet, not a soul would have disagreed with you in matters of your interest.[134]

5. Miqdād ibn ʿAmr

The narrator of the report says,

One day I happened by the mosque of the Messenger of God. I saw a man who was sitting with his knees on the floor, and was wailing with such intensity that it was as if the whole world belonged to him and he had just lost it. While he was in the midst of his sorrows, he said, "What a surprising thing is the way the Quraysh has acted! They have taken away the caliphate from the House of their Prophet, while the first person to attain to faith is among them![135]

6. Nuʿmān ibn ʿAjlān

In response to the verses composed by Umar and ibn al-ʿĀs, Nuʿmān ibn ʿAjlān composed an ode about the events that occurred in the Saqīfa, from which we will quote a few couplets:[136]

وَ قُلتُم حَرامٌ نَصْبُ سَعدٍ وَ نَصْبُكُم   عَتيقَ بنَ عُثمانَ حَلالٌ اَبابَكرٍ

وَ كانَ هَواناً في عَلِيٍّ وَ اِنَّهُ   لَاَهلٌ لَهَا يا عَمْرو مِنْ حَيْثُ لا تَدرِي

وَصِيِّ النَّبِيِّ المُصطفىٰ و ابْنِ عَمِّهِ   و قاتِلِ فُرْسانِ الضَّلالَةِ وَ الكُفرِ

فَلَوْلا اتِّقاءُ اللّهِ لَمْ تَذْهَبُوا بِها   وَلٰكِنَّ هٰذَا الخَيْرَ أَجْمَعُ لِلصَّبْرِ [137]

[134] Ibn Abīʾl-Hadīd, Abdul-Hamīd, *Sharh Nahj al-Balāgha*, 6:31, quoting Jawharī's *Saqīfa*.
[135] Yaʿqūbī, Ahmad ibn Ishāq, *Tārīkh al-Yaʿqūbī*, 2:114.
[136] Ibn Abīʾl-Hadīd, Abdul-Hamīd, *Sharh Nahj al-Balāgha*, 6:31, quoting Zubayr ibn Bakkār's *al-Muwaffaqīāt*.

You said that the appointment of Saʻd (Ibn ʻAbāda) to the caliphate is forbidden to the caliphate and that the appointment of Abū Bakr is correct and lawful. What we wanted was Ali. Ali was more worthy of this office because he was the *waṣī* of the Prophet and the son of his aunt, and he was the one who killed the champions of misguidance and unbelief. Thus, if it hadn't been for fear of God's [retribution], you would never have attained to this office; but attaining to this good (= Islam) is more suitable to longanimity, forbearance, and patience (*sabr*).

7. Umm Mistah ibn Uthātha

Umm Mistah ibn Uthātha recited the following couplets at the Prophet's grave:

قَدْ كَانَ بَعْدَكَ أَنْبَاءٌ وَ هَنْبَثَةٌ   لَوْ كُنْتَ شَاهِدَهَا لَمْ تَكْثُرِ الخَطَبُ

إِنَّا فَقَدْنَاكَ فَقْدَ الأَرْضِ وَابِلَهَا   فَاخْتَلَّ قَوْمُكَ فَاشْهَدْهُمْ وَلَا تَغِبْ

After you, O Prophet, important conversations and events occurred that, if you were still alive, we would have avoided all these troubles.

You left us, and we became like parched land that no longer receives rain and has lost its freshness and vitality. You left us, and the people became corrupted and ruined. Look at them, O Prophet, and bear witness.[138]

---

[137] The importance of the issue warrants quoting Nuʻmān ibn ʻAjlān's verses in greater detail:

وَ قُلْتُمْ حَرَامٌ نَصْبُ سَعْدٍ وَ نَصْبُكُمْ   عَتِيقَ بْنَ عُثْمَانَ حَلَالٌ أَبَابَكْرِ

وَ أَهْلُ أَبِي بَكْرٍ لَهَا خَيْرُ فَائِمٍ   وَ إِنَّ عَلِيّاً كَانَ أَخْلَقَ بِالأَمْرِ

وَ كَانَ هَوَانَا فِي عَلِيٍّ وَ إِنَّهُ   لَأَهْلٌ لَهَا يَا عَمْرُو مِنْ حَيْثُ لَا نَدْرِي

فَذَاكَ بِعَوْنِ اللَّهِ يَدْعُو إِلَى الهُدَى   وَ يَنْهَى عَنِ الفَحْشَاءِ وَ النَّغْيِ وَ النُّكْرِ

وَصِيُّ النَّبِيِّ المُصْطَفَى وَ ابْنُ عَمِّهِ   وَ قَاتِلُ فُرْسَانِ الضَّلَالَةِ وَ الكُفْرِ

وَ هَذَا بِحَمْدِ اللَّهِ يَهْدِي مِنَ العَمَى   وَ يَفْتَحُ آذَاناً ثَقُلْنَ مِنَ الوَقْرِ

نَجِيُّ رَسُولِ اللَّهِ فِي الغَارِ وَخِدْنَهُ   وَ صَاحِبُهُ الصِّدِّيقُ فِي سَالِفِ الدَّهْرِ

فَلَوْلَا اتِّقَاءُ اللَّهِ لَمْ تَذْهَبُوا بِهَا   وَ لَكِنَّ هَذَا الخَيْرَ أَجْمَعُ لِلصَّبْرِ

[138] Ibn Abī'l-Hadīd, Abdul-Hamīd, *Sharḥ Nahj al-Balāgha*, 2:131-132 & 6:17.

8. A Woman from the Banī-Najjār

Once the pledge of allegiance to Abū Bakr was well established, he set a stipend for the women and the Ansār (the Helpers), to be paid out of the treasury. He entrusted the stipend of a woman from the Banī Adī ibn an-Najjār to Zayd bin Thabit to deliver it to her. Zayd came to the woman and gave her stipend to her. The woman asked: "What is this?" Zayd replied, "It is your share of the stipends that Abū Bakr has set for women." The woman replied, "Do you want to take my religion from me by offering me a bribe??

"I swear upon my oath before God that I will not accept anything from him." Zayd bin Thabit then returned her stipend back to Abū Bakr].[139]

9. Abū-Sufyān

The Prophet ﷺ had sent Abū Sufyān outside on an errand, so he was not in Medina at the time of the Prophet's ﷺ death. On the way back, Abū Sufyān came across a man who had left Medina. Abū Sufyān asked, "Did the Prophet die?" When the traveller responded in the affirmative, Abū Sufyān asked, "Who became his successor?" When Abū Sufyān heard that Abū Bakr had succeeded the Prophet ﷺ, he asked how "the two deprived people" Ali and 'Abbās had reacted. The man said, "They have confined themselves in their homes." To this, Abū Sufyān replied, "I swear upon my oath before God, if I am granted a long enough life, I will raise their station to lofty heights." He then added, "I see a cloud of dust which will not settle other than by bloodshed." After having said this, he entered Medina. He wandered its streets and alleys, reciting these verses:

بَنِي هاشمٍ لاَ تُطمِعُوا النّاسَ فيكُم   وَلاَ سِيَّمَا تَيْمُ بْنُ مُرَّةَ اَوْ عَدِيّ

فَمَا الأَمْرُ إلاَّ فيكُمْ وَ إليْكُمْ   وَ لَيْسَ لَها إلاّ أبُو حَسَنٍ عَلىّ "

O House of Hāshim! Blockade the ways of avarice for dominion, especially for the two tribes of the Banu-Taym and Banu-'Adī (the tribes of Abu Bakr and Umar, respectively). The governance of this [political

[139] Ibn Abī'l-Hadīd, Abdul-Hamīd, *Sharh Nahj al-Balāgha*, 2:133, quoting Jawharī's *Saqīfa;* Ibn Sa'd, Abu Abdallah Muhammad, *al-Tabaqāt al-Kubrā*, 2/2nd C:129

order] belongs to you! It was once yours, and it must [perforce] return to you. Noone other than Ab'al Hasan Ali has the competence to rule.[140]

In addition to the above two couplets, Ya'qūbī has added the following two verses:

أَبَا حَسَنٍ فَاشْدُدْ بِهَا كَفَّ حَازِمٍ
فَإِنَّكَ بِالْأَمْرِ الَّذِي يُرْتَجَى مَلِيٌّ
وَ إِنَّ امْرَءاً يَرْمِي قُصَيٌّ وَرَاءَهُ
عَزِيزُ الْحِمَى وَالنَّاسُ مِنْ غَالِبٍ قُصَيٌّ ١٢

O Ab'al Hasan! Grab hold of the reins of the reign with a powerful and decisive hand! Because you are more powerful than that which is expected. And of course, a man who has Qusayy[141] as his support cannot have his rights trodden underfoot, and it is only [the progeny of] Qusayy who are men who are [capable of] predominance.[142]

Tabarī[143] relates that Abū Sufyān spoke up, saying, "... O sons of 'Abd al-Manāf, what business does Abū-Bakr have with your business [i.e. governance]? Where are those two people, Ali and 'Abbās, who have been deprived of what is rightfully theirs?"[144]

Abū Sufyān then paid a visit to Alī ibn Abī-Tālib ﷺ and said, "O Ab'al Hasan! Bring your hand forward so that I can pledge allegiance to you." But Ali demurred, and said, "If I had forty resolute men [i.e. those

---

140 Ibn Abī'l-Hadīd, Abdul-Hamīd, *Sharh Nahj al-Balāgha*, 3:120, quoting Jawharī's *Saqīfa*; Ibn 'Abd Rabbih, *al-'Iqd al-Farīd*, 3:62.

141 The Banī-Hāshim and the Banī-Umayya are both lineages of 'Abd al-Manāf, who was the son of Qusayy.

142 Ya'qūbī, Aḥmad ibn Isḥāq, *Tārīkh al-Ya'qūbī*, 2:105. The story is provided in greater detail in Zubayr ibn Bakkār's *al-Muwaffaqīāt*; cf. Ibn Abī'l-Hadīd, Abdul-Hamīd, *Sharh Nahj al-Balāgha*, 6:7.

143 Tabarī, Muhammad ibn Jarīr, *Tārīkh ar-Rusul wa'l-Mulūk*, 2:449, and 1:1827-28 in the European edition.

144 We can glean from these words of Abū Sufyān that he did not believe in the prophethood of the Prophet or in his mission, because he did not say *rasūlallāh.* He said these words out of his sense of tribal allegiance (believing that his tribe had the right to rule).

who believed in his *wasīa*[t]],[145] I would have confronted [the coup plotters], but I don't.[146 and 147]

---

145 [Ministerial inheritor, legatee, executor, and successor.]
146 Ibn Abī'l-Hadīd, Abdul-Hamīd, *Sharh Nahj al-Balāgha*, 2:47.
147 The question may arise in the minds of some people as to why Ali did not accept Abu Sufyan's offer of allegiance. A detailed answer to this question is given in the book [Askari, Allāma Murtaḍā] *Abdullāh Ibn Sabā*, 1:146-151; but briefly stated, it can be said that after the death of the Messenger of God ﷺ, clannish and tribal allegiances were revived. The gathering of the Ansar at the Saqīfa and their attempt at pledging allegiance to Sa'd ibn 'Ubāda was based solely on these biased allegiances, absent which they themselves knew full well that there were people among the emigrants who were greater and had a higher degree of piety than Sa'd ibn 'Ubāda. Similarly, the Aws tribe's pledge of allegiance to Abu Bakr had no basis other than tribal interests. In doing so, they wanted to prevent the leadership from falling into the hands of the Khazraj tribe. The extent to which Umar was influenced by tribal allegiances in his allegiance to Abu Bakr is also clear in his speech in the Saqīfa (*Sahih Bukhari* 4:120). Abu Sufyan was also entangled in clannish biases, and only demanded that allegiance be pledged to the Commander of the Faithful in order to keep the leadership of the community in the hands of a member of his own tribe, the Bani Abd al-Manāf. In this midst, Ali ibn Abī-Tālib was the only person whose [moral] vision exceeded that of determining the leadership of the community on the basis of clannish and tribal prejudices and allegiances. If Ali demanded the right of rulership for himself, it was because he would establish a government which would be based only on the Qur'an and the religion of the Prophet. He wanted to be supported in this task by people such as Salman, Abu Dharr, Miqdād, and Ammār, men whose only motivation and impetus were revealed tenets and beliefs; unlike Abu Sufyan, who had no other motivation than thoughts of worldly gain and clannish prejudice. Therefore, if the Commander of the Faithful accepted Abu Sufyan offer of allegiance, practically all of the efforts of the Prophet and of Imam Ali himself, in following the Messenger of God ﷺ for 23 years to return society to its primordial, divinely-oriented disposition and orientation, and for ridding society of such tribal biases and allegiances, would have been wasted and destroyed. It is worth mentioning that when Abu Sufyan lost hope in Ali, he was happy to accept the bribe of the rulers, and swore allegiance to Abu Bakr, fully revealing his material and worldly motives. At Umar's suggestion, Abu Bakr entrusted the Zakat of the treasury which was already in Abu Sufyan's hands (Ibn 'Abd Rabbih, *al-'Iqd al-Farīd*, 3:62). Also, Abu Sufyan's son appointed Yazid as the commander of an army that was going to the Levant (Tabarī, Muhammad ibn Jarīr, *Tārīkh ar-Rusul wa'l-Mulūk*, 1:1827). [It is the failure of Western orientalists to be able to see the difference in this moral vision that was at the heart of Ali's disagreement with his opponents that leads them to reduce the issue of contention to a merely political struggle for power. And of course, this failure of theirs, in turn, is due to a deficit of a similar nature in their own moral vision. – Tr.]

10. Khālid ibn Sa'īd (of the Banī-Umayya)

Khālid ibn Sa'īd ibn 'Ās was one of the people from the Banī-Umayya tribe who had entered into Islam at an early stage.[148] He was a member of the group who emigrated to Abyssinia. After Islam was firmly established, the Prophet ﷺ charged him, together with his two brothers (Abān and 'Amr), with the responsibility of collecting the *zakāt*[149] from the Madh'haj tribe. Later, they were assigned as representatives of the Prophet ﷺ in San'ā in Yemen. They were not in Medina at the time of the Prophet's ﷺ passing. When they returned to Medina, they said to Abū-Bakr: "We are the sons of Uhayha. We shall not become the agents of anyone else after the passing of the Prophet.[150] And Khālid came to the Commander of the faithful and said, "O Ali! Bring your hand forward so that I can pledge allegiance to you. I swear upon my oath before God, there is noone more deserving of the caliphate than you.[151] When the Banī-Hāshim pledged alleginace to Abū-Bakr, Khālid also pledged his allegiance at that time.[152]

10. Umar ibn al-Khattāb

In the last year of his life while he was performing the major pilgrimage (hajj), Umar heard 'Ammār say, "The pledge of allegiance to Abu-Bakr was a mistake whose consequences were felt later. If Umar passes away, we will pledge allegiance to Ali His Eminence Alī ibn Abī-Tālib."[153] Umar was taken aback by this, and when he returned to Medina, he climbed the *minbar* (pulpit) in the Prophet's mosque [= the congregational mosque] on the first Friday of his return and said the following: "The pledge of allegiance to Abu-Bakr was a mistake that

---

[148] According to Abd-Allāh ibn Muslim Ibn Qutayba writing in his *al-Ma'ārif* (p. 128), he entered into Islam before Abu Bakr.
[149] *Zakāt* or the "purifying poor due" is about 2.5% (or 1/40) of a Muslim's total savings and wealth above a minimum threshold amount, known as the *nisāb.*
[150] Ibn Abd'al-Birr, Yusuf ibn Abdallah, *al-Istī'āb fī Ma'rifat al-Ashāb*, 1:398-400; Ibn Abī'l-Hadīd, Abdul-Hamīd, *Sharh Nahj al-Balāgha*, 6:13 & 6:16; Ibn Athīr, 'Alī ibn Muḥammad, *Usd al-Ghābah fī Ma'rifat al-Ṣaḥābah*, 2:82; Ibn Hajar, Ahmad ibn Ali al-Asqalāni, *al-Iṣābah fī Tamyīz al-Ṣaḥābah*, 1:406.
[151] Ya'qūbī, Aḥmad ibn Isḥāq, *Tārīkh al-Ya'qūbī*, 2:105.
[152] Ibn Abī'l-Hadīd, Abdul-Hamīd, *Sharh Nahj al-Balāgha*, 1:135, quoting Jawharī's *Saqīfa*; Ibn Athīr, 'Alī ibn Muḥammad, *Usd al-Ghābah fī Ma'rifat al-Ṣaḥābah*, 2:82
[153] Ibn Abī'l-Hadīd, Abdul-Hamīd, *Sharh Nahj al-Balāgha*, 2:123.

took place and is behind us. True, that is what it was, but God protected the people from the ill effects of that mistake."[154]

11. Mu'āwiya

Mu'āwiya wrote the following in a letter to Muhammad ibn Abu-Bakr:

Your father (Abu Bakr) and I knew the virtue and preeminence of the son of Abu-Talib (Ali), and we considered his right [to the succession] as [something that was] necessary for us [to have ourselves]. God chose [to reveal] a matter that was [heretofore] with Him [alone], and kept His promise [by so doing], and revealed his invitation and made clear his unimpeachable authority (*hujja*). And because God blessed His Prophet, may God bless him and grant him peace, and took his spirit [back] unto Himself, your father and his criterion (*fārūq*) 'Umar were the first to usurp Ali's right and to oppose him. The two agreed with each other, and then called Ali to pledge allegiance [to Abu Bakr]. When Ali refused, they made wrongful decisions (they wanted to kill Ali) and harbored dangerous plans for him, as a result of which Ali ultimately pledged allegiance and gave in to them.[155]

12. Sa'd ibn Ubāda

They left Sa'd be for a few days after the events in the Saqīfa, then sent for him to come and pledge his allegiance, telling him that everyone, including your kin, had already done so. Sa'd responded as follows:

Upon my word of honor before God, I will not pledge allegiance to you before I have emptied my quiver of arrows that are aimed towards you,

---

[154] Abdul-Hamīd, *Sharh Nahj al-Balāgha*, 2:22-23, 6:47, 11:13, 12:47; Balādhūrī, Ahmad ibn Yahyā ibn Jābir, *Ansāb al-Ashrāf*, 5:15; Bukhārī, Muḥammad ibn Ismā'īl, *Ṣaḥīḥ al-Bukhārī*, 4:119-120; Ibn Abī'l-Hadīd, Abdul-Hamīd, *Sharh Nahj al-Balāgha*, 2:22-23,
Ibn Hishām, 'Abd al-Malik, *al-Sīrah al-Nabawīyah*, 4:336-338; Muttaqī al-Hindī, *Kanz al-U'mmāl*, 3:139, hadith 2326; Ya'qūbī, Aḥmad ibn Isḥāq, *Tārīkh al-Ya'qūbī*, 2:160. It is worthy of note that Abu Bakr had used this same phrase about his own caliphate: انّ بيعتى كانت فلتة وقى الله شرّه (Abdul-Hamīd, *Sharh Nahj al-Balāgha*, 6:47-50).

[155] Mas'ūdī, Alī ibn al-Ḥusayn, *Murawwij adh-Dhahab*, 2:60; Nasr ibn Muzāhim, *Waq'at Siffīn*, p. 135; Ibn Abī'l-Hadīd, Abdul-Hamīd, *Sharh Nahj al-Balāgha*, 1:248 & 2:65.

and until their arrowheads are colored with your blood. What did you imagine? As long as I have my sword in my hand, I will bring it down on your foreheads and will fight you as much as I can and will not pledge allegiance to you. Upon my word of honor before God, even if you had all the *jinns* and humans take your side with respect to the matter of governance, I would not bow my head down to your rule and would not recognize its [legitimacy] until the Day [of Resurrection], when my account is tried in the court of divine justice.

When Sa'd's words reached Abu Bakr, Umar said to him: "Do not give Sa'd any slack until he pledges allegiance to you. But Bashīr ibn Sa'd said: "He is stubborn and spiteful and will not pledge allegiance to you, even if it kills him. But killing him is not a simple task, for he won't be killed before he takes all his family and dependents with him. Leave him be,[156] for doing so will not harm you, as he is just one person.

They accepted Bashīr ibn Sa'd's counsel and gave up on Sa'd ibn Ubāda and let him be. Sa'd did not participate in any of their public gatherings and never attended the Friday congregational prayers, and was not seen accompanying them in the performance of the Hajj pilgrimage or any other rites. This state of affairs continued until Abu Bakr's demise, when the turn came for Umar's caliphate.[157]

[156] Ibn Athīr Jazarī, 'Alī, *al-Kāmil fī al-Tārīkh*, 2:126; Tabarī, Muhammad ibn Jarīr, *Tārīkh ar-Rusul wa'l-Mulūk*, 3:495. These two sources have cited the hadith report up to this point. The following sources add that Sa'd would not greet (*salām*) any of them when he came across them: Ibn Qutayba, Abd-Allāh ibn Muslim, *al-Imāma wa'l-Siyāsa*, 1:10; Muttaqī al-Hindī, *Kanz al-U'mmāl*, 3:134, hadith #2296; Halabī, Alī ibn Ibrāhīm, *Insān al-'Uyūn fī Sīra al-Amīn al-Ma'mūn* (*as-Sīrat al-Halabīa*), 4:397, and the European edition of Tabarī's *Tārikh*, 1:1844.

[157] The previous sources, as well as Tabarī, Muhibbiddīn, *ar-Riyāḍ an-Naḍra*, 1:168.

4 How the Caliphal Administration dealt with the Opposition outside Medina

1. The Murder of Mālik bin Nuwaira

Mālik bin Nuwaira was a courageous leader of a section of the Banī Tamīm tribe. He was a companion of the Prophet ﷺ as well as his agent, and was a gifted poet as well. Malik demurred from sending the alms he had collected after the death of the Prophet ﷺ to Medina and returned them to their owners, reciting these two couplets:

فَقُلْتُ خُذُوا اَموالَكُمْ غَيرَ خائِفٍ   وَلا ناظِرٍ في ما يَجِيءُ مِنَ الغَدِ

فَإنْ قامَ بِالدّينِ المُحَقَّقِ قائمٌ ۲   أطَعْنا وَ قُلْنا الدّينُ دينُ محمَّدِ

I said, take your property and have no fear or concern about future events;

Just as when someone stands up in [the cause of] the righteous religion, we would obey him and say, "that religion is the religion of Muhammad.[158 and 159]

All of the [major] historians have related this story, including Tabari, Ibn Athir, Ibn Kathir, and Ya'qubi, stating that Abu Bakr sent Khālid ibn Walīd with an army to the tribes who had not pledged allegiance to him after the passing of the Prophet ﷺ, and/ or to those who did not pay the

---

[158] In *Majma' ash-Shu'arā'* (p. 260), the verse appears as فان قام بالامر المخوّف قائم , and in Ibn Abī'l-Hadīd's *Sharh Nahj al-Balāgha* it appears as فان قام بالامر المجدّد قائم , both of which are deliberate distortions or falsifications (*tahrīf*).

[159] Ibn Hajar, Ahmad ibn Ali al-Asqalāni, *al-Iṣābah fī Tamyīz al-Ṣaḥābah*, 3:336.

zakāt (or the purifying dues)[160] to his dues collector, so that Khālid ibn Walīd would force them to pay the *zakāt* due. Umar said to Abu Bakr: "Wait a while on this;" but Abu Bakr said: "No, upon my oath before God ﷻ, if they do not give me the bit and bridle of a camel as they used to give to the Prophet, I will go to war with them." Abu Bakr said this and sent Khālid ibn Walīd with an army to go to war with them.

The land where Mālik bin Nuwaira lived was called Buttāh: Abu Qatāda, one of the companions, reports:

They ambushed that land (even though the Prophet never did so). And because Khālid ibn Walīd's army had surrounded them at night, Malik bin Nuwaira's tribe became terrified. They dressed for war and took up arms and came to confront the enemy. [Abu Qatāda continues:] We told them that we are Muslims. They replied: We too are Muslims. The commander of the army asked them: Then why did you take up arms? They said: Why did you take up arms? [Abu Qatāda said:] We told them that if what you say is true, then lay down your arms. They proceeded to drop their weapons. Then we prayed, and they prayed with us.[161]

In another report, it is stated:

As soon as they laid down their weapons, Khālid's forces tied the hands of the men and marched them to Khālid. Mālik bin Nuwaira's wife was with him. There, Abu Qatāda[162] and Abdullah ibn Umar testified before Khālid that they were Muslims and that they had seen them pray. All of the historians have written that Nuwaira's wife was with him and was very beautiful. Khālid turned to Ḍarrār Ibn Azwar and said: Strike Mālik's neck [with your sword]! At that point, Mālik pointed to his wife and said, "This woman killed me [= unwittingly became the cause of my murder!]" Khālid said: "God killed you because you apostatized from Islam." Mālik said: "I am a Muslim and committed to Islam." Khālid said to Ḍarrār: Strike his neck! And Ḍarrār followed Khālid's order. They

---

[160] *Zakāt* or the "purifying poor due" is about 2.5% (or 1/40) of a Muslim's total savings and wealth above a minimum threshold amount, known as the *nisāb*.
[161] There is consensus regarding this issue among the scholars of the School of the Caliphs.
[162] Askari, Allāma Murtaḍā, *Abdullāh ibn Sabā*, 1:181, quoting Ibn Abī'l-Hadīd, Abdul-Hamīd, *Sharh Nahj al-Balāgha.*

killed the other Muslims too,[163] and Khālid went to bed with Mālik's wife that night.[164]

Abu Qatāda returned to Medina and reported the incident to Abu Bakr, and swore that he would never go on a military expedition under Khālid's command because he had murdered Mālik, who was a Muslim. Umar told Abu Bakr that Khālid was guilty of fornication and should be stoned to death.[165] Abu Bakr said, "I will not stone him because he has applied his *ijtihād* (independent striving for the derivation of law), albeit that he has erred in his *ijtihad.*" Umar said, "He is a murderer, and he killed a Muslim; you should apply *qisās* (just retaliation) in his case." Abu Bakr said, "I will never kill him; he applied his *ijtihād* and erred in doing so."[166] Umar said, "At least dismiss him from his post so that he would no longer be a general." Abu Bakr said, "I will never place the sword that God has drawn for them back in its scabbard." The origins of Khālid ibn Walīd's title Sayfullāh (the Sword of God) comes from this exchange of words.[167] Later, when Khālid came to Medina, Umar again acted harshly towards him in the congregational mosque of Medina. Khālid went to see Abu Bakr, who accepted his apology, and Khālid came back and requited Umar's aggression.[168]

This was an example of the way in which the cabal of the caliphate treated those outside Medina who were unwilling or demurred from pledging allegiance to the caliph.

---

[163] Abū al-Fidā, Ismā'īl ibn Ali, *Tarikh al-Mukhtasar fi Akhbar al-Bashar*, p. 158; Ibn Khallakān, Aḥmad, *Wafyāt al-'Ayān*, 5:66; Ibn Shahna's *Tārīkh*, referred to in the margin of Ibn Athīr Jazarī, 'Alī, *al-Kāmil fī al-Tārīkh*, vol. 11.; *Fuāt al-Wafīāt*, 2:627.

[164] Muttaqī al-Hindī, *Kanz al-U'mmāl*, 3:132; Ya'qūbī, Aḥmad ibn Isḥāq, *Tārīkh al-Ya'qūbī*, 2:110.

[165] Ya'qūbī, Aḥmad ibn Isḥāq, *Tārīkh al-Ya'qūbī*, Ayatī translation, 2:10.

[166] Whenever one of the Caliphate gang did something wrong, they would say that he had applied his *ijtihad* [a personal striving for the derivation of sacred law], and that if the *ijtihad* of a *mujtahid* [one who practices *ijtihad*] turns out to be correct, he will be rewarded [the equivalent of] two good deeds (*hasana*), and that if his *ijtihad* turns out to be incorrect, he will be rewarded one good deed. For a detailed discussion of this matter, refer to the discussion of *ijtihad* in the School of the Caliphs in Askari, Allāma Murtaḍā, *Mu'ālim al-Madrisatayn*, p. 89 ff.

[167] ما كنت اعمد سيفا سلّه الله عليهم., according to Abū al-Fidā, Ismā'īl ibn Ali, *Tarikh al-Mukhtasar fi Akhbar al-Bashar*; and Muttaqī al-Hindī, *Kanz al-U'mmāl*, 3:132, hadith #228.

[168] Askari, Allāma Murtaḍā, *Abdullāh ibn Sabā*, 1:184-185, quoting Tabarī.

2. Some Other Examples

Zīād ibn Labīd, Abu Bakr's representative in Yemen, had gathered the taxes (*sadaqāt*). In those days, they would take camels from camel herders, and among the camels [that had been consigned to be given as tax payment], there was a calf that belonged to a young man who said to Zīād ibn Labīd, "I am fond of this calf. Don't take it from me, and let me give you a [full-grown] camel instead." Abu Bakr's representative said, "No. This [calf] has been counted as part of the gathered taxes, and it is not possible to take it back." The young man complained to Hāritha ibn Surāqa, the tribal chief. Hāritha said to Zīād ibn Labīd, "This young man has grown fond of the calf; take a camel in its stead." When Abu Bakr's representative gave a negatory answer, the exchange became heated and turned violent.[169]

When the residents of the town of Dabā heard about the incident, they ran Abu Bakr's representative out of town. Zīād ibn Labīd surrounded the town with the aid of people from different tribes. The residents of the town of Dabā, along with those with whom Zīād ibn Labīd had clashed, originally fought him and his army but were defeated. The residents of Dabā had walled fortifications, behind which they took refuge, but they were defeated again. Eventually they said to Zīād ibn Labīd, "We will pay the *zakāt* and surrender." Zīād ibn Labīd said, "I will accept your surrender only on the condition that you admit that we are in the right and you were in the wrong; and that our dead

---

[169] Ibn A'tham, *al-Futūh*, 1:48-49. The tribal leader, Hāritha ibn Sarāqa stated something that is very interesting and highly significant. He said,

خذ ناقتك اليك فان كلّمك احد فاحطم انفه بالسّيف! نحن انّما اطعنا رسول الله (ص) اذ كان حيّا' و لو قام رجل من اهل بيته لا طعناه و امّا ابن ابى قحافه فلا و الله ما له فى رقابنا طاعة و لا بيعة.

What this means is, "Take your camel, and if anyone talks to you about it (in protest), sever his nose with a sword. We only obeyed the Messenger of God ﷺ when he was alive, and if a man from his House (*ahl al-bayt*), rose up in insurrection after him against the government, we would obey him at any instant also. As for the son of Abī Qahāfa (Abu Bakr), I swear by God ﷻ that there is no obligation of obedience or allegiance to him upon us. When Hāritha ibn Sarāqa said this, he recited a couplet of poetry:

اطعنا رسول الله اذ كان بيننا   فيا عجبا ممّن يطيع ابا بكر

We obeyed the Messenger of God while he was among us,
So how strange are the deeds of one who obeys Abā Bakr!
(Ibn A'tham, *al-Futūh*, 1:49).

are in Heaven and yours are in Hell, and that you will accept whatever judgment we make about you." The residents of Dabā had no choice but to accept these conditions, which they did. Zīād ibn Labīd then ordered them to exit their town and leave their arms behind, which they did.

When Zīād's soldiery entered the city, they severed the heads of the elders of the town, and took their women and children prisoner, and took their belongings as booty, which they sent to Abu Bakr in Medina. Then they attacked the tribe of Kinda from there. They severed the heads of the elders of that tribe also and sent the rest to Medina. Abu Bakr wanted to sever the heads of the menfolk and take their women as slaves, but Umar prevailed on him not to do so. These people remained as prisoners until the time of Umar's [caliphate], at which time they were freed by Umar and allowed to return to their tribe.[170]

The caliphal authority made no distinction between Muslims and apostates, treating everyone in the same [barbaric] way; the way of the Arabs in the pre-Islamic Era of Ignorance. During the Era of Ignorance, when one side prevailed over another in a battle, the men and women of the vanquished side were taken as slaves, and their property was looted as booty. In any event, the caliphal authority labelled all these people as apostates, and the history books describe them as apostates, even to this day.[171]

---

[170] Ibn A'tham, *al-Futūh*, 1:60-61.

[171] For a more detailed discussion of this issue, cf. *Abdullāh Ibn Sabā* [by Allāma Askarī] 1:165-192 and 2:21-99.

5 How the Caliphate dealt with the Opposition within Medina

1. The Murder of Sa'd ibn 'Abāda

After Umar became caliph, one day he saw Sa'd ibn 'Abāda in one of the alleys of Medīna. He turned to him and said, "Hey, O Sa'd!" To which Sa'd immediately replied, "Hey, O Umar!" The caliph asked, "Was it not you who said such and such?" And Sa'd said, "Yes. I said those things, and now you have become caliph. I swear upon my oath to God that I preferred your friend to you. I swear to God that I am disgusted at being neighbours with you!" To which Umar replied, "Anyone who does not like his neighbor moves somewhere else." Sa'd said, "I am well aware of that; I will move to become neighbors with someone who is better than you."

Not long had passed when Sa'd set off for the lands of the Levant where the Yamānī tribes were located.[172 and 173] It was in the early days of Umar's caliphate. Balādhūrī writes in his *Ansāb al-Ashrāf*: "Sa'd ibn 'Abāda did not pledge allegiance to Abu Bakr [*sic*], and went to the Levant. Umar sent a man after him to the Levant and told him to get Sa'd ibn 'Abāda to pledge allegiance to him using any ruse he could think of, but if none of the tricks worked and if he refused, to kill him with God's help! The agent headed for the Levant and Sa'd ibn 'Abāda in Hawārayn.[174] He immediately brought up the issue of pledging allegiance, and asked Sa'd ibn 'Abāda to pledge allegiance to Umar. In

[172] Ibn Asākir, 'Alī, *at-Tārīkh al-Madīna^t ad-Damishq*, 6:90; Ibn Sa'd, Abu Abdallah Muhammad, *al-Tabaqāt al-Kubrā*, 2/3rd C:145; Muttaqī al-Hindī, *Kanz al-U'mmāl*, 3:134, hadith #2296; Halabī, Alī ibn Ibrāhīm, *Insān al-'Uyūn fī Sīra al-Amīn al-Ma'mūn* (*as-Sīra^t al-Halabīa*), 3:397.
[173] The Ansar were originally from the Yemenite tribe of Sabā'īya. They lived in Yemen until the destruction of the Ma'rib dam, after which they dispersed to the lands of Iraq and Syria, and to Medina.
[174] A well-known hamlet of Aleppo.

response to the man who had been sent by Umar, Sa'd ibn 'Abāda said that he would not pledge allegiance to someone from the tribe of Quraysh. Umar's agent then threatened him with death, saying that if he didn't pledge allegiance, he would kill him. Sa'd ibn 'Abāda said that he would not pledge allegiance even if he tried to kill him. When Umar's man saw Sa'd ibn 'Abāda's determination, he said, "Are you not in accord with the will of this community?" To this, Sa'd ibn 'Abāda said, "With respect to the issue of the pledge of allegiance, yes, my affairs are different than others when it comes to the pledge of allegiance." Having heard Sa'd ibn 'Abāda's die-hard determination not to pledge allegiance, Umar's agent shot Sa'd with an arrow to his heart, which rent his life-vein asunder.[175]

It is stated in the book *Tabserat al-Ulūm* that Muhammad ibn Maslama al-Ansārī had been commissioned to carry out the task. [this source states also states that] Muhammad ibn Maslama went to the Levant and shot Sa'd with an arrow. It is also reported that Khālid ibn Walīd was in the Levant at the time, and that he aided Muhammad ibn Maslama in the murder of Sa'd ibn 'Abāda.[176]

Mas'ūdī reports in his *Murawwij adh-Dhahab* that Sa'd ibn 'Abāda did not pledge allegiance [to Umar]; that he left Medina for the Levant, and was killed in the eleventh year of the Islamic calendar.[177]

Ibn 'Abd Rabbih also states that Sa'd ibn 'Abāda was found dead with an arrow in his heart; and it was rumored that he had urinated in the standing position, and that [therefore] the *jinns* had shot him with two arrows to his heart, and recited this couplet:

قَد قَتَلنا سَيِّدَ الخَزرَج سَعدَ بنَ عُبادَه.

وَ رَمَيناهُ بِسَهمَين فَلَم نُخطِىء فُـؤادَه.

We killed *Sayyid al-Khazraj* [the Chief of the Khazraj tribe] Sa'd ibn 'Abāda; We shot him twice, and his heart gave in.

In response to this effrontery, one of the Ansār recited the following two couplets:

---

[175] Balādhurī, Ahmad ibn Yahyā ibn Jābir, *Ansāb al-Ashrāf*, 1:589; and Ibn 'Abd Rabbih, *al-'Iqd al-Farīd*, 3:64-65, in which it appears with a slight variation relative to that of Balādhurī's.
[176] *Tabsirat al-Ulūm*, p. 32.
[177] Mas'ūdī, Alī ibn al-Husayn, *Murawwij adh-Dhahab*, 1:414 & 2:194.

يَقولُونَ سَعدٌ شَقَّتِ الجِنُّ بَطنَهُ   أَلا رُبَّما حَقَّقتَ فِعلَكَ بِالغَدرِ

وَ ما ذَنبُ سَعدٍ أَنَّهُ بالَ قائِماً   وَلَكِنَّ سَعداً لَمْ يُبايِعْ أَبابَكرٍ ^٨

It is said that the *jinn* tore Saad's belly apart. Beware, for it might be the case that you did your deed with deceit. Sa'd's fault was not that he had urinated in the standing position; his fault was that he refused to pledge allegiance to Abu Bakr.[178]

Thus, the book of Sa'd ibn 'Abāda's life came to a close. But, in so far as the murder of such a determined personality and fearless opponent on the part of the reigning authority was dubious and suspect, it was an event that historians demurred from writing about in their annals. Some of the historians chose to bypass this important event altogether and ignore it.[179] Another group chose to combine the incident of his murder with mythical trappings – as we have already seen – and involve *jinns* into the act![180]

But by positing such fanciful fairy tales, these historians nevertheless fail to state the reason for the *jinns*' reason for their intense hatred and enmity with Sa'd ibn 'Abāda [so that the myth is not even internally consistent or creditable]. Why, pray tell, did the jinn single out poor Sa'd ibn 'Abāda out of all these companions – both from the Emigrants and Helpers – to aim their deadly arrows at?

---

[178] Khoī, *Ma'jam Rijāl al-Hadīth*, 8:73.

[179] Such as Tabarī, Ibn Athīr, and Ibn Kathīr, who have done so in their books of history.

[180] Such as has been done by Ibn Abd'al-Birr in his *al-Istī'āb fi Ma'rifat al-Ashāb*, and by Muhibbiddīn al-Tabarī in his *ar-Riyāḍ an-Naḍra*.

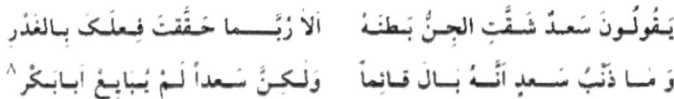

2. The Attempted Enticement of 'Abbās

Abu Bakr formed a council consisting of Umar ibn al-Khattāb, Abu Ubayda ibn al-Jarrāh and Mughira^t ibn Shu'ba that was tasked with deciding what to do with people who did not pledge allegiance to Abu Bakr. The council decided that the best way forward was to go and see 'Abbās and give him and his progeny a stake in the government. They reasoned that in this way, Ali ﷺ would be defeated,[181] and 'Abbās's [subsequent] proclivity towards the caliphal authority would act as a detrimental proof against Ali ﷺ that would be in the hands of the caliphate.[182]

Abu Bakr paid a visit to 'Abbās at night,[183] together with the members of the council. Abu Bakr praised God ﷻ, and then said:

God sent the Prophet, who was the guide and guardian of the believers, and he was among the believers until God preferred the Hereafter for him. And the Prophet, in his turn, did not appoint anyone [to lead his ministry] after his passing[184] and left that [decision] to the people. And the people chose me. Nor should you believe that there is any weakness in me, as I do not fear anyone but God.[185] Those who have not pledged allegiance to me oppose [the will of] the Muslim community at large, and seek refuge in you. Thus, you should either join all the people and

---

[181] In order to belittle Ali, Umar used to aggrandize Ibn Abbās. It was a policy [of the authorities] that Ibn Abbās should narrate hadith reports and explicate and offer his commentary on verses of the Quran. On occasion, Ibn Abbās would say things that were against the interests of the policies of the rulers. For an example of this, see the discussion between Ibn Abbās and Umar as reported by Tabari in Askari, Allāma Murtaḍā, *Abdullāh ibn Sabā*, 1:140-142.

[182] According to Ibn Abī'l-Hadīd, quoting Jawharī's *Saqīfa* in his *Sharh Nahj al-Balāgha*, this meeting took place in the second night after the passing of the Prophet.

[183] All of the prophets used to appoint *awsīā* (plural of *wasī*: legatee, heir, successor). And the Prophet also appointed a *wasī* for himself, like all the other prophets. For a detailed discussion of the issue of legateeship (*wisāya*), see Askari, Allāma Murtaḍā, *Mu'ālim al-Madrisatayn*, 1:289-345 of the fifth edition (1413), as well as Askari, Allāma Murtaḍā, *Aqā'id al-Islam min Qur'ān al-Karīm*, 2:264-285 of the second edition (1418).

[184] When providing reasons for a given position in an argument, it sometimes happens that a reason or reasons are given that are acceptable to the opposite party but which are not acceptable to the person providing them. It seems that Ibn Abbās's words here fall into this category.

[185] Ibn Abī'l-Hadīd, quoting Jawharī's *Saqīfa* in his *Sharh Nahj al-Balāgha*, as well as Ibn Qutayba's *al-Imāma wa'l-Siyāsa* add the following sentence here: "And if it is your own right, we have no need of it."

pledge allegiance [to me], or if you do not join them, you should do something to preclude their fighting us.[186]

We would like to give you a stake in the government that will remain in place for your posterity after your passing because you are the Prophet's ﷺ uncle. And while the people recognized your [lofty spiritual] station as the Prophet's uncle, and recognized Ali's station as well, but they did not choose you for this task. But be that as it may, we are willing to give you a share. Be calm, [O clan of the] Banī Hāshim! For the Apostle of God ﷺ is of both of us! [We are of the tribe of the Quraysh, and the Apostle of God is also of the Quraysh.]

At this juncture, Umar said in a threatening tone,

"We have not come to see you because we are in need of your services. We have come because we do not want to see a disagreement or remonstrance on your part concerning an issue on which the Muslim faithful are agreed, which would only harm both of you. So be careful about how you act."

'Abbās began by praising God ﷻ, and then said,

As you said, God sent the Prophet to be a guide and guardian of the believers. And God blessed the community of the faithful with the blessing of the presence of the Prophet, until He called the Prophet back to Himself and chose for him what He willed; and left it to the Muslim faithful to discern and chose that which is right for themselves, rather than for the faithful to become separated from the truth and what is right by being misguided by the desires and inclinations of the lower desires of their souls. If you have taken on the governance of the community of the faithful in the name of the Prophet, then you have in fact taken a right which is ours, because we are the relatives of the Prophet and have priority over you (*awlā*) in terms of our family bond. But then, if you have taken to the helm of state on the basis that you are one among the believers of the Prophet's [mission and ministry], then

---

186 [This speech of Abu Bakr's is itself evidence of the fact that all of the companions of the Prophet ﷺ had not pledged allegiance to him.] – The note has been added by the original redactor(s).

we too are among such believers. In any event, we have not intervened in the initiative which you took, nor have we interfered with it, but nevertheless continue to object to what you have done. On the other hand, if your position is that the office of leadership has been established for you on the basis of the pledges of allegiance which have been given to you by the believers, and you judge yourself to be worthy of this office on the basis of such pledges, then this is certainly not the case as we too are counted among the believers, and have neither consented to what you claim, nor do we believe that it is anything less than an abomination.

What a great distance there is between the two positions that you have taken. On one hand you say that the people have disagreed and remonstrated with you concerning the matter of leadership; and on the other hand you say that the people have chosen you to be their leader. And how far [from the truth] is this title that you have given yourself: the Successor (Caliph) of the Apostle of God (*khalīfa*ᵗ *rasūl allāh*)! from the fact that you say that "the Prophet ﷺ, in his turn, did not appoint anyone [to lead his ministry] after his passing, and left that [decision] to the people to choose whom they wanted," and that they chose you. For in this case, the Successor of the Apostle of God would be chosen by the people, and not by the Prophet.

As for what you said that if I were to swear allegiance to you, you would give me a stake in the government: if what you are giving me a stake in belongs to the believers, and is their right, then you have no right to give me anything, as you cannot give away something that does not belong to you. But if it is our right, then you must give it all; we do not want a part of what belongs to us, such that you give us a part and keep another part.

And as to what you said about the Apostle of God being "of both of us," the Prophet is indeed a part of a tree of which we are its branches which has grown in your neighborhood.[187]

And as for your statement, O Umar, that you stated you feared that the people would disagree with us. How, then, is it that it is you [and not

[187] This last sentence is Ibn Abbās's way of saying that Umar is not one of them, and has nothing to do with the Prophet.

the people] that are raising this [alleged] disagreement for the first time?

After hearing 'Abbās's response, the company rose and left.[188]

3. The Sit-in at Lady Fātima's House

Umar ibn al-Khattāb has stated the following: "After God ﷻ took His prophet back unto Himself, reports reached us to the effect that Alī ibn Abī-Tālib and Zubayr and their companions have severed ties with us and secluded themselves in Lady Fātima's House as a form of protest against us."[189]

The historians have named the following people as those who refused to pledge allegiance to Abu Bakr and who secluded themselves with Alī ibn Abī-Tālib and Zubayr in Lady Fātima's House: Abbās bin Abdul Muttalib, Utba bin Abī-Lahab, Salman al-Fārsī, Abu Dharr Ghaffārī, Ammār bin Yāsir, Miqdād bin Aswad, Barā' bin 'Āzib, Ubay bin Ka'b, Sa'd ibn Abī-Waqqās, Talha ibn Ubaydallāh, and a number of others from the Banī Hāshim clan, and from among the Emigrants and Helpers.[190]

---

[188] Ya'qūbī, Aḥmad ibn Isḥāq, *Tārīkh al-Ya'qūbī*, 2:103; Ibn Abī'l-Hadīd, quoting Jawharī's *Saqīfa* in his *Sharh Nahj al-Balāgha*, 2:13 & 2:74, as well as 1:220-221; and with phrasing that is close to that of Abī'l-Hadīd's, Ibn Qutayba's *al-Imāma wa'l-Siyāsa*, 1:14.

[189] Ahmad b. Hanbal, *Musnad*, 1:55; Ibn Athīr Jazarī, 'Alī, *al-Kāmil fī al-Tārīkh*, 2:124; Ibn Kathīr, Abu'al-Fiḍā Ismā'īl ibn Umar, *Tārīkh*, 5:246; Tabarī, Muhammad ibn Jarīr, *Tārīkh ar-Rusul wa'l-Mulūk*, 2:466 (and 1:1822 of the European edition); Ibn Jawzī, Abd al-Rahmān b. Ali, *Siffa[t] as-Safwa*, 1:97; Ibn Abī'l-Hadīd, Abdul-Hamīd, *Sharh Nahj al-Balāgha*, 1:123; Ibn Hishām, 'Abd al-Malik, *al-Sīrah al-Nabawīyah*, 4:338; Suyūtī, Jalāladdīn, *Tarikh al-Khulafā*, p. 45; and the digest (*taysīr*) of *al-Wusūl*, 2:41.

[190] The are other sources over and above the ones that have already been mentioned which stipulate that these few people refused to pledge allegiance to Abu Bakr and gathered in Lady Fātima's house in protest. Some of these sources provide the names of a few people who had gathered in Lady Fātima's house in order to pay allegiance to Ali. These sources consist of: Ibn 'Abd Rabbih, *al-'Iqd al-Farīd*, 3:64; Tabarī, Muhibbiddīn, *ar-Riyāḍ an-Naḍra*, 1:167; Abū al-Fidā, Ismā'īl ibn Ali, *Tarikh al-Mukhtasar fī Akhbar al-Bashar*, 1:156; Diyār-Bakri, Husain ibn Muhammad, *Tārīkh al-Khamīs fī Ahwāl an-Nafs an-Nafīs*, 1:188; Ibn Abī'l-Hadīd, quoting Jawharī's *Saqīfa* in his *Sharh Nahj al-Balāgha*, 2:130-134; Halabī, Alī ibn Ibrāhīm, *Insān al-'Uyūn fī Sīra al-Amīn al-Ma'mūn (as-Sīra[t] al-Halabīa)*, 3:394 & 3:397; Ibn Shahna, Muhammad ibn Muhamamd, *al-Kāmil*, in the margins of Ibn Athīr Jazarī, 'Alī, *al-Kāmil fī al-Tārīkh*, 11:112.

The issue of the refusal of Ali and his comrades to pledge allegiance to Abu Bakr and their sit-in in Lady Fātima's ﷺ house has been reported in history books, in hadith compendia, in works of prosopography, in books of theology, and the like to the point of *tawātur*,[191] and there is no doubt about their occurrence. But because the authors of these books preferred not to unveil the events that occurred between the protesters and the victorious party, they have not revealed anything other than what slipped through their penmanship unconsciously.

We will now present an example of this modicum of information that has slipped through Baladhurī's pen regarding this important historical event.

When Ali refused to shoulder the yoke of pledging allegiance to Abu Bakr, Abu Bakr ordered Umar ibn al-Khattāb to bring Ali to his presence, and to use force to do so if necessary. Umar carried out the order, as a consequence of which there was an exchange between him and Ali, until Ali said, "Be sure to milk the Camel of the Caliphate well, for half of it will be your share. Upon my word of honor with God ﷻ, the effort and exertion that you exert today on behalf of Abu Bakr's reign is only expended so that he will consider you more worthy to succeed him tomorrow.[192]

4. The Attack on Lady Fātima's House

The names of the following people have appeared in the books of the historians as those who attacked Lady Fātima's ﷺ house under the orders of Abu Bakr: Umar ibn al-Khattāb, Abdul-Rahmān ibn 'Awf, Thābit ibn Qays ibn Shammās, Ziād ibn Labīd, Muhammad ibn Maslama, Zayd ibn Thābit, Salama ibn Salāma ibn Waqsh, Salama ibn Aslam, Usayd ibn Huḍayr, ...[193]

The details of the attack and how these people entered Lady Fātima's ﷺ house have been described as follows:

---

[191] [To the point where the narrators and transmitters of the reports are so numerous that the occurrence of the event cannot reasonably be in doubt.]
[192] Balādhūrī, Ahmad ibn Yahyā ibn Jābir, *Ansāb al-Ashrāf*, 1:587.
[193] Tabarī, Muhammad ibn Jarīr, *Tārīkh ar-Rusul wa'l-Mulūk*, 2:443-444; Ibn Abī'l-Hadīd, quoting Jawharī's *Saqīfa* in his *Sharh Nahj al-Balāgha*, 2:130-134, and vol. 17 in response to the *Qāḍī al-Quḍḍāt*, ath-Thānī.

A group of the Emigrants that included Ali ibn Abī-Tālib and Zubayr, who had refused to pledge allegiance to Abu Bakr, had gathered in Lady Fātima's house, armed and angry.[194]

Abu Bakr and Umar were informed that a group of Emigrants and Helpers had gathered around Ali ibn Abī-Tālib in Lady Fātima's house, the daughter of the Prophet of God, and intended to pledge allegiance to him concerning the issue of the succession.[195] Abu Bakr ordered Umar to go to Lady Fātima's house[196] and to run them out of the house and disperse the group, and fight them if they resisted.

Umar left for Lady Fātima's house in order to carry out Abu Bakr's orders, holding a fire brand in hand, with which he had determined to set the house on fire.

When Lady Fātima came to the door, she turned to Umar and said: "O son of Kattāb! Have you come to set our house on fire?"

Umar answered, "Yes, unless you join the [rest of] the community and pledge allegiance to Abu Bakr."[197]

Balādhūrī relates the narrative as follows: Abu Bakr sent for Ali in order to get him to pledge allegiance to him, but he refused. Then Umar headed for his house with a firebrand in hand. Fātima confronted Umar at her front door and said, "O son of Kattāb! Have you come to set fire to the door of our house?" Umar replied, "Yes. This act will fortify the religion that your father brought."[198]

The narrative appears in *Kanz al-Ummāl* in the following way: Umar said to Lady Fātima: "No one was more beloved to your father than you, but this fact will not prevent me from ordering your house be burned if this group [remains] gathered in your house."[199]

The narrative appears in the book *al-Imāma wa'l-Siyāsa* as follows: Umar came and called on Ali and the others who had gathered in his house to come out of the house, but they did not do so. Then

---

[194] 162 Tabarī, Muhibbiddīn, *ar-Riyāḍ an-Naḍra*, 1:218; Ibn Abī'l-Hadīd, quoting Jawharī's *Saqīfa* in his *Sharh Nahj al-Balāgha*, 2:130, 2:19, and vol. 17 in response to the *Qāḍī al-Quḍḍāt*, ath-Thānī.

[195] Ya'qūbī, Aḥmad ibn Isḥāq, *Tārīkh al-Ya'qūbī*, 2:105.

[196] Ibn Shahna, Md ibn Md, *al-Kāmil*, in the margins of Ibn Athīr Jazarī, 'Alī, *al-Kāmil fī al-Tārīkh*, 11:113; Ibn Abī'l-Hadīd, Abdul-Hamīd, *Sharh Nahj al-Balāgha*, 2:134.

[197] Ibn Abd al-Rabbih, *al-'Iqd al-Farīd*, 3:64; Abū al-Fidā, Ismā'īl ibn Ali, *Tarikh al-Mukhtasar fi Akhbar al-Bashar*, 1:156.

[198] Balādhūrī, Ahmad ibn Yahyā ibn Jābir, *Ansāb al-Ashrāf*, 1:586.

[199] Muttaqī al-Hindī, *Kanz al-U'mmāl*, 3:140.

Umar said, "I swear unto the God ﷻ in Whose hand my life rests: you will either come out, or I will burn the house down with everyone who is [still] in it." [At that point,] Umar was told that Lady Fātima عليها السلام was in the house, to which he replied that he would burn it down nevertheless.[200]

Hāfiz Ibrāhīm, the Egyptian poet, had composed the following verses concerning these events:[201]

و قولة لعليّ قالها عمر   اكرم بسامعها اعظم بملقيها

حرّقت دارك لا ابقى عليك بها   ان لم تبايع و ابنة المصطفى فيها

ما كان غير ابى حفص يفوه بها   امام فارس عدنان و حاميها

Umar said something to Ali about which both the speaker and the listener are both great and honorable people (*bozorgvār*) and are worthy of veneration and respect. Umar said, "If you do not pledge allegiance, I will burn the house down on your head, and will not let a single soul live, even though the daughter of Mustafā [the Prophet ﷺ] is in the house." Given that these words were spoken before the vanguard of the Warriors of 'Adnān (that is, the great warrior of the tribe of Quraysh), and their leader (Ali ibn Abī-Tālib عليه السلام), they could not have been spoken by anyone other than Umar.

Ya'qūbī states in his *Tārikh*: They, together with a group, attacked Ali's house. In the clash that ensued, Ali's sword broke,[202] and the attackers dared to enter Ali's house and entered it.[203]

Tabari too states in his *Tārikh*: Umar came to Ali's house while Talha and Zubayr and a number of others of the Emigrants were

---

[200] Ibn Qutayba, Abd-Allāh ibn Muslim, *al-Imāma wa'l-Siyāsa*, 1:12.

[201] The *Dīwān* of Hāfiẓ Ibrāhīm, p. 82 (Egypt, 1987 CE). It is interesting to note that these verses appear in an ode (*qasīda*) in which the poet has composed with the intent of eulogizing Umar ibn al-Khattāb. Cf. Aminī, Allāma, *al-Ghadīr*, 8:86.

[202] This hadith report is not true, for two reasons: (1) The Most Noble Prophet had told His Eminence to wait (Majlisī, Allāma Muhammad Bāqir, *Bihār al-Anwār*, 22:527-528; Ibn Shahrāshūb, Muhammad ibn Ali, *Manāqib Āl Abi-Tālib*, 3:336), and drawing a sword went against that command; and (2) His Eminence's having drawn his sword and no one having died is incommensurate with His Eminence's bravery [and martial skills] in the battles. The person who drew his sword was Zubayr.

[203] Ya'qūbī, Aḥmad ibn Isḥāq, *Tārīkh al-Ya'qūbī*, 2:105.

sequestered there. Zubayr (Ali's paternal cousin) rushed to confront him with a drawn sword, but his foot gave way, and his sword fell to the ground. The attackers then rushed forth and arrested him.[204]

Therefore, the false meme (*shobhe*) that is put out nowadays that the houses of the time of the Prophet ﷺ did not have doors for Umar to set fire to is demonstrably incorrect. Given what has been written in the books of the School of the Caliphs, and on the basis of what the caliphs themselves admit, including Umar and Abu Bakr, they set the door of Lady Fātima's عليها السلام house on fire and entered the house by force. We shall point to two reasons here.

5. What Abu Bakr said on his Deathbed

Abu Bakr said the following on his deathbed:

أمّا انّى لا آسى على شىء من الدّنيا الّا على ثلاث فعلتهنّ وددت انّى تركتهنّ.[205] فأمّا الثلاث اللّاتى وددت انّى تركتهنّ فوددت انّى لم اكشف بيت فاطمة (س) عن شىء و ان كانوا قد غلّقوه علىّ الحرب.[206]

I am not bothered by anything [that I have done] in the *dunya* (the lower realm of being; the earthly plane) other than three things which I

---

[204] Tabarī, Muhammad ibn Jarīr, *Tārīkh ar-Rusul wa'l-Mulūk*, 2:443-444, 2:446, and 1:1819-1820 of the European edition; Tabarī, Muhibbiddīn, *ar-Riyāḍ an-Naḍra*, 1:168; Dayār-Bakrī, Ḥusayn Ibn Md., *Tārīkh al-Khamīs fī Ahwāl Anfus an-Nafīs*, 1:188; Ibn Abī'l-Hadīd, Abdul-Hamīd, *Sharh Nahj al-Balāgha*, 2:122, 2;132, 2:134, 2:58, & 2:6; Muttaqī al-Hindī, *Kanz al-U'mmāl*, 3:128. The text in Tabari is as follows:

«بايع النّاس و استشبتوا للبيعة و تخلّف علىّ و الزّبير و اخترط الزّبير سيفه و قال لا اغمده حتّى يبايع علىّ. فبلغ ذلك ابا بكر و عمر. فقال عمر: خذوا سيف الزّبير فاضربوا به الحجر»

[205] In Arabic, the midrail of the door is called the *ghalaq*. Now they make small ones that slide from one leaf of the door to the other. Thus, the houses at the time of the Prophet had doors, and according to Abu Bakr himself, they broke down the door and entered the house with men that were armed with weapons of war.

[206] Dhahabī, Shams al-Dīn Muhammad ibn Ahmad, *Tārīkh al-Islam*, 1:388; Ibn 'Abd Rabbih, *al-'Iqd al-Farīd*, 3:69; Ibn Abī'l-Hadīd, Abdul-Hamīd, *Sharh Nahj al-Balāgha*, 9:130; Lisān al-Mīzān, 4:189; Ibn Asākir, 'Alī, *at-Tārīkh al-Madīna*ᵗ *ad-Damishq*, under the heading of Abū Bakr; Ibn Qutayba, Abd-Allāh ibn Muslim, *al-Imāma wa'l-Siyāsa*, 1:18; Mas'ūdī, Alī ibn al-Ḥusain, *Murawwij adh-Dhahab*, 1:414; Tabarī, Muhammad ibn Jarīr, *Tārīkh ar-Rusul wa'l-Mulūk*, 4:52

How the Caliphal Admin dealt with the Opposition within Medina

have done. And would that I had not done these three things. Would that I had never forced open the door of [Lady] Fāṭima's house, although they had closed it to me in order to wage war against me...

Ya'qūbī presents Abu Bakr's words in this regard as follows in his *Tārīkh*: "Would that I had not forced open [the door] of [Lady] Fāṭima, the daughter of the Prophet ﷺ, and not let my forces enter into her house, although the door of that house had been closed in order to wage war against me.²⁰⁷

6. What 'Umar ibn al-Khaṭṭāb said to His Eminence Alī ibn Abī-Ṭālib

In the book *Kanz al-'Ummāl*, it is stated that Umar said,

ان امرتهم ان يحرقوا عليك الباب

This means, "I would order them to set the door of your house on fire." This phrase suffices to prove our claim.

The story of the burning down of Lady Fāṭima's ﷺ house was infamous. After many years had passed from this episode, Abdullah Ibn Zubayr put pressure on the Bani Hashim for them to submit to his rule and dominion in Mecca, and when they refused to pledge allegiance to him, he ordered them to be imprisoned in the crook of a mountain valley, and for its entrance to be blocked by a large pile of firewood in order to burn them all in its flames. 'Urwa, Abdullah Ibn Zubayr's brother, justified his brother's action by referring to Umar's setting fire to Lady Fāṭima's ﷺ house when Ali ﷺ and his followers refused to pledge allegiance to Abu Bakr, saying, "My brother did this only in order to prevent dissension from arising between the Muslims and the destruction of their unity. He wanted everyone to become a unitary front by obeying him, just as Umar ibn al-Khaṭṭāb had done with the Banī Hāshim before him when they refused to pledge allegiance to Abu Bakr. He too prepared firewood in order to burn them in their house.²⁰⁸

---

²⁰⁷ Ya'qūbī, Aḥmad ibn Isḥāq, *Tārīkh al-Ya'qūbī*, 2:115. The text of Abu Bakr's speech as it appears in Yaqūbī is as follows:

«و ليتنى لم افتّش بيت فاطمة بنت رسول الله و ادخله الرجال و لو كان اغلق على حرب».

²⁰⁸ Mas'ūdī, Alī ibn al-Ḥusayn, *Murawwij adh-Dhahab*, 3:86; Ibn Abī'l-Hadīd, Abdul-Hamīd, *Sharh Nahj al-Balāgha*, 20:481.

7. How the Caliphate dealt with His Eminence Alī ibn Abī-Tālib

Abu Bakr al-Jawhar has related that when Ali was being taken against his will to the Mosque in order for him to pledge allegiance to Abu Bakr, he said,

انا عبد الله و اخو رسول الله (ص)

Which means, "I am the servant of God and the brother of God's apostle."[209] His eminence was ultimately made to appear before Abu Bakr, and was asked to pledge allegiance to him. In response, Ali said, "I am worthier of the office of rulership than you. Therefore, I will not pledge allegiance to you. Rather, it is you who should pledge allegiance to me. You took this office away from the Helpers (*ansār*) on the basis of your kinship with the Prophet; and they consented to give you the reins of power for the same reason. I, in turn, present you with the same reason. Thus, if you do not follow your lower [= self-serving] desires, and you fear God, treat us [of the *ahl al-bayt*] with fairness, and give to us our right of rulership, just as the Helpers gave that right to you, and formally recognize our right to rule. For if you do not do so, and commit this injustice against us, it will come back to haunt you."

Umar said, "You will not be freed until you pledge allegiance."

Ali replied, "O Umar, you are milking a cow, half of whose milk will be your share. Strengthen the foundation of his [= Abu Bakr's] reign so that he will vouchsafe it to you tomorrow. I swear to God, neither will I accept what you say, nor will I follow him."

Abu Bakr said, "If you do not pledge allegiance to me, I will not force you to do so."

Abu Ubaydā al-Jarrāh said, "O Abu'l-Hasan. You are young, and these are old men who are your Qurayshite kin! You neither have their experience, nor do you have their experience and mastery of [the] affairs [of state]. For a matter of such grave importance, I consider Abu Bakr to be more capable, more knowledgeable, and with greater longanimity and forbearance. So agree with him and entrust the matter of the rule to him. For if you remain [alive] and live a long life, you will be more deserving than anyone of being vested in this position, both in terms of your wisdom, as well as in terms of your kinship with the

---

[209] Ibn Abī'l-Hadīd, Abdul-Hamīd, *Sharh Nahj al-Balāgha,* quoting Jawharī's *Saqīfa* 6:285; Ibn ʿAbd Rabbih, *al-ʿIqd al-Farīd,* 4:248; *Subh al-Iʿshī,* 1:128.

Messenger of God, and in terms of your priority in Islam and your efforts for establishing Islam."

Ali ﷺ said: "O group of Emigrants! Take God into consideration in your thoughts and do not take rulership and [the] government [of the community] out of the House of Muhammad, placing it instead in [the possession of] your own clans and tribes. Do not remove the House of the Prophet from the position and station that they have among the people, and do not trample on their right. I swear by God, O Emigrants, as long as there exists in us, the Ahl al-Bayt of the Prophet, those who recite the Quran and are knowledgeable in matters of religion and with the exemplary model of the Prophet, we will be worthier than you for taking the helm of the ship of state of this community in hand. I swear by God that all of these signs are present in us. So do not follow the bidding of your lower desires, as step by step you will become ever more distant from the path of that which is right."

Having heard the words of the Imam, Bashīr ibn Sa'd turned to his eminence and said: "If the Helpers had heard these words from you before they pledged allegiance to Abu Bakr, not even two of them would have disagreed with each other in accepting your rule and sovereignty [over them]. But what can be done now that they have pledged allegiance to Abu Bakr and it is too late to do anything about it." Verily, Ali did not pledge allegiance to Abu Bakr at that time, and returned to his home without doing so. [210]

Abu Bakr al-Jawhari has also related: When Lady Fātima saw what they did with Ali and Zubayr, she stood in the portal of her quarters[211] and, facing Abu Bakr, said, "O Abu Bakr! How soon did you become a deceiver with the family of the Prophet ﷺ of God! I swear by God ﷻ that I will not speak to Umar again for as long as I live."

In another hadith report, it is stated that Lady Fātima ﷺ exited her house while she was weeping bitterly, and pushed the people [who had come for her husband] away from her house.[212]

Ya'qūbī also writes in his *Tārīkh*: Fātima ﷺ came out of her house and said to the people who had invaded her home, "You will leave my house [immediately], or, by God, I will bare my head and take

[210] Ibn Abī'l-Hadīd, quoting Jawharī's *Saqīfa* in his *Sharh Nahj al-Balāgha*, 6:285.

[211] The door to Lady Fātima's ^^ house opened onto the mosque. Ibn Abī'l-Hadīd, quoting Jawharī's *Saqīfa* in his *Sharh Nahj al-Balāgha*, 2:134 & 6:284.

[212] Ibid.

my complaint to God." Having heard this threat, the invaders left the house, together with the others that were there.[213]

Mas'ūdī also writes in his *Tārīkh*: When people had finished pledging allegiance to Abu Bakr in the Saqīfa, and pledges of allegiance to him were renewed on Tuesday in the mosque, Ali came out of his house and, facing Abu Bakr, said to him, "You have ruined the affairs of the Muslims, failed to make any consultations, and ignored our right." Abu Bakr replied: "Yes, this is true, but I was afraid that sedition and chaos would [otherwise] arise."[214]

8. The Reaction of the House of the Prophet after the Saqīfa

Ya'qūbī says: A group of people surrounded Ali and wanted to pledge allegiance to him. His Eminence said to them: "Show up here tomorrow morning with shaved heads." But when morning came, only three of those present showed up.[215]

From then on, Ali would take Lady Fātima with him and sit her on a stool at the doors of the houses of the Emigrants and would ask them to help her regain the right that was taken from her; and Lady Fātima would also call on them to help Ali. But the Emigrants would reply, "O daughter of the Prophet ﷺ, we have pledged allegiance to Abu Bakr, and the deed is done. If your cousin had surpassed Abu Bakr in taking the reins of the succession in hand, we would, of course, not have accepted Abu Bakr."

In response to them, Ali said,

أ فكنت اترك رسول الله ميتا فى بيته لم اجهّزه و اخرج الى النّاس
انازعهم فى سلطانه؟

"Did you [expect me to] abandon [the body of] the Messenger of God in his house without [performing the ritual] cleansing [of his body] and [preparing it for burial by] enshrouding [it with a burial

---

213 Ya'qūbī, Aḥmad ibn Isḥāq, *Tārīkh al-Ya'qūbī*, 2:105.
214 Mas'ūdī, Alī ibn al-Ḥusayn, *Murawwij adh-Dhahab*, 1:414; and slightly differently in Ibn Qutayba, Abd-Allāh ibn Muslim, *al-Imāma wa'l-Siyāsa*, 1:12-14 (Askari, Allāma Murtaḍā, *Abdullāh ibn Sabā*, 1:136)
215 Ya'qūbī, Aḥmad ibn Isḥāq, *Tārīkh al-Ya'qūbī*, 2:126; Ibn Abī'l-Hadīd, Abdul-Hamīd, *Sharh Nahj al-Balāgha*, 2:4.

shroud], and go and get into an altercation with people in order to secure [my succession to] his reign??

Lady Fātima ﷺ added: "Abu'l-Hasan did what was right and proper, but the people did something for which they will be held accountable by God years later, and for which they will have to answer."[216]

Referring to this in a letter he sent to Ali, Mu'āwiyah writes:

I remember how yesterday you would sit the occupier of your inner sanctum [reference to Lady Fātima] on a stool and would [stand] holding al-Hasan and al-Husayn's hands in your own when pledges of allegiance had been given to Abu Bakr the Truthful (*as-Siddīq*). And you did not leave out a single [veteran] of [the Battle of] Badr or the [other] pioneers of Islam in your efforts to call to aid you [in your cause]. You would go to their doors with your wife, and present your two children as testimony and proofs, and call them to help you against the companion of the Prophet [reference to Abu Bakr]. But in the end, no one responded to the call, other than four or five people. Because, I swear upon my own soul, if you were in the right, they would undoubtedly have turned to you and responded to your call. But the claim that you made was false and baseless, and said things that no one believed, and you intended to do the impossible. And although I have a forgetful memory, I have not forgotten your words to Abu Sufyan - who incited you to rise up [in insurrection] – to whom you said: "If I had forty determined and steadfast men with me, I would rise up against them."[217]

---

[216] Ibn Abī'l-Hadīd, quoting Jawharī's *Saqīfa* in his *Sharh Nahj al-Balāgha*, 6:28; Ibn Qutayba, Abd-Allāh ibn Muslim, *al-Imāma wa'l-Siyāsa*, 1:12.

[217] Ibn Abī'l-Hadīd, quoting Jawharī's *Saqīfa* in his *Sharh Nahj al-Balāgha*, 2:47 & 1:131. The Commander of the Faithful responded as follows to these words of Mu'āwiya's: «لقد اردت ان تذمّ فمدحت و ان تفضح فافتضحت و ما على المسلم من غضاضة فى ان يكون مظلوما ما لم يكن شاكّا فى دينه و لا مرتابا بيقينه»
"I swear by God, you wanted to reproach him, but you [actually] praised him, and you wanted to disgrace him, but you yourself was disgraced {because, by saying this, you have made the transgression of my rights manifest, because you confessed to the fact that I pledged allegiance to [the forces of] oppression, reluctantly and under duress. So you in fact reproached the caliphs, and have disgraced yourself], and no reproach can be validly levelled against the Muslims while they do not harbor doubts about their religion and beliefs." (*Nahj al-Balāgha*, Letter #28, pp. 899-900.) In addition to this, Mu'āwiya explicitly confesses to Abu Bakr's and Umar's preplanned usurpation of Ali's

9. The Guidance of the Prophet

The Prophet ﷺ had carefully laid out plans for the guidance of the Muslim faithful after his passing – plans that could not be surpassed [in their excellence]. One of the instances of this planning is the story of the revelation of the Verse of Purification (*Āya^t at-Tathīr*). Umm Salāma has narrated the story as follows:

One day the Prophet was in my quarters when he received indications of God's mercy. He said: "Tell my *ahl al-bayt* (the People of my House) to come here." I asked, "Who are your *ahl al-bayt*?" He said: "Ali, Fātima, Hasan and Husain." When they arrived, the Prophet placed Hasan and Husain on his two knees, and sat Ali and Fātima before and behind himself. He then took the Yemenese mantle from the bed and spread it over his and their heads, and said,

إِنَّمَا يُرِيدُ اللَّهُ لِيُذْهِبَ عَنكُمُ الرِّجْسَ أَهْلَ الْبَيْتِ وَيُطَهِّرَكُمْ تَطْهِيرًا ﴿٣٣﴾

[33:33] And God desires to remove from you *ar-rijs* (all that might be loathsome; sin), O you members of the [Prophet's] Household, and to purify you to utmost purity.

(Umm Salāma relates:) I said, "O Apostle of God am I not of your *ahl al-bayt*?" The Apostle of God said, "You are a righteous lady, but you are not of my *ahl al-bayt*. You are a wife of the Prophet ."[218]

After the revelation of this verse, the Prophet ﷺ would pass by the door of Ali and Fātima's house (which opened into the mosque), and would place his hand on their door and call out: "Peace be with

---

right [to the succession]. (Mas'ūdī, Alī ibn al-Ḥusayn, *Murawwij adh-Dhahab*, 2:60; Nasr ibn Muzāhim, *Waq'at Siffīn*, p. 135; Ibn Abī'l-Hadīd, Abdul-Hamīd, *Sharh Nahj al-Balāgha*, 2:65 & 1:284.)

[218] Ahmad b. Hanbal, *Musnad*, 6:306; And according to a hadith report in Hākim al-Haskānī an-Neyshāpūrī, *al-Mustadrak 'Alā's-Sahīhayn*, 2:416 & 3:147; Ibn Athīr, 'Alī ibn Muḥammad, *Usd al-Ghābah fī Ma'rifat al-Ṣaḥābah*, 4:29 & 2:297 & 5:521 & 5:589; Suyūṭī, Jalāl al-Dīn 'Abd al-Raḥmān, *al-Durr al-Manthūr fī al-Tafsīr bi-al-Ma'thūr*, 5:198-199; and in a different hadith report in Tirmidhī, Muḥammad ibn 'Īsá, *Sunan al-Tirmidhī*, 13:248; Tabarī, Muhammad ibn Jarīr, *Tārīkh ar-Rusul wa'l-Mulūk*, 6:22, under the āya in question; Ibn Hajar, Ahmad ibn Ali al-Asqalāni, *Taqrīb al-Tahdhīb*, 2:297; Bayhaqī, Ahmad ibn Husayn, *Sunan al-Kubrā*, 2:150; Khatīb al-Baghdādī, Ahmad ibn Ali, *Tarīkh al-Baghdād*, 9:126.

you, O People of the House!" And he would then recite the Āya of Purification." He would then call them to the communal devotions, saying, "*as-salāh, as-salāh.*" Because the door of Ali ﷺ and Fātima's ﷺ house opened into the mosque, all of the Prophet's companions would see what the Prophet ﷺ did with this house and its inhabitants five times a day.[219] This act of the Prophet's caused the light of truth to shine [in the souls of those who witnessed it]. Still, we saw the odium of what some of the companions of the Prophet ﷺ did with this house and with its inhabitants.[220]

---

[219] Suyūṭī, Jalāl al-Dīn 'Abd al-Raḥmān, *al-Durr al-Manthūr fī al-Tafsīr bi-al-Ma'thūr,* 5:199, under the āya in question, and according to a hadith report, in Ibn Abd'al-Birr, Yusuf ibn Abdallah, *al-Istī'āb fī Ma'rifat al-Ashāb,* 2:598; Ibn Athīr, 'Alī ibn Muḥammad, *Usd al-Ghābah fī Ma'rifat al-Ṣaḥābah,* 5:174; Haythamī, Ahmad Ibn-Hajar, *Majma' az-Zawāid wa Manba' al-Fawā'id,* 9:168; and according to a hadith report narrated by Anas ibn Mālik in Hākim al-Haskānī an-Neyshāpūrī, *al-Mustadrak 'Alā's-Sahīhayn,* 3:158, which Hākim has deemed to be a 'sound' or authoritative (*sahīh*) report, using Muslim's criteria. Ahmad b. Hanbal, *Musnad,* 3:258; Ibn Athīr, 'Alī ibn Muḥammad, *Usd al-Ghābah fī Ma'rifat al-Ṣaḥābah,* 5:521; Ibn Kathīr, Abu'al-Fiḍā Ismā'īl ibn Umar, *Tārīkh,* 3:483; Suyūṭī, Jalāl al-Dīn 'Abd al-Raḥmān, *al-Durr al-Manthūr fī al-Tafsīr bi-al-Ma'thūr,* 5:199; Tabarī, Muhammad ibn Jarīr, *Tārīkh ar-Rusul wa'l-Mulūk,* 22:5; Tayālasī, Sulaymān ibn Dāwūd, *Musnad,* 8:274; Muttaqī al-Hindī, *Kanz al-U'mmāl,* 7:103; Tirmidhī, Muḥammad ibn 'Īsá, *Sunan al-Tirmidhī,* 12:85; *Jāmi' al-Usūl,* 10:101, hadith #6691; and the digest (*tīsīr*) of *al-Wusūl,* 3:297. For an extended bibliography on the sources of this topic, cf. Askari, Allāma Murtaḍā, *Hadīth al-Kisā fī Kutub Madrisat al-Khulafā' wa Madrisat Ahl al-Bayt.*

[220] To gain a better understanding of the odium of this event, which also appears in the books of the School of the Caliphs [= Sunnis], cf. Askari, Allāma Murtaḍā, *Abdullāh ibn Sabā,* 1:128-139; and احراق بيت فاطمة (س) فى الكتب المعتبرة عند اهل السنّة' شيخ حسين غيب غلامى' اوّل' ها' ق' ه 1417 .

6 Economic Warfare against the House of the Prophet

The caliphal authority needed to carry out a military campaign in order to obtain the pledges of allegiance of the tribes outside Medina. And it needed [to disburse public] treasure and property in order to be able to carry out its other functions. On the other hand, those who were in Medina and around the Commander of the Faithful Ali posed a danger to the caliphal power. In fact, this is where the real danger lay. Therefore, in order to disperse them, the property and wealth of the *Ahl al-Bayt* (which included the Fadak lands and their share of the *khums*, and the Prophet's inheritance) was confiscated so as to impoverish the family of the Prophet ﷺ and to drive people away from them.

1. Sources of the Prophet's property and how they were acquired

(1) We can attain an understanding of the financial sources of the Prophet ﷺ and his *Ahl al-Bayt* from the following two verses:

مَّا أَفَاءَ اللَّهُ عَلَىٰ رَسُولِهِ مِنْ أَهْلِ الْقُرَىٰ فَلِلَّهِ وَلِلرَّسُولِ وَلِذِي الْقُرْبَىٰ
وَالْيَتَامَىٰ وَالْمَسَاكِينِ وَابْنِ السَّبِيلِ كَيْ لَا يَكُونَ دُولَةً بَيْنَ الْأَغْنِيَاءِ
مِنكُمْ ﴿٧﴾

[59:7] Whatever [spoils taken] from the people of those villages [of the unbelievers] God has turned over to His Apostle - [all of it] belongs to God and the Apostle, the near of kin [of the Prophet], the orphans, the needy, and the wayfarer [of the Banī Hāshim, who are the progeny of his eminence 'Abd al-Mutallib] ...

The name of these properties [when referred to collectively] is *fī*.[221] And *fī* refers to the property of unbelievers which falls into the hands of the Muslim community without any warfare having taken place. The Fadak lands are a case in point, though not the only case, of course.[222] This property rightfully belonged to the Prophet ﷺ, who gave of it in charity to his near of kin, to orphans, to the indigent, and to the stranded wayfarer (*ibn as-sabīl*)[223] of the Banī Hāshim. The stranded wayfarer who is not of the Banī Hāshim is paid out of the more general *zakāt* (alms or 'purifying dues') funds.

(2) Here is the second verse in evidence:

وَاعْلَمُوا أَنَّمَا غَنِمْتُم مِّن شَيْءٍ فَأَنَّ لِلَّهِ خُمُسَهُ وَلِلرَّسُولِ وَلِذِي الْقُرْبَىٰ وَالْيَتَامَىٰ وَالْمَسَاكِينِ وَابْنِ السَّبِيلِ إِن كُنتُمْ آمَنتُم بِاللَّهِ وَمَا أَنزَلْنَا عَلَىٰ عَبْدِنَا يَوْمَ الْفُرْقَانِ يَوْمَ الْتَقَى الْجَمْعَانِ ۗ وَاللَّهُ عَلَىٰ كُلِّ شَيْءٍ قَدِيرٌ ﴿٤١﴾

8:41] And know that whatever booty you acquire [in war], one-fifth [thereof belongs to God and the Apostle, the near of kin, and the orphans, and the needy, and the stranded wayfarer [of the kin of the Apostle of God; of the Banī Hāshim]. [This you must observe] if you believe in God...

On this basis, the Shi'a pay a fifth of whatever they make in profits as *khums*.

(3, 4, & 5) Three of the forts of Khaybar. Khaybar consisted of seven or eight forts, three of which belonged to the Prophet ﷺ.

(6) Fadak, which was one of the forts of Khaybar. And the residents of Fadak surrendered to the Prophet ﷺwithout putting up any resistance.

(7) Wādī al-Qurā. The villages between Medina and the Levant were called Wādī al-Qurā. Their number was seventy villages (or hamlets) and all their inhabitants were Jews. They had rebelled, and when the Prophet ﷺcame, they surrendered and made an agreement

[221] *Lisān al-'Arab*, under the word *al-fī'*.
[222] For a detailed discussion of the issue of Fadak, cf. Askari, Allāma Murtaḍā, *Mu'ālim al-Madrisatayn*.
[223] [*Ibn as-sabīl* are wayfarers who are not indigent in their home towns, but who have fallen on hard times outside their normal place of residence for some reason or other, such as there having been robbed of their money by thieves.]

with him that they could keep one third of the product [of their lands] for themselves, but would give two thirds of it to the Prophet ﷺor to a person designated by him.[224]

(8) The Helpers donated lands that had no natural water catchment to the Prophet ﷺ,[225] and all of these lands were the property of the Prophet ﷺ.

2. The Context of Revelation of Verse 17:26

وَآتِ ذَا الْقُرْبَىٰ حَقَّهُ وَالْمِسْكِينَ وَابْنَ السَّبِيلِ وَلَا تُبَذِّرْ تَبْذِيرًا ﴿٢٦﴾

[17:26] And give what is due to the near of kin, as well as to the needy and the stranded wayfarer [of the Banī Hāshim], but do not squander [thy substance] senselessly.

The Prophet ﷺ had gifted some of the lands he had to Abu Bakr, Umar, Uthmān, 'Āisha, Hafsa,[226] and to others. And he said to one of his companions[227] in Wādī al-Qurā, Stand and shoot your arrow; wherever it falls will be the limit of your property."[228] But the Prophet ﷺ had not gifted anything to Lady Fātima ؑ, which is why verse 17:26 was revealed.

Her eminence Lady Khadīja ؑ, Lady Fātima's mother, had given all of her worldly possessions in the cause of Islam, which is why God ﷻ commanded the Prophet ﷺ to give Lady Fātima ؑ the Fadak fortifications and lands in return for these sacrifices. The Prophet ﷺ duly complied, calling Lady Fātima ؑ to him and giving her Fadak.[229]

---

[224] Wāqidī, *al-Maghāzī*, pp. 710-711; *Futūh al-Baldān*, 1:39-40; *Imtā' al-Asmā'*, p. 332; Māwardī, *al-Ahkām al-Sultānīa*, p. 170; Abū Ya'lā, *al-Ahkām al-Sultānīa*, p. 185.

[225] Abū 'Ubaida, *Amwāl*, p. 282.

[226] Ibn Sa'd, Abu Abdallah Muhammad, *al-Tabaqāt al-Kubrā*, 2:58; *Futūh al-Baldān*, 1:18-22.

[227] Hamzat ibn Nu'mān al-'Udhrī.

[228] *Futūh al-Baldān*, 1:40.

[229] A letter of the Prophet's is extant in which he stipulates the ownership of Fadak as belonging to Lady Fātima. (Majlisī, Allāma Muhammad Bāqir, *Bihār al-Anwār*, 8:93 & 8:105).

3. The Usurpation of Fadak by the Caliphs

As we stated above, the Prophet ﷺ had given some of his property to various Muslims who were in possession of these properties. There is a ruling of the sacred law (the *sharī'a*) that a person who is in possession of a given property is its legal owner according to the sacred law. This ruling is called the rule of possession (*qāida dhū al-yad*).

The Prophet ﷺ had given Fadak to Lady Fātima عليها السلام, who had taken possession of it, so it fell under the *dhū al-yad* ruling.[230] Nevertheless, Abu Bakr took Fadak from Lady Fātima عليها السلام. Lady Fātima عليها السلام said, "Return Fadak to me, because it was given to me by the Prophet ﷺ." She was told to bring witnesses; but they had not asked the others to produce witnesses for the properties that the Prophet ﷺ had given them during his lifetime! Lady Fātima عليها السلام said, "At the time the Prophet ﷺgave me this property, these two witnesses were present: Ali عليه السلام and Umm Ayman.[231] Abu Bakr replied, "That will not do. In the testimony of witnesses, there must either be two men, or one man and two women."[232]

Another hadith report tells us that the caliph decided to return Fadak to Lady Fātima عليها السلام after she produced her witnesses. He thus deeded Fadak to Lady Fātima عليها السلام on some parchment, but then Umar showed up and tore the parchment up.[233]

---

230 When the order for the confiscation of Fadak was issued by Abu Bakr, Lady Fātima's workers were occupied in working its fields. (Ibn Abī'l-Hadīd, Abdul-Hamīd, *Sharh Nahj al-Balāgha*, 11:211)

231 According to Mas'ūdī's *Murawwij adh-Dhahab*, 2:200, Lady Fātima presented the Hasnayn (Hasan and Husain) as witnesses in addion to Ali and Umm Amīn. Ali and Umm Amīn testified that the Prophet had given Fadak to Lady Fātima while he was alive (*Wafā' al-Wifā'*, 2:160). According to Balādhūrī, one of the Prophet's slaves who was named Ribāh also testified to the truth of Lady Fatima's assertion. (*Futūh al-Baldān*, p. 43).

232 Halabī, Alī ibn Ibrāhīm, *Insān al-'Uyūn fī Sīra al-Amīn al-Ma'mūn* (*as-Sīra[t] al-Halabīa*), 2:400; Balādhūrī, Ahmad ibn Yahyā ibn Jābir, *Futūh al-Baldān*, p. 43; *Ma'jam al-Baldān*, Vol. 4, under the heading 'Fadak'.

233 Halabī, Alī ibn Ibrāhīm, *Insān al-'Uyūn fī Sīra al-Amīn al-Ma'mūn* (*as-Sīra[t] al-Halabīa*), 3:400; Ibn Abī'l-Hadīd, Abdul-Hamīd, *Sharh Nahj al-Balāgha*, 16:274.

4. The Usurpation of the Prophet's Inheritance

The inheritance of the Prophet ﷺ was also taken away from the Ahl al-Bayt.[234] Lady Fāṭima ؑ said to Abu Bakr: "Return my inheritance from the Prophet ﷺ." Abu Bakr said, "Do you want the furniture and belongings of the house, or the fields and gardens that belonged to the Prophet?" Lady Fāṭima ؑ said, "Both. I inherit these from the Prophet, just as your daughters will inherit from you after your death." Abu Bakr said: "By God, the Prophet was better than me, and you are better than my daughters, but what can I do when the Prophet said, 'No one inherits from us prophets; whatever we leave behind is [to be given away in??] charity.[235]

5. Lady Fāṭima's Speech in the Mosque

Ten days after the death of the Prophet ﷺ,[236] after Lady Fāṭima ؑ had presented all of her reasons and produced her witnesses in support of her inheritance rights, and Abu Bakr refused to accept them and return her property to her, Lady Fāṭima ؑ sought the help of her father's friends. To this aim, as we are told by the historians and hadith scholars, she headed for the Mosque of the Prophet ﷺ. This subject

---

[234] Umar said, "When the Prophet of God died, I went to Ali with Abu Bakr and said, 'What do you say about what the Messenger of God has left behind?' Ali said, 'We are more deserving than anyone else (to take possession of) what the Messenger of God has left behind.' I said, 'And with respect to [the] Khaybar [properties]?' He said, 'Yes, with respect to [the] Khaybar [properties] also.' I said, 'What about [the] Fadak [lands]?' He said, 'Yes, [the] Fadak [lands] also.' I said, 'Know that, by God, even if you sever our heads with a sword, such a thing would not be possible. In other words, it would be impossible for us to give these to you.'" (Haythamī, Ahmad Ibn-Hajar, *Majma' az-Zawāid wa Manba' al-Fawā'id*, 9:39).

[235] Ibn Abī'l-Hadīd writes in his *Sharh Nahj al-Balāgha* (4:82) that the majority opinion (*mashhūr ān ast ke*) that no one other than Abu Bakr has narrated the hadith report that states that the Prophet said that prophets do not leave any belongings as inheritance. On page 85 [of the same volume,] he writes, "most hadith reports indicate that the hadith report has not been narrated by anyone other than Abu Bakr himself." Jalāladdīn Suyūtī also writes on p. 89 of his *Tarikh al-Khulafā* where he counts the hadith reports narrated by Abu Bakr, saying that the hadith report that states that the Prophet said that prophets do not leave any belongings as inheritance is the 29th. But irrespective of all this, hadith reports were fabricated later whose origin was attributed to persons other than Abu Bakr in order for it to be able to be claimed that people other than Abu Bakr also narrated this particular hadith report. See also, Ibn Sa'd, Abu Abdallah Muhammad, *al-Tabaqāt al-Kubrā*, 2:316 as well as Askari, Allāma Murtaḍā, *Mu'ālim al-Madrisatayn*.

[236] Ibn Abī'l-Hadīd, Abdul-Hamīd, *Sharh Nahj al-Balāgha*, 4:97.

appears in Abu Bakr Jawharī's *Saqīfa,* who cites the narrative of the Mu'tazilite scholar Ibn Abī'l-Hadīd. It also appears in Ahmad ibn Abī-Tayfūr's *Balāghāt an-Nisā'*.[237] We shall present Abu Bakr Jawharī's report, which states:

When Fātima realized that Abu Bakr had decided not to return the Fadak property to her, she put on a headscarf,[238] wrapped herself in a *chādor,*[239] and went to the mosque among a cluster of her female relatives, while her skirt covered her noble legs, whose strides were like those of the Prophet's. She entered the mosque and came upon Abu Bakr, who was sitting among a crowded group of the Emigrants and the Helpers, and some others. Then a veil was set up before her, after which Lady Fātima uttered a heartfelt wail that affected those present very deeply and made them weep bitterly, and made the atmosphere tense. She tarried a little while for the weeping of the crowd to settle, and for their wails and moans to calm down. She then started her speech by praising God, the Almighty and Majestic, and by sending blessings unto His Prophet, and then said:

I am Fātima, the daughter of the Apostle; [9:128] an Apostle from among yourselves upon whom weighs heavily [the thought] that you might suffer [in this life and in the life to come]; full of concern for you [is he, and] full of compassion and mercy towards the believers. If you look unto him and consider his lineage, you will find that he is my father and not yours. And that he is the brother of my cousin, and he is not the brother of your menfolk. ... And you now think that we do not to inherit from the Prophet? [5:50] Do they, perchance, desire [to be

---

237 In addition to this, this matter appears in Majlisī, Allāma Muhammad Bāqir, *Bihār al-Anwār,* 8:108 ff. and Tabarsī's *al-Ihtijāj,* 1:253 as well.

238 What is meant by a headscarf here is a *jamār,* which is a piece of cloth with which women covered their heads, necks, and breasts, and which was thus larger than a regular headscarf which only covers the head. The following Quranic verse refers to this same article of clothing: [24:31] *And tell the believing women to lower their gaze and to be mindful of their chastity, and not to display their charms [in public] beyond what may [decently] be apparent thereof; hence, let them draw their head-coverings over their bosoms.*

239 A *chādor* is a full body-length cloth that is worn over a woman's head and which comes down to the ankles. It is open in front but is held closed with the hands.

ruled by] the law of pagan ignorance? But for people who have inner certainty, who could be a better law-giver than God?
O son of Abu Qahāfa! [Is this truly what you propose? That] you should inherit from your father, but that I should not inherit from mine?? Truly, yours is an astounding and horrifying claim! Let Fadak, then, be your lot, like a camel that has [already] been saddled and tethered, which will revisit you on the Day of Requital; for God ﷻ is a righteous judge, and the Prophet ﷺ is a worthy claimant, in the court of the Day of Requital. That is the Day when the criminals will suffer a [grave] loss.

Lady Fātima عليها السلام then turned toward her father's grave and recited these two verses:

قد كان بعدك أنباء و هنبثة   لو كنت شاهدها لم تكثر الخطب
انّا فقدناك فقد الارض و ابلها   و اختلّ قومك فاشهدهم لقد نكبو

[O Prophet!] Verily, after your passing, hardships arose which would be curtailed had you been present. We lost you, and it is as if the Earth has lost all of its bounteous men. Your tribe became debased and turned away from righteousness. So bear witness.[240]

[The narrator says that until that day, he had not seen those people, men and women both, weeping and wailing as much as they were.] Then Lady Fātima عليها السلام turned to the Helpers and said:

O group of those who were chosen! O arms of the nation and guardians of Islam! Why are you so slack in coming to my aid? Why do you not help me? Why do you ignore [the trampling of] my rights and my grievance? Did not the Messenger of God say that honoring a man's

[240] The end of the second couplet in most of the sources appears as *wa lā taghibī*, similar to *Bilāghat an-Nasā*, p. 14, as well as Ibn Abī'l-Hadīd, Abdul-Hamīd, *Sharh Nahj al-Balāgha*, 16:251; Majlisī, Allāma Muhammad Bāqir, *Bihār al-Anwār*, 43:195; and Tabarsī's *al-Ihtijāj*, 1:106. But *laqad nakabū* has been used [instead] for rhyming purposes, as well as for making the meaning more appropriate. Cf. Askari, Allāma Murtaḍā, *al-Qurān al-Karīm wa Riwāyāt al-Madrisatayn*, 2:229.

offspring is tantamount to honoring the father? How soon have you changed God's religion and hastened to establish reprehensible innovations! Now that the Prophet has passed away, will you then also destroy his religion?! I swear upon my soul that his death is a great tragedy and a deep, ever-widening rift that will never be closed. After his passing, hopes were dashed, and the Earth became dark and opaque, and the mountains were shattered asunder. After his passing, [all] limits were lifted and the veil of sanctity was torn, and safety and security were lost. All of this had been announced in the Quran before the death of the Prophet, and made you aware of it, where it says:

وَمَا مُحَمَّدٌ إِلَّا رَسُولٌ قَدْ خَلَتْ مِن قَبْلِهِ الرُّسُلُ ۚ أَفَإِن مَّاتَ أَوْ قُتِلَ انقَلَبْتُمْ
عَلَىٰ أَعْقَابِكُمْ ۚ وَمَن يَنقَلِبْ عَلَىٰ عَقِبَيْهِ فَلَن يَضُرَّ اللَّهَ شَيْئًا ۗ وَسَيَجْزِي
اللَّهُ الشَّاكِرِينَ ﴿١٤٤﴾

[3:144] And Muhammad is only an apostle; all the [other] apostles have passed away before him: if, then, he dies or is slain, will you turn about on your heels? But he that turns about on his heels can in no wise harm God - whereas God will requite all who are grateful [to Him].

I am speaking to you, O sons of the tribe! They usurp my father's inheritance before your very eyes, and you hear my cry for justice, but you do nothing, even though you have the wherewithal and understand [the meaning of] honor and respect! You are the best and the most righteous [men] that have been chosen by God! You fell out with the Arabs [infidels], and you accepted the hardships [that all that entailed], and you engaged them in a struggle and vanquished them, to the point that the millstone of Islam was put in motion thanks to your spiritual will and commitment, and victories were gained, and the conflagration of war subsided, and the sound and the fury of idolatry dwindled, and [moral] chaos disappeared, and God's order was established. But now, after all this progress, you have retreated, and after all this stewardship and support, you have failed. After all this courage, do you then fear a handful of retrograde people, (who have thrown away their faith with the covenant they discarded, and who mock your religion and sense of morality)? Have you then gone and slunk away in some corner after such courage? [9:12] *But if they break their solemn pledges after having concluded a covenant, and revile your religion, then fight against these*

archetypes of faithlessness who, behold, have no [regard for their own] pledges, so that they might desist [from aggression].
But I see that you have turned to abjection and ease, and to self-satisfaction and self-indulgence, and have negated your beliefs, and you have squandered what had been easily gained. But know that "if you and all the people on Earth turn to unbelief, that God will surely be needless of you."[241]
I have shared with you that which needed to be said, although I had become aware of your wretchedness and moral retrogression. Let this [property; Fadak], then, be your lot. Hold it in hand as a peaceful, calm, obedient and beneficial [creature], with all the odium and disgrace [that such unlawful possession entails], and with its inextricable link to the divinely-lit fire that will inevitably lap at the hearts [of those who hold it]. For God sees everything that you do, [26:227] *and [trust in God's promise that] those who are bent on wrongdoing will in time come to know how evil a turn their destinies are bound to take.*

The narrator states: Muhammad ibn Zakarīa has reported (from Muhammad ibn Zahhāk), [who has reported] from Hishām ibn Muhammad, [who has reported] from 'Awāna ibn al-Hakam, that when Lady Fātima said what she intended to say to Abu Bakr, Abu Bakr praised and thanked God ﷻ, and sent blessings unto His Prophet ﷺ, and then said,

O the best of ladies, and O daughter of the best of fathers! I swear by God that I have done nothing against the wishes of the Messenger of God, and I have done nothing other than to follow his command. The leader of the caravan does not lie to the caravan. You said what you had to say and conveyed your message, and you spoke in anger, then turned away. Then may God have mercy on us both. But to move on (*ammā ba'd*), I handed over the arms and armor of the Prophet, his shoes, and riding animals to Ali! But other than these, I myself heard the Prophet of God say, "We prophets do not leave any gold or silver or land or property or housing as inheritance. Rather, our inheritance is faith and wisdom and knowledge and our example." And all I did was to implement the words of his eminence [the Prophet], and the extent to

[241] Quranic reference not given and not found – translator.

which I have succeeded in doing so comes only from God, to Whom I take recourse, and to Whom I mention my needs.

According to the report which appears in *Balāghāt an-Nisā'*,[242] Lady Fātima responded to Abu Bakr's words as follows:

O people! I am Fātima and my father is Muhammad. Just as I said earlier, [he was] [9:128] *an Apostle from among yourselves* ... You have purposefully ignored God's sacred writ and ignored its commandments, whereas God has stated, [27:16] *Solomon inherited from David*; and in the story of John the son of Zakariya, Zakariya says, [19:5] ... *Bestow, then, upon me, out of Thy grace, the gift of a successor* [19:6] *who can inherit from me and inherit from the House of Jacob.* And God has also stated that [8:75] blood relatives are more entitled to inherit from one another according to God's sacred writ. And God has also stated that [2:180] *It is ordained for you, when death approaches any of you and he is leaving behind much wealth, to make bequests in favor of his parents and [other] near of kin in accordance with what is fair: this is binding on all who are conscious of God.* Despite all this, you say that I have no inheritance rights with respect to my father, and that there is no such bond between us?!
Has God revealed a verse especially for you, excepting His prophet [from the general rules cited above]? Or are you saying that we follow two different religions, and that is why we do not inherit from one another? Are my father and I not of the same religion? Perhaps you are more aware of the verses of the Quran and its general and particular applications than the Prophet! Are you looking to revive the laws of the era of pre-Islamic ignorance? ... I said what had to be said. And I know how feeble you are and how you do not want to help. The substance of your spears has become frail, and your certainty has waned. Let this [property; Fadak], then, be your lot. This camel you are riding on has a wounded leg [and will not take you to your desired destination]. This disgrace will remain on your foreheads until it joins the Fire of God on the Day of Resurrection, for God sees all that you do; [26:227] *and those who are bent on wrongdoing will in time come to know how evil a turn their destinies are bound to take.*

---

[242] Pages 12-17; and Ibn Abī'l-Hadīd, Abdul-Hamīd, *Sharh Nahj al-Balāgha*, 4:78-79 & 4:93.

Ibn Abi'l-Hadīd writes, "The story of Fadak and the appearance of [Lady] Fātima before Abu Bakr took place ten days after the death of the Prophet. And it is true to say that none of the people, be they men or women, uttered a single word about the inheritance of that Lady after she returned [home] from that gathering.[243]

6. The Conversation of Lady Fātima with Imam Ali

After returning from the mosque, Lady Fātima addressed Imam Ali and said:

يا بن ابى طالب إشتملت شملة الجنين قعدت حجرة الظّنين. نقضت قادمة الاجدل فخانك ريش الاعزل. اضرعت خدّك يوم اضعت جدّك. افترست الذّئاب و افترشت التّراب. هذا ابن ابى قحافة يبتزّنى نحيلة ابى و بليغة ابنى. جهد فى خصامى و الفيته الدّ فى كلامى. حتّى منعتنى القيلة نصرها و المهاجرة وصلها. ويلاى فى كلّ شارق؛ ويلاى فى كلّ غارب؛ مات العمد و وهنت العضد و غضّت الجماعة دونى طرفها فلا دافع و لا مانع خرجت كاظمة و عدت راغمة و لا خيار لى ليتنى مت قبل ذلّتى عذيرى الله منك عاديا و منك حاميا شكواى الى ربّى و عدواى الى ابى اللّهمّ انت اشدّ قوّة

O Son of Abī-Tālib.[244] You have been placed in a sack like a fetal sac in a mother's womb, and you have covered yourself [from the people], hiding yourself in a room like the room where the accused are sequestered. You broke the hand of a warrior ram such as 'Amr ibn Abdwūd, but now the featherless bird who can only hop [reference to the ruler of the time] has betrayed you. You humiliated your face when you let your sword out of the palm of your hand. You hunted wolves, tearing them to pieces, but now you are wallowing in the dust. It was this son of Abī Qahāfa [Abu Bakr] who took from me by force that which my father had given me, and which would have been the source of a satisfactory livelihood for my two sons.[245] He strove in enmity

---

[243] Ibn Abī'l-Hadīd, Abdul-Hamīd, *Sharh Nahj al-Balāgha*, 4:97

[244] It is a point of pride for Ali to have been named 'the son of Abū-Tālib.

[245] Lady Fātima does not speak of *khums* here, because the Commander of the Faithful has a share in the *khums*. She also does not speak of inheritance; what

towards me, and in talking with him, I found him to have extreme enmity towards me, so that the Helpers withheld their help from me, and the Emigrants (who should have closer relations due to their bonds of blood) cut off their relations. Woe to me every morning and every evening. My support [the Prophet] is gone, and my arm has become frail. All of the Muslims have ignored me. [Now] there is no one to defend me and no one to repulse [my enemies]. I left my house in anger, and returned with a broken nose. Would that I had died before being humiliated like this. Would that God would come to my aid and support me rather than your help and support, O ferocious lion! I shall take my complaint to my Lord and Sustainer, and will tell my father the condition that I am in. You, O Lord, are more powerful [than these usurpers of Fadak and of the succession].

In response, Imam Ali said,

لا ويل لك بل الويل لشانئك. نهنهى عن وجدك يا ابنة الصّفوة و بقيّة النّبوة فما ونيت عن ديني و لا اخطأت مقدوري فان كنت تريدين البلغة فرزقك مضمون و كفيلك مأمون و ما اعدّ لك خير ممّا قطع عنك فاحتسبي الله

Woe is not on you but on your enemies. Bear this difficulty with forbearance and longanimity, O daughter who is the chosen of God and the remnant of prophethood. I have not slackened in my faith, and have not erred or fallen short of that which is in my power to perform. If you are content with a minimal standard of living, your livelihood is guaranteed. And your guarantor is God. What God has in store for you is better than that which they cut off from you. So account with God that which befell you.

Lady Fātima replied: "God is sufficient for me, and He is the best advocate."[246]

---

she means are the lands of Fadak which the Prophet had given to her [while he was still alive], which she was claiming for her sons, Hasan and Husain.
[246] Majlisī, Allāma Muhammad Bāqir, *Bihār al-Anwār*, 43:148; and Tabarsī's *al-Ihtijāj*, 1:107-108, with slight variations in the wording.

7 Lady Fātima's Illness

Lady Fātima عليها السلام became ill. The first person to visit her was Umm Salama. She said, "O daughter of the Apostle of God. How were you last night?" Lady Fātima عليها السلام responded:

Grief and sorrow filled my heart because of the death of the Prophet and the injustice committed against the Prophet's *wasī* (legatee, heir, executor, and successor). Ali's sanctity was desecrated [reference to what was done to herself]; by the same one who usurped his imamate, contrary to that which God revealed in the Quran and what the Prophet had stated. The reason for this was the hatred they harbored [in their hearts towards Ali] from [the Battle of] Badr, and revenge and reprisal for the blood he had shed at [the Battle of] Uhud.[247] These hypocrites hid the enmity they had for Ali in their hearts, and when they took [control of] the caliphate and reached their goal, the raincloud of the schismatics suddenly burst and rained calamity down on us. The bowstring of faith was cut from their breasts, and they inflicted on us whatever their hearts desired in worldly pride. All of this was because Ali had killed their fathers in fierce battles and stations of martyred.[248]

---

247 Out of the seventy greater warriors [on the side of the Meccan polytheists] that had been killed in the Battle of Badr, thirty-five of them had been killed by Ali. Similarly, eleven of the Qurayshite warriors had been slain by Ali in the Battle of Uhud.

248 Ibn Shahrāshūb, Muhammad ibn Ali, *Manāqib Āl Abi-Tālib*, quoted in Majlisī, Allāma Muhammad Bāqir, *Bihār al-Anwār*, 43:156, hadith #5. This is the text of the hadith report:

دخلت ام سلمة على فاطمة (س) فقالت لها: كيف اصبحت عن ليلتك يا بنت رسول الله؟

قالت: اصبحت بين كمد و كرب، فقد النّبى و ظلم الوصىّ.

هتك و الله حجابه، من اصبحت امامته مغصوبة على غير ما شرع الله فى التّنزيل و سنّها النّبىّ فى التأويل و لكنّها أحقاد بدريّة و تزات احديّة، كانت عليها قلوب النّفاق مكتمنة. فلما استهدف الامر.

1. The Passion of Lady Fātima in Hearing Bilal's Call to Prayer

Ever since the Prophet ﷺ passed away, Bilal had been silent and had not made the call to prayer. One day, Lady Fātima ؑ desired to hear the sound of the call to prayer of her father's muazzin. When this news reached Bilal, he came over to the mosque and recited the call to prayer. Hearing the sound of Bilal's call to prayer reminded Lady Fātima of her father and of the days when he was alive. This caused her to let out a moan, after which she fainted and fell to the ground. The people told Bilal to stop, as the daughter of the Prophet ﷺ had passed away. They had thought that Lady Fātima ؑ had passed away. Bilal stopped his recitation of the call to prayer. When Lady Fātima ؑ gained consciousness, she asked Bilal to finish the call to prayer, but he refused and said, "I fear for your well-being because of what passes through your mind when you hear me making the call to prayer." Hearing this, Lady Fātima ؑ excused Bilal from having to make the call to prayer.[249]

2. The Womenfolk of the Emigrants and the Helpers pay Lady Fātima a Visit

When Lady Fātima ؑ was afflicted by the illness that led to her death, the women of the Emigrants and the Helpers paid her a visit and

---

ارسلت علينا شآبيب الآثار، من مخيلة الشّقاق. فيقطع وتر الايمان من قسى صدورها على ما وعد الله من حفظ الرّسالة و كفالة المؤمنين أحرزوا عائدتهم غرور الدّنيا، بعد استنصار ممّن فتك بآبائهم فى مواطن الكرب و منازل الشّهادات.

[249] Saddūq, Shaykh Abu-Ja'far Muhammad ibn Ali ibn Bābawayh, *Man lā Yahdharahū al-Faqīh*, 1:297-298, hadith #907; Majlisī, Allāma Muhammad Bāqir, *Bihār al-Anwār*, 43:157. Here is the text of the hadith report:

لمّا قبض النبيّ امتنع بلال من الأذان و قال: لا اؤذّن لاحد بعد رسول الله (ص). و انّ فاطمة (س) قالت ذات يوم: انّى اشتهى ان اسمع صوت مؤذّن ابى بالأذان. فاخذ فى الأذان. فلمّا قال «الله اكبر» ذكرت اباها و ايّامه فلم تتمالك من البكاء. فلمّا بلغ الى قوله «اشهد انّ محمّدا رسول الله» شهقت فاطمة شهقة و سقطت لوجهها و غشى عليها.

فقال النّاس لبلال امسك يا بلال، فقد فارقت ابنة رسول الله (ص) الدنيا، و ظنّوا انّها قد ماتت. فقطع اذانه و لم يتمّه. فافاقت فاطمة و سألته ان يتمّ الأذان. قال يا سيّدة النّسوان انّى اخشى عليك ممّا تنزلينه بنفسك اذا سمعت صوتى بالأذان. فاعفته عن ذلك.

asked her how she was coping with her illness. Lady Fātima ﷺ praised God ﷻ and sent blessings on her father, and then said:

I have had my fill of your world. I abhor your menfolk, and I threw them away after having tested them:[250] the odium of their inaction, the futility of their broken swords, the fragility of their spears, and the abomination of their [moral] stance. I cast the rope of their sin around their own necks and threw the opprobrium of what they did onto themselves.[251]
May all oppressors be warded off at a distance, and may their ears and noses be severed! Woe to them who tore the successor to the Prophet from his [rightful] place, and removed him from the base of the prophetic ministry; [removed] the lofty and constant mountain of the House of the Prophet, the station of prophethood and the locus of revelation, and those who are knowledgeable in worldly matters as well as those of religion. Verily, this is an obvious loss.[252] What [rightful] objection could they possibly have had to Abu'l-Hasan? True, they did not like the effectiveness of Ali's sword, his invincibility in battle, his severity in punishing [wrongful] deeds, and his being uncompromising in the Way of God. These are the things that made them hostile to Ali. If they had not kept their distance from the rope that the Prophet had vouchsafed them to, he would have ruled them with a gentle hand, so that the nose of the camel of governance would not be injured, and its rider would not be put through violent motions [= would have a comfortable ride under all conditions].[253] And he would have led them to a watering place with crystal clear water gushing forth at both ends,

---

250 فقلن لها: ' اجتمع اليها نساء المهاجرين و الانصار' لمّا مرضت فاطمة (س) المرضة الّتى توفّيت فيها ثمّ قالت: اصبحت و الله 'كيف اصبحت من علّتك يا ابنة رسول الله؟ فحمدت الله و صلّت على ابيها .عائفة لدنيا كنّ قالية لرجالكنّ لفظتهم بعد ان عجمتهم و شنأتهم بعد ان سبرتهم

251 فقبحا لفلول الحدّ و اللعب بعد الجد و خور القناة و خطل الرّأى. لا جرم لقد قلّدتهم ربقتها و شننت عليهم عارها.

252 فجدعا و عقرا و سحقا للقوم الظّالمين. ويحهم' انّى زخزحوها عن رواسى الرّسالة و قواعد النبوّة و مهبط الوحى و الطّبين بامر الدّنيا و الدّين. الا ذلك هو الخسران المبين.

253 و ما نقموا من ابى الحسن؟ ما نقموا و الله منه الّا نكير سيفه و شدّة وطئه و نكال وقعته و تنمّره فى ذات الله. و الله لو تكافّوا عن زمام نبذه رسول الله (ص) اليه لاعتلقه و لساربهم سيرا سجحا لا يكلم خشاشه و لا يتعتع راكبه

and the portals of the grace of heaven and earth will have opened up to them. [But not that this did not occur,] God will rebuke and punish them for what they have done.[254]

So come hither and listen. If you survive, the times will show you strange things. If you are one to be surprised, then be surprised by this occurrence. What kind of support did they lean on [reference to Abu Bakr]? To what rope did they hold fast to? Instead of the animal's head, they clung to its tail [this is an Arabic proverb]. May the noses be cut off of the group that thinks it has done something that is rightful.[255] [2:12] *Oh, verily, it is they, they who are spreading corruption; but they perceive it not.* [10:35] *Does the one who guides to the truth deserve to be followed and obeyed, or the one who cannot guide unless he is himself guided? What, then, is amiss with you and your judgment?* I swear by God ﷻ, this act of yours will breed sedition and corruption; wait a while to see the results. You will milk blood in this milk bowl. That is where the survivors will understand what their antecedents did.[256] Get ready for acts of sedition. I give you tidings of drawn swords and an all-encompassing chaos that pervades all, and the tyranny of oppressors who will take from you what you have. The future generations [= your children] will reap what you have sown, and the future will reap. [Her ladyship is referring to what will happen to the Helpers afterwards.] So let grief and sorrow be upon you. Which side are you on? The Way of truth and righteousness (*al-haqq*) and God's mercy is lost on you. Should we force you to [the Way that entails] God's mercy, even though you hate it?[257]

---

254 و لاوردهم منهلا نميرا فضفاضا، تطفح ضفّتاه، قد تحيّر بهم الرّى، و لفتحت عليهم - بركات من السّماء و الارض. و سيأخذهم الله بما كانوا يكسبون.

255 الا هلمّ فاسمع و ما عشت اراك الدّهر العجب. و ان تعجب فقد اعجبك الحادث. الى اىّ سناد استندوا و باىّ عروة تمسّكوا. استبدلوا الذّنابى و الله بالقوادم و العجز بالكاهل.
فرغما لمعاطس قوم يحسبون انّهم يحسنون صنعا.

256 . أَلا إِنَّهُمْ هُمُ الْمُفْسِدُونَ وَ لكِنْ لا يَشْعُرُونَ. أَ فَمَنْ يَهْدِى إِلَى الْحَقِّ أَحَقُّ أَنْ يُتَّبَعَ أَمَّنْ لا يَهِدِّى إِلَّا أَنْ يُهْدى فَما لَكُمْ كَيْفَ تَحْكُمُونَ اما لعمر الهكنّ لقد لقحت، فنظرة ريثما تنتج، ثمّ احتلبوا طلاع القعب دما عبيطا و ذعافا ممقرا. هنالك يخسر المبطلون و يعرف التّالون غبّ ما اسّس الاوّلون.

257 ثمّ طيبوا عن انفسكم انفسا و اطمئنّوا للفتنة جأشا، و ابشروا بسيف صارم و استبداد من الظّالمين يدع فيئكم زهيدا و زرعكم حصيدا. فيا حسرتى لكم و انّى بكم و قد عميت قلوبكم عليكم. انلزمكموها و انتم لها كارهون.

The womenfolk of the Emigrants and the Helpers retold what they had heard from Lady Fātima to their husbands. After this, a group of the elders of the Emigrants and the Helpers came to apologize to Lady Fātima, and said, "O master of [all] women, if Abu'l-Hasan [= Imam Ali] had pointed these things out to us before we had pledged our allegiance and covenanted with Abu Bakr, we would never have left him and turned to anyone else. Lady Fātima said, "Leave me, for no pretexts remains after [your] insincere pretexts. Nor is there anything left to do after your culpability [and sin].[258] [In other words, after you fell short of your duties and obligations, the failure of which drove Ali into seclusion in his home, and you considered the outrages that were performed against the House of the Prophet ﷺ to be acceptable (and Abu Bakr's agent brought a firebrand to Lady Fātima's عليها السلام house in order to burn it down...), then it is too late, and apologies cannot be accepted, as the era of tyranny and ruination have begun.

3. Abu Bakr and Umar pay Lady Fātima a Visit

When Lady Fātima's عليها السلام condition worsened, and her illness became severe, Abu Bakr and Umar wanted to make a good show for themselves and say that they had gone and visited her, and that they had made peace with each other and that Lady Fātima عليها السلام forgave them. To this purpose they asked Imam Ali عليه السلام to obtain Lady Fātima's عليها السلام permission for them to come and pay her a visit.

But Lady Fātima عليها السلام was unwilling to give her permission. When Imam Ali عليه السلام insisted, she said, "The house is yours, and the lady [of the house] is also your lady."[259] Abu Bakr and Umar came over, and when they did, Lady Zahra عليها السلام turned her back to them and faced the wall. They said, "We have come to obtain your consent." Lady Fātima عليها السلام said, "I will not speak to you unless you promise that you will bear witness to what I say, if what I say is true." When Abu Bakr and Umar accepted Lady Fātima's عليها السلام condition, she said, "Do you remember that

---

Saddūq, Shaykh Abu-Ja'far Muhammad ibn Ali ibn Bābawayh, *Ma'ānī al-Akhbār*, quoted in Majlisī, Allāma Muhammad Bāqir, *Bihār al-Anwār*, 43:158-159; Tabresī, Abu-Ali Fadl ibn Hasan, *al-Ihtijāj*, 1:108-109; Irbilī, *Kashf al-Ghamma*, p. 147; Umar Ridā Kahāla, *I'lām an-Nasā*, 4:123; Ibn Abī'l-Hadīd, quoting Jawharī's *Saqīfa* in his *Sharh Nahj al-Balāgha*,16:233-234;

258 Tabresī, Abu-Ali Fadl ibn Hasan, *al-Ihtijāj*, 1:109.

259 البيت بيتك و الحرّة حرّتك

the Prophet ﷺ said. 'Fātima's pleasure is God's pleasure, God becomes angry[260] when Fātima is angered'?" The two said that they remembered. Then Lady Fātima said, "Bear witness, O Lord, that I am angry with these two people! And that I am not pleased with them!"[261]

Abu Bakr, as always, pretended to cry. Umar rebuked him, after which they got up and left. This was the last thing they did [with respect to Lady Fātima].[262]

4. Lady Fātima's Will and her Burial by Night

Lady Fātima ﷺ said: "I hereby make a will that Abu Bakr and Umar do not pray over my body and do not attend my funeral, and that my body should be buried at night."[263] Imam Ali acted on Lady Fātima's will[264] and buried her in her own house.[265] He then made the forms of several graves in the Baqī [cemetery] and sprinkled water over them to make them look like newly dug graves.[266]

In the morning, the people of Medina learned that the Prophet's daughter had been buried at night. They thought that Lady Fātima's ﷺ grave was in the Baqī [cemetery]. [Umar and his companions] came and said, "We will bring the women and have these graves dug up to see where lady Fātima's ﷺ body is buried, and we will then [be able to] pray for it. Imam Ali ﷺ came in anger to the cemetery and said, "If any one of you touches these graves, I will stain the earth with his blood."

---

260 رضا الله من رضا فاطمة. انّ الله يغضب لغضب فاطمة و يرضى لرضا فاطمة.

261, Muhammad ibn Ismā'īl al-Bukhārī writes in his *Ṣaḥīḥ* (5:177) that after the daughter of the Prophet asked the caliph for her inheritance, and the Abu Bakr replied that he had heard from the Prophet that we prophets do not leave anything by way of inheritance, Lady Fātima no longer spoke to Abu Bakr until her death.

262 Majlisī, Allāma Muhammad Bāqir, *Bihār al-Anwār*, quoting *Dalāil al-Imāma*. Also see Saddūq, Shaykh Abu-Ja'far Muhammad ibn Ali ibn Bābawayh, *Ilal ash-Sharā'i*, 1:178; Ibn Qutayba, Abd-Allāh ibn Muslim, *al-Imāma wa'l-Siyāsa*, 1:14; Umar Riḍā Kahāla, *I'lām an-Nasā*, 3:1214; Ibn Abī'l-Hadīd, Abdul-Hamīd, *Sharh Nahj al-Balāgha*, 16:273.

263 Ibn Shahrāshūb, Muhammad ibn Ali, *Manāqib Āl Abi-Tālib*, 1:504; Majlisī, Allāma Muhammad Bāqir, *Bihār al-Anwār*, 43:159, 43:182-183.

264 Balādhūrī, Ahmad ibn Yahyā ibn Jābir, *Ansāb al-Ashrāf*, p. 405; Bukhārī, Muḥammad ibn Ismā'īl, *Ṣaḥīḥ al-Bukhārī*, 5:77; Ibn Sa'd, Abu Abdallah Muḥammad, *al-Tabaqāt al-Kubrā*, 8:18-19.

265 Ibn Shahrāshūb, Muhammad ibn Ali, *Manāqib Āl Abi-Tālib*, 3:365; Koleynī, Shaykh Muhammad b. Ya'qūb, *'Usūl al-Kāfī*, 1:461.

266 Majlisī, Allāma Muhammad Bāqir, *Bihār al-Anwār*, 43:183.

And seeing Ali ﷺ in this mood, the crowd that had gathered there dispersed.[267]

Asbagh ibn Nubāta asked the Commander of the Faithful why he had buried Lady Fātima ﷺ at night. His eminence the Imam said,

انّها كانت ساخطة على قوم كرهت حضورهم جنازتها و حرام على من يتولّاهم ان يصلّى على احد من ولدها

Because Lady Fātima was angry with those people, she did not want them or anyone who followed them to be present at [the burial of] her body. It is not permitted (*harām*) for any one of them to pray for any of the progeny of Lady Fātima."[268]

Indeed, keeping the location of the grave of the daughter of the Prophet ﷺ secret is a clear indication of her dissatisfaction with certain people, and it is obvious that with this will, she wanted others to be aware of this dissatisfaction.

5. The Situation of Medina after the Martyrdom of Lady Fātima, and the Fulfillment of her Prophecies

After the martyrdom of Lady Fātima ﷺ, the caliphal authority sent some troops to confront those who had not pledged allegiance to Abu Bakr outside Medina, a group of which were apostate tribes. In those campaigns, none of the Helpers was appointed to head the Muslim forces, and the caliphal authority became thoroughly Qurayshite in its makeup.[269] The Quraysh was given precedence over any non-Quraysh element in everything. In the cities they conquered, the commanders of the divisions and the governors of the cities were all appointed from the Quraysh tribe.[270] As a result, the Ansar became

[267] Majlisī, Allāma Muhammad Bāqir, *Bihār al-Anwār*, 43:171-172.
[268] Majlisī, Allāma Muhammad Bāqir, *Bihār al-Anwār*, 43:183.
[269] The Quraysh even resorted to fabricating hadith reports for the purposes of consolidating their hold on power, attributing them to the Prophet. [The author gives several examples in the footnote of the original, with references to many of the authoritative Sunnite sources, from Bokhārī and Muslim on down.]
[270] Needless to say, this monopoly of the Quraysh's on the governance of the community was broken when Imam Ali acceded to the caliphate. He divided the treasury among the people and, like the Most Noble Prophet ﷺ, did not differentiate between the Quraysh and non-Quraysh Muslims. Like every other

impoverished and fell by the wayside to the point that they went hungry. When we read in the biographies of their eminences of the Imams as-Sajjād, al-Bāqir, and as-Sādiq that these Imams would visit the houses of the indigent of Medina at night and give them bread and money, the people they were visiting were the children of Helpers.

Mu'allā ibn Khunays, who was one of the companions of Imam Sādiq, says: "I saw the Imam came out of his house in the dark night with a burden on his shoulders. I said: 'O son of the Messenger of God, allow me to help you.' He said: 'This is a load that I must take myself.' Having said this, he set off, and I proceeded to follow him. After a while, something fell to the ground from that load. His eminence bent down and said, 'Let me find this [thing that has fallen]'. He found it momentarily and placed it into a bag that he had on his shoulder, and proceeded to the portico (*saqīfa*) of the Bani Sā'ida, and put two loaves of bread beside the head of each person who was sleeping there."

When he returned, Mu'allā ibn Khunays asked the Imam: "O son of the Messenger of God, do these people recognize the truth [about your right to the Imamate]?" And the Imam responded, "If they knew the truth, we would even share the salt that is ground in our own homes with them; no, they do not recognize the truth."[271]

Imam Sajjād ﷺ also used to take food to the houses [of the indigent]. The residents of the houses he used to call on would stand at their front doors in anticipation of the person who visited them at night and would take the food from him. While ritually bathing the body of Imam Sajjād ﷺ [in preparation for burial], it was noticed that his back had become callused. When [his son] Imam Bāqir ﷺ was asked the reason for it, he said, "It is [the result] of the loads [of food] that he

---

Muslim, he took only three dinars [for himself] and gave three dinars to his slave Qambar. He also appointed non-Qurayshites to positions of authority, and appointed members of the Ansar as governors of the Provinces. For example, he made ''Uthmān ibn Hanif the governor of Basra, and his brother the governor of Medina, and Qais ibn Sa'd ibn' Abadah, and after him Mālik Ashtar, the governor of Egypt and the other the governor of Alexandria. In contrast, Mu'awiyah deposed the Quraysh from the governorship of the Levant, and rejected Talha and Zubayr's request for office. He also appointed one or two Qurayshites too, of course, but he abolished the Quraysh's monopoly on governance. (For greater details concerning this issue, cf. Askari, Allāma Murtaḍā, *Naqsh-e A'imma dar ihyā'-e dīn*, 14:159 ff.

[271] Majlisī, Allāma Muhammad Bāqir, *Bihār al-Anwār*, 47:20, hadith #17.

used to carry at night.[272] When Imam Sajjād ﷺ passed away, the aid that was given to the indigent at night came to a halt. That is when it was realized that the person who used to bring the food to their houses was the Imam.[273]

All of these indigents were of [the Medinan tribes of] the 'Helpers' (*ansār*). But the Quraysh were possessed much wealth and slaves and had prestige and lived in luxury. When Abd al-Rahmān ibn 'Awf passed away (during Uthmān's caliphate), the gold he brought was brought to Uthmān so that he could divide it among Abd al-Rahmān's heirs. There was so much gold piled up in the assembly of the caliphal court that it filled the gap between the two sides of the assembly in such a way that the two sides of the assembly could not see each other![274]

These were some examples of that which Lady Fātima had predicted to the womenfolk of the Helpers, stating that this is how things would end up. And indeed, that is what happened, and things became even worse than that.

When Yazid's army came to Medina and massacred the Medinans at the Battle of Harra,[275] Yazid had ordered that the army [be allowed] to do whatever they wanted for three days.[276] The Ansar were massacred, such that blood flowed in the mosque of the Prophet ﷺ. Whatever was in people's houses was looted, and thousands of unmarried girls became pregnant as a consequence [of the rape and pillage] of this massacre.[277]

---

272 Abū Naīm Isfahānī, *Hilyat al-Awliā*, 3:136; Irbilī, *Kashf al-Ghamma*, 2:289; Ibn Shahrāshūb, Muhammad ibn Ali, *Manāqib Āl Abi-Tālib*, 4:154; Saddūq, Shaykh Abu-Ja'far Muhammad ibn Ali ibn Bābawayh, *al-Khisāl*, pp. 517-518.
273 31 Irbilī, *Kashf al-Ghamma*, 2:289; *Nur al-Absār fī Manāqib Al al-Bayt an-Nabī al-Mukhtār*, p. 140 (Cairo); Majlisī, Allāma Muhammad Bāqir, *Bihār al-Anwār*, 46:88; Ibn Shahrāshūb, Muhammad ibn Ali, *Manāqib Āl Abi-Tālib*, 4:154; Ibn Sa'd, Abu Abdallah Muhammad, *al-Tabaqāt al-Kubrā*, 5:222.
274 Mas'ūdī, Alī ibn al-Ḥusayn, *Murawwij adh-Dhahab*, 2:340
275 The Battle of al-Harra was fought between the Syrian army of the Umayyad caliph Yazid I (r. 680–683) led by Muslim ibn Uqba and the local defenders of Medina, namely the Ansar and Muhajirun factions, who had not accepted Yazid as their caliph. The battle took place at the lava field of Harrat Waqim in the northeastern outskirts of Medina on 26 August 683.
276 Ibn Athīr Jazarī, 'Alī, *al-Kāmil fī al-Tārīkh*, 3:47; Ibn Kathīr, Abu'al-Fiḍā Ismā'īl ibn Umar, *Tārīkh*, 8:220; Tabarī, Muhammad ibn Jarīr, *Tārīkh ar-Rusul wa'l-Mulūk*, 7:11.
277 Ibn Kathīr, Abu'al-Fiḍā Ismā'īl ibn Umar, *Tārīkh*, 6:234 & 8:32.

6. The Pledging of Allegiance[278] of the Commander of the Faithful [Imam Ali to Abu Bakr] after the martyrdom of Lady Fātima, and the reason for it

In Bokhārī's *Sahīh*, a hadith report is narrated by Zuhrī from Āisha in which the story between Abu Bakr and Lady Fātima's inheritance from the Messenger of God is discussed, at the end of which report Āisha says,

Fātima turned her back on Abu Bakr and did not speak [again] until she died. She lived for six months after the passing of the Messenger of God, and after she passed away, her husband Ali performed the ritual supplications for her and buried her [at night] without informing Abu Bakr [of her burial]. Fātima was a source of honor and respect for Ali. As long as Fātima was alive, Ali enjoyed a position of honor among the people, but when she passed away, the people turned away from him.

At this point in the report, someone asked Zuhri, "Did Ali not pledge allegiance to Abu Bakr during these six months?" Zuhri said, "Neither he nor anyone of the Banī Hāshim [clan did so] until Ali pledged allegiance to Abu Bakr [after Lady Fātima's passing].[279]

---

[278] A correct and valid pledge of allegiance is one that is offered and entered into voluntarily and with the consent of the person who is making the pledge. Failing this, it is not an actual pledging of one's allegiance but a [meaningless] shaking of the hands, and is nothing but a superficial and specious act. This is similar to a transaction of buying and selling, in which the *bay'* or the contract is only valid if it is entered into voluntarily, and which would be nothing but [a form of] iniquitous usurpation if the element of voluntary volition were absent. Thus, the "pledge of allegiance" of the Commander of the Faithful, which was given after six months only for the sake of [the greater good of] saving Islam and without the least bit of consent, was nothing more than a superficial and specious pledge of allegiance. The hadith report of the Imams that states that, "There is none among us [Imams] who does not have [the yoke of the opprobrium of] a superficial and specious pledge of allegiance around our necks, other than the Lord of the Age," has the same signification, as it means that a real pledge of allegiance has not been given or entered into, and that what has taken place is specious.

[279] Bukhārī, Muhammad ibn Ismā'īl, *Sahīh al-Bukhārī*, 3:38; Ibn Abī'l-Hadīd, Abdul-Hamīd, *Sharh Nahj al-Balāgha*, 2:122; Ibn Kathīr, Abu'al-Fidā Ismā'īl ibn Umar, *Tārīkh*

Mas'ūdī, Alī ibn al-Husain, *al-Tanbīh wa'l-Ishrāf*, p. 250; Mas'ūdī, Alī ibn al-Husayn, *Murawwij adh-Dhahab*, 2:414; Muslim ibn al-Hajjāj, *Sahīh Muslim*, 1:72 & 5:153;

Tabarī, Muhammad ibn Jarīr, *Tārīkh ar-Rusul wa'l-Mulūk*, 2:448 & 1:1825 of the European edition); Abū al-Fidā, Ismā'īl ibn Ali, *Tarikh al-Mukhtasar fi Akhbar*

Outside Medina, there was a group who was against pledging allegiance to Abu Bakr. When a group heard the news of the Prophet's death, they apostatized from Islam, and these are referred to as the *murtadīn* (the apostates) in the annals of history. The most important of these was Musaylama in Yamāma, who claimed to be a Prophet ﷺ. Forty thousand soldiers had gathered near Yemen and were prepared to attack Medina, and would have destroyed Medina if they had come. In other words, the problem was larger than that of [the pending attack on Medina by the Meccan idolaters at] the Battle of the Trench, for the enemy consisted of ten thousand men in that battle, whereas this force was forty thousand strong. If they had attacked and conquered Medina, no trace of Islam would have been left. They would even have destroyed the tomb of the Prophet ﷺ. Therefore, Uthmān came to the Commander of the Faithful [Imam Ali] and said, "O paternal cousin,[280] while your allegiance to Abu Bakr remains unpledged, no one can be mustered to fight these enemies. Uthmān went on about this matter until he convinced Imam Ali to come with him; and he took him to Abu Bakr, and the Imam pledged allegiance to him. Ali's pledge of allegiance to Abu Bakr gladdened the Muslims, after which they prepared to go to war with the apostates on the war against the apostates, and an army was mustered from all quarters and moved [on Musaylama's forces in Yamāma].[281]

It is also stated in the *Nahj al-Balāgha* that the Imam said:

«فامسكت يدى حتّى رأيت راجعة النّاس قد رجعت عن الاسلام
يدعون الى محق دين محمّد (ص) فخشيت ان لم انصر الاسلام و اهله
ان ارى فيه ثلما أو هدما تكون المصيبة به علىّ اعظم من فوت

---

al-Bashar, 1:156; Dayār-Bakrī, Ḥusayn Ibn Md., *Tārīkh al-Khamīs fī Ahwāl Anfus an-Nafīs*, 1:193;
Haythamī, Ahmad Ibn-Hajar, al-*Sawā'iq al-Muhriqa*, 1:12; Ibn Abd'al-Birr, Yusuf ibn Abdallah, *al-Istī'āb fī Ma'rifat al-Ashāb*, 2:244; Balādhūrī, Ahmad ibn Yahyā ibn Jābir, *Ansāb al-Ashrāf*, 1:586; Aminī, Allāma, *al-Ghadīr*, 3:102; Ibn Athīr, 'Alī ibn Muḥammad, *Usd al-Ghābah fī Ma'rifat al-Ṣaḥābah*, 3:222; Ya'qūbī, Aḥmad ibn Isḥāq, *Tārīkh al-Ya'qūbī*, 2:105.

[280] He used the expression 'paternal cousin' because the Commander of the Faithful was from the Banī Hāshim [branch of the Bani Abd Manāf tribe] and 'Uthmān was from the Bani Umayyah side, and Hashim and Umayyah were both sons of Abd Manāf.

[281] Balādhūrī, Ahmad ibn Yahyā ibn Jābir, *Ansāb al-Ashrāf*, 1:587.

ولايتكم الّتى هى متاع أيام قلائل يزول منها ما كان كما يزول
السّراب و كما يتقشّع السّحاب، فنهضت فى تلك الأحداث، حتّى
زاغ الباطل و زهق و اطمأنّ الدّين و تنهنه

So I withheld my hand [and did not pledge allegiance] until I became certain that I was more deserving of the office [of leadership] held by Muhammad among the people than those who took over the government after his passing. So I delayed [making any pledge] until God willed [that I do so, which was] the time at which I saw that a group of people had apostatized and turned from Islam, and were calling for the destruction of the religion of God and the religion of the Prophet. I was thus concerned that if I did not come to the aid of Islam and the Muslims, I would see a breach in Islam and a devastation, and [saw that] the suffering that would be caused by these two [factors] would be much greater for me than the loss of my guardianship and rule over your affairs. [For it was] a government that was no more a few days in the making, and anything that it yielded would disappear like a mirage or a cloud that is scattered. So I went to Abu Bakr at this time and pledged allegiance to him, and it was during these events that I stood up in order to destroy falsehood, and so that the Word of God [= Islam] was able to maintain its dominant position, even though the unbelievers hated this.[282]

[282] Ibn Abī'l-Hadīd, Abdul-Hamīd, *Sharh Nahj al-Balāgha*, 6:94.

8 The Situation of the Islamic Territories and the Behavior of the Imams

The Islamic territories had several main capitals whose governors were appointed by the caliph. Alexandria was one such capital, under whose aegis the whole of Islamic Africa was ruled. The governor of Alexandria, in turn, appointed for the whole of Islamic Africa and appointed governors for each city. The tribute of all of the cities came to the governor, who would march on the cities that had not as yet been conquered, and conquer them, and so on.

Another one of these capitals was Kufa. When it is said that Walīd became [a] governor of Kufa, this does not mean that he was the only governor of Kufa. To the contrary; the seat of government for the governor of Kufa was the city of Kufa, but [present day] Iraq up to [the city of] Madain, which existed in those days, and from Baghdad to Mosul, and Kermanshah and Rey and Khorasan, all the way to some cities in Central Asia - which were called the East Islamic cities - were all under the rule of the governor of Kufa. Walīd appointed governors for all of those cities, appointed Friday prayer leaders, and sent troops to the border cities of the Islamic territories.

The capital city of Basra was likewise the seat of the governorate of Basra, whose jurisdiction included the cities of southwestern Iran and the present-day Persian Gulf countries, other than parts of Saudi Arabia. All the vast lands of Saudi Arabia today, except Mecca, Medina, Jeddah and Riyāḍ, were also part of the governorate of Basra. The governor of Basra was also responsible for ruling over the Persian Gulf all the way out to the Sea of Oman, and the Indian Ocean as far as India. The Indian cities that were conquered became part of the governorate of Basra. Basra was called the port of India because the connection of this region with India took place from this port.

The Levant had two centers of government: Damascus and Homs. And what is meant by the Levant (ash-Shām) is Trans-Jordan, Lebanon, [occupied] Palestine, and Syria. All of these lands were part of the territory of those two governmental centers. This region used to be called the Eastern Roman empire [or Byzantium]. In all these lands, there were five cities that acted as garrisons for the Muslim army: Kufa, Basra, Damascus, Homs, and Alexandria. In addition to being centers of government, these cities were also garrisons for the Muslim army.

It is noteworthy that the [Shī'a] Imams did not take part in any of the campaigns and battles that took place during the reigns of Abu Bakr, Umar, or Uthmān, including Imam Ali, Imam Hasan, and Imam Husain. And the other Imams, from Imam Sajjad to Imam Hassan Askari also followed the same tradition and example of their righteous predecessors and pure forefathers.

9 Abu Bakr's Will and Umar's Caliphate

Abu Bakr became ill in the month of Jamādi ath-Thāni of the year 13 AH. He asked for Uthmān to write his will while he was on his deathbed. Abu Bakr said: "Write: In the name of God, the Compassionate, the Merciful. This is the will of Abu Bakr ibn Abī Quhāfa to the Muslims." After having spoken this sentence, he fainted from the severity of his malady. 'Uthmān concluded the will as follows: "I have chosen Umar ibn al-Khattab to be my successor and to be your caliph. In this way, I have not fallen short of my benevolence towards you."

At this juncture, Abu Bakr opened his eyes and said to Uthmān: "Let me see what you have written." When Abu Bakr heard what Uthmān read to him, he said: "I agree with what you have written. May God reward Islam and the Muslims." He then signed what Uthmān had written.[283]

Tabari writes at the end of this story:

'Umar was sitting among the people in the mosque of the Prophet while holding a stick from the frond of a palm tree. Shadīd, a freedman of Abu Bakr's, who held the order of Abu Bakr's appointment of Umar as his successor, was present at the gathering. Umar turned to the people and said: "O people, listen to the words and orders of the Caliph of the Messenger of God, and pay heed to his command. He says, "I have not fallen short of my benevolence towards you."[284]

In the story of the passing of the Prophet ﷺ, when the Prophet said:

[283] Tabarī, Muhammad ibn Jarīr, *Tārīkh ar-Rusul wa'l-Mulūk*, 3:52.
[284] Tabarī, Muhammad ibn Jarīr, *Tārīkh ar-Rusul wa'l-Mulūk*, 3:52.

اتونی بدوات و قرطاس اکتب لکم کتابا لن تضلّوا بعده

['Bring [me] a scroll and inkpot so that I can write an inscription for you after which you will never go astray.] Those present said: "The Prophet's illness has prevailed over him." Umar said, "[Among you is the Book of God, and] the Book of God is sufficient unto us!" Some of those present in the room wanted to go and get a scroll and an inkpot, at which point Umar said, "This man is delirious!"[285]

How different Umar's behavior and words were during the writing of the will of the Most Noble Prophet before his passing, from his behavior and words about the will of Abu Bakr, which was written while he was unconscious!

[285] Ahmad b. Hanbal, *Musnad*, hadith #2,992; Bukhārī, Muḥammad ibn Ismā'īl, *Ṣaḥīḥ al-Bukhārī*, 1:22; Ibn Sa'd, Abu Abdallah Muhammad, *al-Tabaqāt al-Kubrā*, 2:244. See also, Tabarī, Muhammad ibn Jarīr, *Tārīkh ar-Rusul wa'l-Mulūk*, 3:193; Bukhārī, Muḥammad ibn Ismā'īl, *Ṣaḥīḥ al-Bukhārī*, 2:120; Muslim ibn al-Ḥajjāj, *Ṣaḥīḥ Muslim*, 5:76.

10 Governance during Umar's Caliphate

Umar's reign was an Arab reign, and Umar had forbidden non-Arabs from taking up residence in Medina, which was the capital of 'Islamdom' (the dominion of Islam). He had made exceptions to this rule of his for only two people. One of these was Hormozān, the former king of Shūsh and Shūshtar (or Tostar), who had become Muslim, and who advised Umar how to conquer the cities of Iran.[286] And the other one was Abū Lu'lu'a, who was the manservant of Mughira ibn Shu'ba. Abū Lu'lu'a was a skilled craftsman, and was highly skilled in painting, ironwork, and carpentry. Mughira had asked Umar's permission for Abū Lu'lu'a to remain in Medina, and Umar granted his request.[287] Verily, this was indeed the measure of Arab pride: no non-Arab was permitted to reside in the capital of the dominions of Islam.[288] Umar has also forbidden non-Arabs from marrying Arab women, and non-Quraysh men from marrying women of the Quraysh tribe.[289] Thus, Umar transformed Islamic society into a class society.

Mālik ibn Anas states in his *al-Mu'atta'* that Umar had decreed – and it should be noted that Umar's decrees were tantamount to sacred law from the perspective of the [majority of the] people – that if a non-Arab man married an Arab woman, and that marriage produced offspring, if the offspring were to be born in Arab lands, he shall inherit

[286] For an example of this kind of counsel, cf. Suyūtī, Jalāladdīn, *Tarikh al-Khulafā*, pp. 143-144.
[287] Mas'ūdī, Alī ibn al-Ḥusayn, *Murawwij adh-Dhahab*, 2:322.
[288] Suyūtī, Jalāladdīn, *Tarikh al-Khulafā*, p. 133. There was Salmān and Bilāl, too, of course, who were resident in Medina from the time of the presence of the Prophet ﷺ, and who were considered to be the Prophet's companions.
[289] Askari, Allāma Murtaḍā, *Mu'ālim al-Madrisatayn*, 2:364, quoting *Wāfī*.

from his father, but if he were to be born in non-Arab lands, he shall not inherit from his father![290]

Umar's reign was a Qurayshite-Arab reign. Umar never appointed a non-Qurayshite governor to any city or commander to any army. There was, of course, an exception to this rule, which was that he never appointed anyone [to these positions of responsibility] from the clan of the Banī Hāshim, [which was the clan of the Prophet ﷺ, of course]. We shall relate three episodes from Tabari's *History* that involved Umar and Ibn Abbās.[291]

Umar's conversation with Ibn Abbās

1. One day, Umar said to Ibn Abbās, "What was it that made the Quraysh prevent you[292] from attaining power?"

Ibn Abbās said, "I do not know."

Umar said, "I know. The Quraysh did not want to have you rule over them."

Ibn Abbās said, "Why? We were good for them." He said this on account of the fact that the Prophet ﷺ was of the Bani Hāshim.

Umar said, "They did not want to have [the institutions of] prophethood and the succession (*khilāfa*) both to be yours, and for you to become haughty and rule it over them. You might think that it was Abu Bakr's doing. But by God ﷻ, that is not the case. Abu Bakr chose what he thought was the wisest path."[293]

---

[290] Mālik ibn Anas, *al-Muwatta*, 2:60: ابى عمر بن الخطاب ان يورث احدا من الاعاجم الّا احدا ولد فى ارض العرب.

[291] The Arabs were divided into two groups: the Adnāni and the Qahtāni. The Qahtānis were originally from Yemen, and included the Ansar; The Adnānis, from whom the Quraysh hailed, were from Mecca and Najd. Umar's policy was to bring Ibn Abbās closer to himself and had him accompany him in order to aggrandize him relative to Imam Ali. After Imam Ali, Ibn Abbas was the strong among the Banī Hāshim in terms of his rhetorical and debating skills. For more information on this subject, see Ibn Sa'd, Abu Abdallah Muhammad, *al-Tabaqāt al-Kubrā*, 2:2nd C:120, and Ibn Abī'l-Hadīd, Abdul-Hamīd, *Sharh Nahj al-Balāgha.*

[292] [The you is plural here, and refers, of course, to the Bani Hāshim overall, rather than to Ibn Abbās personally.]

[293] Tabarī, Muhammad ibn Jarīr, *Tārīkh ar-Rusul wa'l-Mulūk*, 5:2768 of the European edition.

2. In another hadith report, Umar says to Ibn Abbās, "Do you know why your tribe (meaning the Quraysh) prevented you from attaining power after the passing of the Prophet?"

Ibn Abbās says, "I did not want to respond to Umar; I said, 'Will you tell me if I say that I do not know?'"

He said, "They did not want to have [the institutions of] prophethood and the succession (*khilāfa*) both to be yours..."

We stated earlier that their stated policy was to rotate the reins of power within the hands of the Quraysh so as to have all of its clans benefit from the accession to power. And they acted accordingly: when they took power from the House of the Prophet ﷺ, it benefitted the Taym, 'Adiyy, and Bani 'Umayyah clans.

Umar said, "The Quraysh decided to take this path, and their decision was the right one and succeeded."

Ibn Abbās says, "I said, 'O Commander of the Faithful! If you will permit me, and will not become angry at me, I will say something; otherwise, I will remain quiet.'"

Umar said, "Speak."

I said, "O Commander of the Faithful! When you say that 'The Quraysh decided to take this path, and their decision was the right one, and succeeded,' [surely] the Quraysh would have been [truly] successful if they had chosen the person whom God ﷻ had chosen (i.e. Ali). But as to what you said about the Quraysh not wanting to have [the institutions of] prophethood and the succession (*khilāfa*) both to be in our hands,' verily God ﷻ the Mighty and Majestic describes a tribe who had such a dislike, where He says,

ذَٰلِكَ بِأَنَّهُمْ كَرِهُوا مَا أَنزَلَ اللَّهُ فَأَحْبَطَ أَعْمَالَهُمْ ۝٩

[47:9] this, because they hate [the very thought of] what God has bestowed from on high and thus He causes all their deeds to come to naught!

"They hated what God had revealed to them in the Quran (which stipulated the heir and successor (*wasī*[294]) of the Prophet); and so God *caused all of their deeds to come to naught.*"

---

[294] *Wasī*: ministerial inheritor, legatee, executor, and successor.

Umar said, "Things that have been ascribed to you have reached me, but I didn't want to accept that you had said them lest your station be diminished [in my eyes]."

Ibn Abbās said, "If I have spoken the truth, then my station should not be diminished in your eyes; and if what has been ascribed to me are lies, then I am someone who is capable of defending myself against lies that have been attributed to me."

Umar said, "I have been told that you have said that the succession (*khilāfa*) was taken from you unjustly and out of covetousness."

Ibn Abbās replied, "As to an injustice having been done to us, that is something that everyone understands, whether he be a wise man or a fool.[295] But as to your point that I said that it was out of covetousness and envy, well, Iblīs also envied Adam, and we are the children of Adam.[296]

Umar said, "The hearts of the Bani Hashim are far [from the truth]. There is nothing in your hears but a residing envy that does not diminish in time and which will always remain with you."

Ibn Abbās said, "O Commander of the Faithful! Be calm. You say that this is the way the Bani Hāshim are. The Prophet ﷺ was from the Bani Hāshim, and God ﷻ has stated:

إِنَّمَا يُرِيدُ اللَّهُ لِيُذْهِبَ عَنكُمُ الرِّجْسَ أَهْلَ الْبَيْتِ وَيُطَهِّرَكُمْ تَطْهِيرًا ﴿٣٣﴾

[33:33] ... for God only wants to remove from you all that might be loathsome, O you members of the [Prophet's] household, and to purify you to utmost purity.

Umar said, "Leave my presence, Ibn Abbās!"

Ibn Abbās said, "I will certainly do that." And he rose to leave.

---

[295] Given the things that Lady Fātima did [between the time of her father's death] until her burial, the truth could not have been hidden from anyone living in that era to whom news [of her reaction] reached.

[296] He compared Abu Bakr and Umar to Iblīs (Satan).

Umar felt ashamed and said, "Sit back down.[297] Upon my word of honor before God, I respect your rights, and I like and desire that which makes you happy."

Ibn Abbās said, "O Commander of the Faithful! I have a right over you and over every Muslim. Anyone who respects that right will have attained his fortune, and anyone who disrespects it will have lost his fortune."

Umar could stand no more of this, and got up and left.[298]

3. Another report states that Umar sent for Ibn Abbās, and when Ibn Abbās arrived, he said to him, "The governor of Hims was a good man, and has left the world. I am thinking of sending you there, but I am concerned."

Ibn Abbās said, "What are you concerned about?"

Umar said, "I fear that you will [still] be there [installed as its governor] when I die,[299] and to call the people towards you (the Bani Hāshim). And this the people must not do. I want to be assured about this [concern]."

Ibn Abbās said, "It would be best if you appointed a governor about whom you would have no such concerns."[300]

Verily, the general policy of the political order during Umar's reign was for it to be an Arab and Qurayshite order, to the exclusion of the Bani Hāshim.[301]

---

[297] It would not have been good for Umar if the Bani Hashim became aware of this. The Bani Hāshim were a large clan, and it was not the policy of the rulers to have bad relations with them.

[298] Ṭabarī, Muḥammad ibn Jarīr, *Tārīkh ar-Rusul wa'l-Mulūk*, 2:321-322 of the European edition.

[299] Hims [or Homs] was a garrison town, and like Kufa, Basra, Alexandria, and Damascus, and housed a military base. As such, the governor of these cities was also the commander of the armies that were based in those towns, and would be in a position to muster his army after the death of the caliph to attain to power, just as Mu'āwiya did against his eminence Ali after the death of Uthmān.

[300] Mas'ūdī, Alī ibn al-Ḥusain, *Murawwij adh-Dhahab*, 2:321-322.

[301] Imam Ali has stated the following concerning the six-man consultative council that was formed to determine the next caliph after the death of Umar: "The people look to the Quraysh and await to see what they will do, and the Quraysh tribe ponders what it is to do and says, 'If the Banī Hāshim accede to power, the caliphate will never be taken away from them; and if the caliphate goes to a clan of the Quraysh other than the Banī Hāshim, it will revolve around those clans and will benefit all of them.'" (Ṭabarī, Muḥammad ibn Jarīr, *Tārīkh ar-Rusul wa'l-Mulūk*, 5:2787 of the European edition.)

Mu'āwiya during Umar's reign

When Umar journeyed to the Levant, Mu'āwiya received him with the pomp and glory of a kingly court. When Umar saw Mu'āwiya's house in its full regalia from afar, he said, "Here is an Arab King." And when he approached Mu'āwiya, he said to him, "This is your state, whereas I hear that those who are in need [of your ministrations] lie in [endless] wait in your court! Why do you carry on like this?!"

Mu'āwiya apologized and said, "We live in a land in which the spies of the enemy (Byzantium) are numerous. Thus, it is imperative to expose the majesty of our reign [to public view] so that they fear us."[302]

During Umar's reign, Mu'āwiya participated in one of the battles between the Muslim forces and Byzantium. The Muslims were victorious in that Battle, and some spoils were acquired as a result. There was some silverware among the spoils which were offered for sale, so that the proceeds would then be divvied up among the populace. The people showed up to purchase the silverware, each ounce of which sold for two ounces of silver coinage. This was a usurious price, and illicit under the sacred law. The news of the incident reached Ubāda[t] ibn Sāmit, the great Companion of the Prophet ﷺ who resided in the Levant (*shām*, what is meant in all probability is Damascus). Ubāda rose up and cried, "I have heard from the Apostle of God ﷺ that he forbade the buying and selling of gold and silver with anything other than an equal amount of gold or silver, and that anyone who trades in gold and silver in anything other than their equal amounts has committed usury."

Upon hearing what Ubāda said, the people returned everything that they had purchased. When Mu'āwiya heard about this, he became disconcerted and delivered a sermon in which he said, "How is it that the people recount sayings of the Prophet ﷺ, whom we knew and whom we accompanied, and whom we never once heard say any such thing!" Ubāda rose up and repeated what he had said earlier, then added, "We shall repeat what we have heard the Apostle of God ﷺ say, even if Mu'āwiya is not happy about it."

Mu'āwiya expelled Ubāda from the army, and Ubāda returned to Medina. Umar asked him why he had returned from the Levant, as

---

[302] Ibn Abd'al-Birr, Yusuf ibn Abdallah, *al-Istī'āb fi Ma'rifat al-Ashāb*, 1:253; Ibn Hajar, Ahmad ibn Ali al-Asqalāni, *al-Iṣābah fī Tamyīz al-Ṣaḥābah*, 3:413; Ibn Kathīr, Abu'al-Fiḍā Ismā'īl ibn Umar, *Tārīkh*, 8:120.

he had sent him there to teach the Levantines the Quran. Ubāda recounted Mu'āwiya's unbecoming behavior to Umar, who said, "Go back to where you came from. May God cover the face of a land with ignominy where you and the likes of you cannot live. Mu'āwiya will never be able to rule over you."[303]

Ubāda returned to the Levant, but Umar did not reprimand Mu'āwiya in any way.

Umar's Confession, the Consultative Council, and the Pledge of Allegiance to Uthmān

During the last year, when Umar had made the major pilgrimage (*hajj*), 'Ammār ibn Yāsir told his friends in Mina that making the pledge of allegiance [on the part of the community as a whole] was a hasty affair or mistake (*falta*) that happened on the spur of the moment, and that we would pledge allegiance to Ali ﷺ when Umar died.[304]

This news reached Umar in Mina at a time when he was heading towards Medina. On the first Friday that he went to the pulpit in the Mosque of the Prophet ﷺ in Medina, Umar delivered a lengthy sermon, at the end of which he said that the pledge of allegiance to Abu Bakr was a hasty affair or mistake (*falta*) which occurred, but whose ill God ﷻ removed from the Muslim [community], and that after this, the pledging of allegiance [to the caliph] must take place through a process of consultation, and if anyone pledges allegiance to anyone else without [due] consultation, both of their necks should be severed with a sword.[305]

During the time when Abu Lu'lu' stabbed Umar with a dagger, Umar was given some water to drink. When the water came out of the stab wound and it became evident that his entrails had been severed and that he would soon die, he was asked to appoint a successor. Umar said, "If Abu Ubayda al-Jarrāh is alive, I appoint him as my successor. And if God were to ask me the reason [for my choice], I would say that your apostle used to say that he was the trustee of the community. And if Sālim, the freedman of Abu Hudhayfa is alive, I would undoubtedly

---

303 Ahmad b. Hanbal, *Musnad*, 5:319; Ibn 'Asākir, 'Alī, *Tahdhīb*, 5:212; Muslim ibn al-Ḥajjāj, *Ṣaḥīḥ Muslim*, 5:46; Nasā'ī, Aḥmad ibn Shu'ayb, *al-Sunan*, 20:222.
304 Ibn Abī'l-Hadīd, Abdul-Hamīd, *Sharh Nahj al-Balāgha*, 2:123.
305 Balādhūrī, Ahmad ibn Yahyā ibn Jābir, *Ansāb al-Ashrāf*, 1:583-584; Ibn Hishām, 'Abd al-Malik, *al-Sīrah al-Nabawīyah*, 4:336-337; see also, Askari, Allāma Murtaḍā, *Abdullāh ibn Sabā*, 1:159 for a more detailed bibliography of the sources on this issue.

appoint him to succeed me. And if God were to ask me the reason [for my choice], I would say that I had heard your apostle say that Sālim's love for God is to such an extent that even if he did not fear God, he would still not disobey Him."

Umar was told, "O Commander of the Faithful, in any event, appoint someone to succeed you."

Umar responded, "I had thought about appointing someone to rule over you who would undoubtedly lead you toward that which is right and just [reference to Ali], but I did not want [the burden of the responsibility of] your affairs to be on my shoulders during my lifetime and after my death."[306]

Balādhūrī states in his *Ansāb al-Ashrāf*: "On the day Umar was stabbed, he gave instructions for Ali, Uthmān, Talha, Zubayr, Abd al-Rahmān ibn 'Awf, and S'ad ibn Abi Waqqās to be brought into his presence. Then he did not speak to anyone but Ali and 'Uthmān. He said to Ali, 'O Ali, it may be that this group (the men that made up the consultative council) will take into account the right [that you have by virtue] of your ties of kinship with the Prophet, and the fact that you were his son in law, and the degree of your knowledge and understanding [of the teachings of Islam] which God has endowed you with, and choose you to rule over them. In that case, do not forget God!'

"Umar then turned to 'Uthmān and said, 'O Uthmān, it may be that they will take your seniority into account, and the fact that you were the Prophet's son in law, [and choose you to rule over them]. So if you acceed to power, fear God and do not place [the yoke of] the House of Abū Mu'ayt on the people's neck. He then had Suhayb brought into Umar's presence, and he told him, 'You shall perform your ritual devotions for a period of three days, and these [six] people will be gathered inside a house and will work on determining who the next caliph will be. If they agree on the appointment of a single person, then sever the neck of anyone who disagrees with their decision.' When that group left Umar's presence, he said, 'If the people choose the *ajlah* [to acceed] to the caliphate,[307] he will guide them to the right path.'"[308]

---

[306] Ibn 'Abd Rabbih, *al-'Iqd al-Farīd*, 4:260.

[307] *Ajlah* is a word used to describe a man who has lost his hair at his crown [or what we would call 'male pattern baldness' nowadays], and who has a little hair left on either side of his head. Umar's use of this word is a reference to Ali.

Quoting Wāqidī in his *Ansāb al-Ashrāf*, Balādhūrī states:

Umar asked those who were around him about whom he should choose to succeed him. He was asked, "What do you think about Uthmān?" He replied, "If I choose him, he will place the House of Abū Mu'ayt (= the Bani Umayya) on the neck of the people." They said, "What about Zubayr?" Umar replied, "He is a true believer (*mu'min*) when he is happy, but becomes an infidel at heart when he is angry." They said, "What about Talha?" Umar replied, "He is an arrogant and selfish person whose nose is pointed upward and whose seat is in water."[309] They said, "What about Sa' ibn Abi Waqqās?" Umar said, "As a commander of the cavalry, he is peerless; but the governance of a hamlet is too big of a burden for him." They then asked him, "What do you say about Abd ar-Rahmān ibn 'Awf?" Umar said, "It suffices him just to be able to manage his own household!"[310]

Elsewhere [in his *Ansāb al-Ashrāf*,] Balādhūrī states:

When Umar ibn al-Khattab was stabbed, he instructed Suhayb, the freedman of Abdallāh ibn Jud'ān to gather the leaders of the Emigrants and the Ansār and bring them to him. When they entered into his presence, Umar said, "I have placed [the decision concerning] the succession and reign [over the community] in the decision of a consultative council (*shawrā*) consisting of six of the initial Emigrants

---

[308] Balādhūrī, Ahmad ibn Yahyā ibn Jābir, *Ansāb al-Ashrāf*, 5:16; as well as Ibn Sa'd, Abu Abdallah Muhammad, *al-Tabaqāt al-Kubrā*, 3:1st C:247, where wording close to this appears. Cf. also Ibn Abd'al-Birr, Yusuf ibn Abdallah, *al-Istī'āb fi Ma'rifat al-Ashāb*, and Muttaqī al-Hindī, *Kanz al-U'mmāl*, 4:429. It is noteworthy that according to Tabarī, Muhibbiddīn, *ar-Riyāḍ an-Naḍra*, 2:72, Aḥmad ibn Shu'ayb an-Nasā'ī cites this hadith report in his *as-Sunan*, and therein adds that Umar said, «لله درّهم» چه نيك مردانى هستند «ان ولوها الاصيلع» meaning, If they leave the leadership of the caliphate in the hands of that man with a raised forehead (i.e. to Ali), then they will see how he will make them abide by that which is right (كيف يحملهم على الحقّ و إن كان السّيف على عنقه), even if it means that he has always to carry a sword around with him. Muhammad ibn Ka'b said to Umar, "You have had a meritorious experience such as this from him (i.e. Ali), and yet you do not hand the caliphate over to him?" Umar replied, If I leave the people be as they are, it is because someone before me (i.e. Abu Bakr) did the same thing (ان تركتهم فقد تركهم من هو خير منّي).

[309] An Arab saying that alludes to haughtiness and arrogance.

[310] Balādhūrī, Ahmad ibn Yahyā ibn Jābir, *Ansāb al-Ashrāf*, 5:17.

with whom the Prophet was well pleased at the time of his passing. These six men are to choose one person from among themselves as the leader who is to lead you and the community." He then named each of the six members of the consultative council, then faced Abu Talha Zayd ibn Sahl al-Khazrajī and said, "Choose fifty men of the Ansār to accompany you, and when I have passed, and have them make these [six] people choose one person from among themselves as your leader and as the leader of the community." Umar then instructed Suhayb to lead the public ritual devotions while the selection process was still taking place.

Talha ibn 'Ubayd-Allāh was not present [in Medina] at that time, and was at his property in Surāh.[311] Umar said, "If Talha shows up within the space of these three days, then so be it. Otherwise, do not wait for him and pursue the matter of determining who is to succeed to the caliphate with all seriousness, and pledge your allegiance to the person on whom you have agreed. And sever the necks of anyone who disagrees with your decision."[312]

Umar instructed the members of the consultative council to consult each other for a period of no more than three days concerning the issue of the succession. He said that if two men chose one person to lead, and two others chose someone else, they should return to their consultations; but that if four people agreed on one person, and the fifth disagreed, the fifth person should fall in line behind the decision of the four. And in the event that the votes turn out to be three votes for each, the vote of the three that includes Abd ar-Rahmān ibn 'Awf shall prevail, as his religiosity and [his discernment of] expedience can be trusted, and his vote is acceptable and trusted by the Muslims.[313]

Quoting Muhammad ibn Jubayr (who is quoting his father) in his *Kanz al-U'mmāl,* Muttaqī al-Hindī narrates that Umar stated, "If

---

[311] *As-Surā* was the name of a mountain around the city of Tāif. The name has also been attributed to other locations as well. ([Yāqūt Shihāb al-Dīn ibn-'Abdullāh al-Hamāwī], *Mu'jam al-Buldān*).

[312] Balādhurī, Aḥmad ibn Yaḥyā ibn Jabir, *Ansāb al-Ashrāf* [Lineages of the Nobles], 5:18. . It is worth noting that Talha came to Medina later; that is, after the death of Umar and the establishment of the council and after allegiance had been pledged to 'Uthmān, and ultimately pledged allegiance to him (Balādhūrī, *Ansāb al-Ashrāf,* 5:20).

[313] Balādhurī, Aḥmad ibn Yaḥyā ibn Jabir, *Ansāb al-Ashrāf,* 5:19. Something close to this also appears in Ibn Abd al-Rabbih's *al-'Iqd al-Farīd,* 3:74.

Abd ar-Rahmān ibn 'Awf places one of his hands on the other as a gesture of having pledged allegiance [to himself], obey him and pledge allegiance to him."[314]

What we can glean from this matter is that Umar placed the decision concerning the succession in the hands of Abd ar-Rahmān ibn 'Awf based on a [previously determined] policy, and vested him with a special authority which he could yield when necessary. And it is clear that he had an arrangement with Abd ar-Rahmān ibn 'Awf which conditioned the appointment to the caliphate on the acceptance of the ways in which the *shaykhayn* [i.e. Abu Bakr and Umar] acted, knowing that Imam Ali would refrain from accepting the ways of the *shaykhayn* as being tantamount to acting in accordance with God's sacred writ and the exemplary model of His prophet; but that Uthmān would accept this condition, as a consequence of which he would accede to the caliphate. Thus, Umar had already issued the order that opposed Ali's [candidacy].

The reason for the statement, in addition to what we have already mentioned, is a passage that Ibn Sa'd cites in his *al-Tabaqāt al-Kubrā*, quoting Sa'īd ibn 'Ās (the Umayyad):

Sa'īd ibn 'Ās asked Umar to add a little to the area of the property his house was on so that he could add an addition to it. The caliph gave him the glad tidings that he would fulfil his request after offering his morning ritual devotions. Umar kept his promise and went to Sa'īd's house that morning and ...
[Sa'īd ibn 'Ās himself adds:] The caliph drew a line with his feet and added to the area of my property. But I said, "O Commander of the Faithful, grant some more, as my family has grown, and I have big ones and little ones among them." Umar said, "For now, this much suffice you. And keep this secret, that after me, someone will acceed to the caliphate who will honour his bonds of kinship with you and fulfil your needs!"

[Sa'īd ibn 'Ās said:] Much time passed after this incident, and Umar's caliphate came to an end, and Uthmān acceded to the caliphate out of Umar's consultative assembly. From the very beginning, he [Uthmān]

[314] Muttaqī al-Hindī, *Kanz al-U'mmāl*, 3:160.

made sure to see I was contented, and saw that my request was fulfilled handsomely...[315]

What can be concluded from this dialogue is that the charter and certainty of Uthmān's caliphate were drawn and signed with Umar's hand during his lifetime, and that the appointment of the six-man council was only a facade with which the [supposed] neutrality of the caliphate in electing the next caliph was put on display in a way that would be popular and acceptable to the general populace.

In addition, the plan to incite people to assassinate and eliminate the Imam is yet another important point that Ibn Sa'd includes in his *al-Tabaqāt al-Kubrā*, in Tabaqat, quoting Sa'īd ibn 'Ās again:

One day Umar ibn al-Khattāb told Sa'īd ibn 'Ās, "Why do you turn away from me and keep your distance from me? Perhaps it is because you think that I was the one who killed your father. But it was not I who killed your father. Your father was killed by Ali ibn Abī Tālib."[316]

Did Umar not intend to incite Sa'īd ibn 'Ās to revenge his father's killer, Ali ibn Abī Tālib ﷺ?

The way Uthmān was elected to the Caliphate

Balādhurī quotes Abu Mikhnaf in his *Ansāb al-Ashrāf* as follows:

On the day of Umar's burial, the members of the consultative council did not do anything. Following Umar's instructions, Abu Talha led the ritual devotions, and nothing happened. On the morning of the next day, Abu Talha gathered the men of the council in the area of the Treasury (*bayt al-māl*) so that they could consult with each other. Umar's funeral took place on a Sunday, which was the fourth day after he had sustained his fatal injury; and Suhayb ibn Sinān lead the prayer ceremony.

When 'Abd al-Rahmān saw the members of the council arguing and that each wanted to eliminate his own rival from the running, he said to them, "Look, Sa'd and I will withdraw [our candidacy], on the condition

[315] Ibn Sa'd, Abu Abdallah Muhammad, *al-Tabaqāt al-Kubrā*, 5:20-22 of the European edition.

[316] Ibid. Imam Ali had killed Sa'īd's father in the Battle of Badr.

that the choice between you four is left to me; because your whispering consultations have taken a long time, and people are waiting to know who their caliph and leader will be. And the sojourn of the residents of other cities who have been staying in Medina to find out what the outcome of this affair will be, have had their stay extended, and should be able to return to their cities and homes."
Everyone agreed with the suggestion of 'Abd al-Rahmān ibn 'Awf, except Ali, who said: "Let us see [what will transpire]." At this time, Abu Talha entered the conclave and Abd al-Rahmān informed him of what he had suggested, and everyone but Ali accepted his suggestion. So, Abu Talha turned to Ali and said: "O Abu'l-Hasan, Abd al-Rahman is trusted by all Muslims; why do you oppose him? He has withdrawn his candidacy, nor will he be a burden the onus of sin for the sake of anyone else." At this point, Ali swore Abd al-Rahman to ignore the desires of his heart and to act in accordance with what is right and for the benefit of the community as a whole, and not to allow his familiar ties to make him veer from his doing the right thing. Abd al-Rahman ibn Awf accepted all of these conditions and swore his oath. After this, Ali turned to him and said, "Now choose with peace of mind."

This event took place in the treasury, or, according to a different narrative, in the house of Miswar ibn Makhrama.[317] Then Abd al-Rahman came forward and took Ali's hand in his own and said to him, "Swear an oath to God that if I pledge allegiance to you, you will not place [the yoke of] the House of Abd al-Muttalib on the people's neck. And swear an oath that you will abide by the exemplary model of the Apostle of God and of the *shaykhayn* (Abu Bakr and Umar) and will not deviate from them." Ali replied, "My behavior towards you will be in accordance with God's sacred writ and the exemplary model of His apostle, to the best of my abilities."

---

[317] Ibn Hajar al-Asqalāni writes in his *Fath al-Bārī fī Sharh Sahīh al-Bukhārī*, (a commentary on *Ṣaḥīḥ al-Bukhārī*) 16:321-322: Mas'ūr ibn Mukhrama narrated that Abd al-Rahmān came to my house and woke me up in order for me to go and inform the people of the council. When I did this, they gathered at the pulpit و اجتمع اولئك الرّهط عند المنبر. Thus, the place of the gathering of the council was the Mosque of the Prophet ﷺ, and this is incorrect, considering what has been stated, and what appears in Balādhūrī's *Ansāb al-Ashrāf*, 5:21, and in Ibn Abī'l-Hadīd's *Sharh Nahj al-Balāgha*, 1:240-241, both of which state that the place of the assembly of the council was the treasury.

Then Abd al-Rahman said to 'Uthmān, "May God bear witness for us against you not to place [the yoke of] the House of the Bani Umayya on the people's neck if you take the reins of power in your hands, and swear an oath that you will abide by God's sacred writ and the exemplary model of the Apostle of God ﷺ and of the *shaykhayn,* and will not deviate from them."

Uthmān replied, "I shall treat you in accordance with God's sacred writ and the exemplary model of the Apostle of God ﷺ and of Abu Bakr and Umar."

Once again, Abd al-Rahman turned to Ali and repeated his earlier words to him, and Ali responded again as he had done earlier. Then he drew 'Uthmān aside and repeated what he had said earlier, and heard the same favorable response from Uthmān. When Abd al-Rahman repeated his suggestion to Ali for the third time, Imam Ali said to him, "God's sacred writ and the exemplary model of the Apostle of God ﷺ do not stand in need of a third or any other method. What you are [actually] doing is taking the succession away from me by whatever means are at your disposal!"

Abd al-Rahman did not pay any attention to the Imam's objection, and turned to 'Uthmān and repeated his initial phrases for the third time, and heard the same answer from 'Uthmān. So he took Uthmān's hand in his and pledged allegiance to him.[318]

Additionally, Tabari and Ibn Athīr write the following as part of their descriptions of the events of the year 23 AH:

When Abd al-Rahman pledged allegiance to 'Uthmān on the third day [of the conclave], Ali said to Abd al-Rahman, "You have arranged the world in accordance with his desires. This is not the first day that you have acted in unison and with each other's support against us. [Then Imam Ali quoted the following phrase from the Quran:]

فَصَبْرٌ جَمِيلٌ ۖ وَاللَّهُ الْمُسْتَعَانُ عَلَىٰ مَا تَصِفُونَ ﴿١٨﴾

[12:18] But [as for myself,] patience in adversity is most goodly [in the sight of God]; and it is to God [alone] that I pray to give me strength to bear the misfortune which you have described to me."

318 Ya'qūbī, Aḥmad ibn Isḥāq, *Tārīkh al-Ya'qūbī,* 1:162; and with slight variations in Balādhūrī, Aḥmad ibn Yahyā ibn Jābir, *Ansāb al-Ashrāf,* 5:21.

[Imam Ali continues:] I swear by God, you have not appointed Uthmān to the caliphate without [knowing that] he will appoint you to the caliphate after him. But every day is subject to God's destined will (*taqdīr*)."[319]

After Abd al-Rahman's pledge of allegiance to Uthmān, the other members of the council also pledged allegiance to him. Ali, who was standing watching what was taking place, sat on the ground. Addressing him, Abd al-Rahman said, "Pledge [your] allegiance, otherwise I will sever your neck [with my sword]!" But none of those present carried a sword with them on that day.[320] It is also reported that Ali exited the conclave of the council in anger, and that the other members of the council caught up with him and said, "Pledge your allegiance or we will fight you." And that therefore he returned with them and pledged allegiance to Uthmān.[321]

The reason for Imam Ali's participation in Umar's six-man council

Imam Ali knew full well that the caliphate would not be given to him, but he participated in the council with the rest of them so that it would not be said of him that he did not want to succeed to the caliphate. Balādhurī writes in his *Ansāb al-Ashrāf*:

Before the convocation of the council's conclave, Ali told his uncle Abbas, "The caliphate has slipped through our hands [yet again]."

Abbas said: "Why do you say that?"

[Imam Ali] responded, "Sa'd will not oppose his cousin Abd al-Rahman, and Abd al-Rahman is 'Uthmān's son-in-law; the three of them are together. Even if Talha and Zubayr were to be with me, it would be of

[319] Ibn Athīr Jazarī, 'Alī, *al-Kāmil fī al-Tārīkh*, 3:73 and Tabarī, Muhammad ibn Jarīr, *Tārīkh ar-Rusul wa'l-Mulūk*, 3:297. See also, Ibn ʿAbd Rabbih, *al-ʿIqd al-Farīd*, 3:76.

[320] [For what it's worth, the Noor software application that is a digitized compendium of most of Allāma Askari's work adds the following ending to this sentence: "... other than Abd al-Rahman."]

[321] Balādhūrī, Ahmad ibn Yahyā ibn Jābir, *Ansāb al-Ashrāf*, 5:21 ff.

no use because of what Umar has said about Abd al-Rahman casting the deciding vote."[322]

Therefore, Imam Ali knew; and if he had not participated in the council, the people would not have pledged allegiance to him after [the death of] Uthmān, because the words of the Prophet ﷺ had been forgotten, and Umar's words were present [in the public's memory]. Umar had grown to such great proportions that his position with them was higher than that of all of the prophets, (God forbid!).

[322] Balādhūrī, Ahmad ibn Yahyā ibn Jābir, *Ansāb al-Ashrāf,* 5:19.

11 Uthmān's Caliphate

Abu Sufyan's Words

On the first day after 'Uthmān's accession to the caliphate, Abu Sufyan, whose eyes had gone blind by that time, came to 'Uthmān and said, "Is there anyone present other than Umayyads?" When they told him that there wasn't, he said, "O Umayyads! From the time that the caliphate fell into the hands of the Taym and 'Adiyy [clans of the Quraysh], I have yearned for it to reach you. Now that it has come to you, [treat it] like children who pass a ball [back and forth] to each other in the game: pass the caliphate to each other [like a ball] and do not let it go out of your hands; as neither is there a Heaven nor a Hell." 'Uthmān yelled at him, but the Umayyads acted on his instructions.[323]

Another hadith report stated puts it this way: Abu Sufyan came unto 'Uthmān while he was an old man and his eyes had lost their sight. After he settled down, he asked, "Is there anyone here that is not one of us who would spread my words to others?" 'Uthmān said, "No." Abu Sufyan said, "This matter of the caliphate is a worldly matter, and this political order is of the kind [that we had] prior to the advent of Islam. Therefore, appoint the governors and authorities of the vast territories of the dominion of Islam from among the Umayya [clan]."[324]

[323] Isfahānī, Abī'l-Faraj, *al-Aghānī*, 6:355-356; see also, Ibn Abd'al-Birr, Yusuf ibn Abdallah, *al-Istī'āb fi Ma'rifat al-Ashāb*, p. 690; and Mughīrī's *al-Nizā' wa'l-Tahāsum*, p. 20; and Mas'ūdī, Ālī ibn al-Ḥusayn, *Murawwij adh-Dhahab*, citing marginalia in Ibn Athīr Jazarī, 'Alī, *al-Kāmil fī al-Tārīkh*, 5:165-166.

[324] Isfahānī, Abī'l-Faraj, *al-Aghānī*, 6:323. The text appears as follows in Ibn 'Asākir's *al-Tahdhīb* (6:409): انّ ابا سفيان دخل على عثمان بعد ما عمى فقال: هاهنا احد؟ فقالوا: لا. فقال: اللّهمّ اجعل الامر امر الجاهليّة و الملك ملك غاصبيّة و اجعل اوتاد الارض لبنى اميّة.

It was during that same time that one day Abu Sufyan went to the grave of Hamza, the great martyr of Islam, and stamped his foot on the grave of that great nobleman and said, "O Abu Umara, that which we drew swords over yesterday is today in the hands of our children, who are busy playing with it.[325]

Walīd, 'Uthmān's Governor in Kūfa

Walid was the son of 'Uqbat ibn Abī Mu'īt. He became a Muslim on the day that Mecca was conquered and came under the control of the Apostle of God ﷺ, after which there was no longer any escape for the polytheists and misguided idolaters of Mecca. After a while, the Prophet of God commissioned him to collect the *zakāt* of the Bani Mustalaq tribe. Walīd went to the land of the Bani Mustalaq and reported that the members of the tribe had apostatized and were refusing to pay *zakāt.* This report was false, and the reason Walīd made this false report was due to the fact that a number of people of the Bani Mustalaq tribe had come out to greet Walīd when they heard the news of the arrival of the representative of the Apostle of God, and wanted to see him up close. But Walīd mistook their intentions, fearing that they had gathered with ill intent toward him. Thus, he returned hastily to Medina and gave that false report.

The Messenger of God commissioned Khālid ibn Walīd to go to that tribe and investigate and report the truth of the matter. In his report, Khālid stressed that the tribe were committed to Islam and had not at all apostatized. During this incident, the following verse was revealed about Walīd and his adventure, wherein God ﷻ characterized Walīd as a corrupt person:[326]

يا أَيُّهَا الَّذِينَ آمَنُوا إِنْ جاءَكُمْ فاسِقٌ بِنَبَإٍ فَتَبَيَّنُوا أَنْ تُصِيبُوا قَوْماً
بِجَهالَةٍ فَتُصْبِحُوا عَلى ما فَعَلْتُمْ نادِمِينَ ٦

---

[325] Ibn Abī'l-Hadīd, Abdul-Hamīd, *Sharh Nahj al-Balāgha*, 4:51.

[326] For biographical sketches of Walīd, see the following sources:
Ibn Abd'al-Birr, Yusuf ibn Abdallah, *al-Istī'āb fi Ma'rifat al-Ashāb*
Ibn Athīr, 'Alī ibn Muḥammad, *Usd al-Ghābah fī Ma'rifat al-Ṣaḥābah*
Ibn Hajar, Ahmad ibn Ali al-Asqalāni, *al-Iṣābah fī Tamyīz al-Ṣaḥābah*
Ibn Sa'd, Abu Abdallah Muhammad, *al-Tabaqāt al-Kubrā*
Muttaqī al-Hindī, *Kanz al-U'mmāl*

49:6 O you who have attained to faith! If any corrupt person comes to you with a [slanderous] tale, use your discernment, lest you hurt people unwittingly and afterwards be filled with remorse for what you have done

Now we see 'Uthmān, who is the caliph of the Muslims, and who considers himself to be the successor of the Apostle of God, appoints such an infamous and corrupt person to the governorship of Kufa merely because of his familial ties and kinship with himself.

Walīd's rule over Kufa lasted for five years, during which time he was engaged in fighting the polytheists in the regions of Azerbaijan. But because he lacked faith, he committed a transgression that was subject to punishment under the sacred law (*hadd*) despite being in a position of high public responsibility and despite being the commander in chief of the Muslim forces who were facing the enemy at the time.[327] The leaders of the community gathered to impose the punishment according to sharia law on him, but Hudhayfah opposed the implementation of this the punishment against Walīd, because he was in charge of the Muslim forces who were up against the enemy; thus, he was let off.[328]

The story of Walīd's drinking while he was the governor of Kufa

Abī'l-Faraj al-Isfahānī (writing in his *Kitāb al-Aghānī*[329]) and Ali ibn al-Husayn al-Mas'ūdī (writing in his *Murawwij adh-Dhahab*[330]) state:

Walid drank with Nadimān and his entertainers from night until morning. Once, when the morning call to prayer was called, he went to the mosque in a drunken state, dressed in his festive clothing and stood in the prayer niche [at the front of the congregation] to pray.

---

[327] The nature of the transgression that Walīd committed is not clear. He was, of course, infamous as a fornicator and wine drinker, and was famously subjected to punishment as determined by the sacred law during 'Uthmān's caliphate at the hands of Ali ibn Abi Tālib (Balādhūrī, Ahmad ibn Yahyā ibn Jābir, *Ansāb al-Ashrāf*, 5:35; and Mas'ūdī, Alī ibn al-Ḥusayn, *Murawwij adh-Dhahab*, 1:449). But withal, I do not know whether or not Walid committed the sin of drinking wine in Azarbāijān, or whether he got up to some other mischief.

[328] Balādhūrī, Ahmad ibn Yahyā ibn Jābir, *Ansāb al-Ashrāf*, 5:31.

[329] Isfahānī, Abī'l-Faraj, *Kitāb al-Aghānī*, 4:176-177 (Dusāsī).

[330] Mas'ūdī, Ali ibn al-Husayn, *Murawwij adh-Dhahab*, 2:335 (Dār al-Andalus).

He prayed four cycles (*rak'ats*) for the morning prayer [instead of two], and said to the people: "Would you like me to add a few more *rak'ats* to the morning prayer?" After which he threw up all he had eaten in the prayer niche of the mosque.

Atab Saghafi, who was in the front row of the worshipers and behind Walid, shouted at him: "May God curse you, what is to become of you?? I swear by God that I am not surprised by anyone other than the Caliph of the Muslims, who has appointed someone such as you as ruler [over us]. The people who were present in the mosque threw what stones and pebbles that were in the mosque at Walīd.

The brother of the caliph and governor of Kufa, who found himself to be in a tight spot, staggered back and made his way to his palace, while reciting these verses under his breath:

> I shall never turn away from wine and beautiful bondmaidens, and shall never deprive myself of their goodness and pleasure. Rather, I will drink enough wine to quench my mind of it, after which I shall pass among the people dragging my robe behind me.

The people said bitterly, "Let us go and tell the caliph ('Uthmān) [about this]." The man who went to Medina came back and said that 'Uthmān beat him.

On another occasion, four people went to Walid's house at night while he was drinking wine, and removed his [signet] ring from his finger. Because Walid was drunk, he did not realize this had occurred. They took the ring with them to 'Uthmān, who asked, "How do you know that Walid had drunk wine?" They said, "This is the same wine that we drank in the era of [pre-Islamic] ignorance. He has drunk wine, and this is his ring!" 'Uthmān, who was furious, threatened the witnesses and the plaintiffs and promised to punish them and pushed them away from his presence.

The plaintiffs, who had been beaten and flogged at 'Uthmān's behest, appealed to Ali ﷺ and asked him to intervene to resolve the matter. Ali ﷺ went to 'Uthmān and spoke to him about them and remonstrated, "Do you neglect to enforce the punishments provided by the sacred law and beat those who testify against your brother, and change the law of God?"[331]

The Mother of the Faithful (Umm al-Mu'minin) 'Āisha, to whom the witnesses had [also] appealed, called out to 'Uthmān, "Have you violated the punishments set out by the divine law? And have you insulted the witnesses?"[332]

The group took refuge in 'Āisha's house for fear of 'Uthmān's wrath, and when 'Uthmān heard words [spoken against him] from 'Āisha's house in the morning that was harsh and aggressive, he cried out involuntarily, "Did the wicked rebels from Iraq not find refuge in any house other than 'Āisha's?!"

When 'Āisha heard these insulting and unforgivable words of 'Uthmān's that were addressed to her, she took the sandals of the Messenger of God and raised them in her hands and shouted in a loud voice, "How soon you have abandoned the tradition and ways of the Messenger of God!" 'Āisha's words quickly spread by word of mouth and filled [the atmosphere of] the mosque, in which one group was heard praising her words, saying that she had done well to express them. Another group reproached her, saying, "What business do women have interfering in political matters?" The situation escalated to the point where words were exchanged, and they started throwing pebbles at each other and hitting each other with their sandals.[333] This was the first encounter between two groups of Muslims after the passing of the Prophet ﷺ.[334]

After this incident, Talha and Zubayr went to 'Uthmān and rebuked him and said, "We advised you from the start not to appoint Walid to any position of authority over the affairs of the Muslims, but you did not heed our advice. But it is not too late now. Now that a group has testified to his drunkenness and debauchery, it is in your best interest to dismiss him." Ali ؑ also said to 'Uthmān, "Dismiss Walid, and if witnesses testify against him in his presence, apply the provisions of the divine law to him as well."[335]

---

[331] *Murrawwij adh-Dhahab*, 2:336.
[332] Balādhūrī, Ahmad ibn Yahyā ibn Jābir, *Ansāb al-Ashrāf*, 5:34.
[333] *A'ānī*, 4:178.
[334] Balādhūrī, Ahmad ibn Yahyā ibn Jābir, *Ansāb al-Ashrāf*, 5:33.
[335] Balādhūrī, Ahmad ibn Yahyā ibn Jābir, *Ansāb al-Ashrāf*, 5:35.

Walīd's Dismissal

'Uthmān had no choice but to dismiss Walid ibn Uqayba from his post as governor of Kūfa, and appointed Sa'īd ibn Ās as the new governor of Kūfa, with the instruction to send Walid ibn Uqayba back to Madina. When Sa'īd ibn Ās entered Kūfa, he refused to mount the pulpit of Kūfa's congregational mosque, saying that the pulpit was ritually unclean (*najis*), and that it must be cleansed and that the government building (the *dār al-imāra*) also needed to be cleaned. A number of the notables of the Banī Umayya clan who had come to Kūfa with Sa'īd beseeched him to refrain from cleaning the pulpit of Kūfa's congregational mosque, reminding him that if anyone else took to doing such a thing, it would be his responsibility to prevent the person from carrying out such an act, as it would impose an ever-lasting stigma on Walīd.

Sa'īd ibn al-Ās ultimately ordered the pulpit of Kūfa's congregational mosque and the government building to be cleaned with water, and ordered Walīd to return to Madīna. When he came into the presence of Uthmān and witnesses testified to his drinking wine, 'Uthmān had no choice but to subject him to the punishment for this transgression of the sacred law (*hadd*), [which consisted of 80 lashes with a whip]. Before he did so, however, Uthmān had a thick gown draped across Walīd's back so that he would not feel the effects of the whip. Walid would tell anyone who went to whip him, "Think of my familial ties and do not sever your relationship with me by whipping me and making the Commander of the Faithful 'Uthmān angry at you." Thus, the person would drop the whip and leave, as he was not willing to bring the ire of 'Uthmān onto himself.

When Ali ibn Abī-Tālib ﷺ saw what was happening, he picked up the whip himself while his son Hasan was also present.[336] Walīd implored him by God ﷻ and by the right of the familial ties that they had not to whip him. His Eminence Ali ﷺ said, "Be silent, O Walīd! The reason for the perdition of the Children of Israel was that they stopped enforcing the punishments that had been set out in the sacred law of God..."[337]

Walīd fled to the right and to the left from Ali's ﷺ administration of his punishment, who caught up with him and threw him to the ground. When 'Uthmān protested, Ali ﷺ said, "He has

[336] Balādhūrī, Ahmad ibn Yahyā ibn Jābir, *Ansāb al-Ashrāf*, 5:35.
[337] Isfahānī, Abī'l-Faraj, *Kitāb al-Aghānī*, 4:177 (Dusāsī).

committed an immoral act; he has drunk wine and resists being punished for it,"[338] after which he administered 40 lashes with a two-pronged whip. His Eminence Ali ﷺ did not raise his arm to such an extent that his underarm would be exposed;[339] in other words, he did not administer the punishment severely.

The custom at the time was that they shaved the head of anyone who was whipped. When 'Uthmān was told to shave Walīd's head, he refused to do so.[340] Later, 'Uthmān made Walīd responsible for collecting the *zakāt* tax of the tribes of Kalb and Balqayn![341]

The Situation in Kūfa during 'Uthmān's Reign.

The situation of the Muslims during 'Uthmān's reign was very chaotic. 'Uthmān appointed his brother[342] Walid as governor of Kufa. The territory that was under the governorship of Kufa extended up to Madain, the imperial capital of Iran, and up to Kermanshah, Rey, central Iran, i.e. Qom and Kāshān, and eastern Iran up to the countries of Central Asia. Kufa was one of the five military centers of the domain of Islam. 'Uthmān had delegated the rule of all of these countries to Walid.

'Uthmān removed Sa'd ibn Abi-Waqqās from the governorship of Kufa. Sa'd was one of the earliest companions of the Prophet ﷺ and one of the first Muslims to emigrate to Madina. The decision to set up camp in this area was taken during the reign of the second caliph. Sa'd ibn Abi-Waqqās had built Kufa [from nothing as a garrison outpost], and had become its governor by order of Umar. The second caliph had also appointed Sa'd ibn Abi-Waqqās to the six-member council that was to be convened after Umar's death as one of the six candidates for the caliphate. This appointment had increased the Muslims' respect for Sa'd. He treated the Kufans well and they in turn were satisfied with him.

When Walid came to Kufa, bringing with him the order for the removal of Sa'd, Sa'd said to him in surprise, "I do not know whether

---

338 Balādhūrī, Ahmad ibn Yahyā ibn Jābir, *Ansāb al-Ashrāf*
Mas'ūdī, Alī ibn al-Ḥusayn, *Murawwij adh-Dhahab, 1:449.*
339 Balādhūrī, Ahmad ibn Yahyā ibn Jābir, *Ansāb al-Ashrāf,* 5:35.
340 Balādhūrī, Ahmad ibn Yahyā ibn Jābir, *Ansāb al-Ashrāf,* 5:35.
341 Balqayn was originally Banū al-Qayn. Ya'qūbī, Aḥmad ibn Isḥāq, *Tārīkh al-Ya'qūbī,* 2:142.
342 Walid and 'Uthmān had the same mother, namely, Arwā bint Karīz ibn Rabī'a.

you have become a smarter and better person after us, or whether I have become an idiot." [This was said because the Qur'an characterized Walid as a sinner, stating the following about him:]

يَا أَيُّهَا الَّذِينَ آمَنُوا إِن جَاءَكُمْ فَاسِقٌ بِنَبَإٍ فَتَبَيَّنُوا أَن تُصِيبُوا قَوْمًا
بِجَهَالَةٍ فَتُصْبِحُوا عَلَىٰ مَا فَعَلْتُمْ نَادِمِينَ ۝٦

[49:6] O you who have attained to faith! If any iniquitous person comes to you with a [slanderous] tale, use your discernment, lest you hurt people unwittingly and afterwards be filled with remorse for what you have done.

Walid responded: "Do not be upset. Such is [the nature of] governance. Some eat at its table for lunch, while others eat its dinner."[343] Sa'd said: "By God, I see that you treat this governorship over the Muslim community as if it were a kingdom!" He said this and returned from Kufa to Medina.[344]

The Story of Ibn Mas'ud

Ibn Mas'ud[345] was the first of the companions of the Prophet ﷺ to recite the Qur'an aloud in the House of God ﷻ before the Quraysh idolaters. The Quraysh asked him, "What are you reciting?" He told them, "The revelation that has been revealed to Muhammad ﷺ." After this, the Meccan idolaters ganged up on him and gave him a beating. Ibn Mas'ud then went to the presence of the Prophet ﷺ, who instructed him to recite the revelation again, which Ibn Mas'ud did.

Ibn Mas'ud was one of the Muslims who emigrated to Abyssinia with Ja'far ibn Abi Talib. He also participated in the Battle of Badr. Ibn Mas'ud was sent to Kufa by the second caliph for the purposes of "[Quranic] recitation" (*iqrā'*), which at that time equated to the teach and explication of the meaning of the Qur'an and teaching the ordinances of Islam's sacred law. Ibn Mas'ud was also sent to Kufa to

---

[343] انّما هو الملك يتغدّاه قوم و يتعشّاه آخرون

[344] Balādhūrī, Ahmad ibn Yahyā ibn Jābir, *Ansāb al-Ashrāf*, 5:29 & 5:31; Ibn Abd'al-Birr, Yusuf ibn Abdallah, *al-Istī'āb fī Ma'rifat al-Ashāb*, 2:604.

[345] Abū Abd ar-Rahmān ibn Mas'ūd ibn Ghāfil ibn Habīb al-Hadhalī. His mother was Umm 'Abd Wadd al-Hadhalī, and his father was Halīf (an ally) of the Banī Zuhra.

act as its treasurer. He was the trustee of the treasury, and its key was entrusted to him. When Umar sent him to Kufa, he wrote to the Kufans: "I considered your [rights] to be prior to mine, which is why I sent Ibn Mas'ud to you."[346]

When Walid became the governor of Kufa, he borrowed one hundred thousand dirhams from the treasury. Other than Ali ﷺ, the caliphs used to do this, and the trustee of the treasury received receipts from them in return for the loan. When the time came for Walid to repay the loan, Ibn Mas'ud demanded that Walid do so. Walid reported the matter to ''Uthmān, who wrote to Ibn Mas'ud, saying, "You are our treasurer. Leave Walid be. So what if he took some money from the treasury?" In reply to the caliph, Ibn Mas'ud said, "I thought I was the treasurer of the Muslims and that the treasury belonged to the Muslims; if the treasury is yours, I will not be your treasurer." He said this and threw the keys away].[347]

Ibn Mas'ud then stayed in Kufa, and began to expose 'Uthmān. Walid wrote to ''Uthmān stating that Ibn Mas'ud was pointing the finger of blame at them. [Upon learning of this,] 'Uthmān ordered Ibn Mas'ud to be sent to Medina. When Walid ordered Ibn Mas'ud to leave Kufa, the people of Kufa gathered around him and said, "Stay in Kufa, for we will defend you." Ibn Mas'ud said: "There will be seditions that will follow after this, and I do not want to be the first to open the door to sedition." The people of Kufa followed him; and he counselled them to piety and righteousness, and to read the Qur'an, and the people prayed for him and told him, "You have taught the ignorant among us, made the learned among us firmer in knowledge, and you have taught us lessons from the Qur'an."

When Ibn Mas'ud arrived in Medina, he entered the mosque of the Prophet ﷺ while 'Uthmān was in the midst of delivering a sermon at the pulpit. Some of the Companions of the Prophet ﷺwere also present in the Mosque. When 'Uthmān saw Ibn Mas'ud, he said: "Now a lowly and worthless insect has come upon you people; his [character] is such that if you extend a hand to him to offer him some food, he will vomit whatever he has eaten and disgorge it from his stomach." In response to

[346] Ibn Athīr, 'Alī ibn Muḥammad, *Usd al-Ghābah fī Ma'rifat al-Ṣaḥābah*, 3:258.
[347] Balādhūrī, Ahmad ibn Yahyā ibn Jābir, *Ansāb al-Ashrāf*, 5:36.

'Uthmān's caustic remark, Ibn Mas'ud, said: "No, 'Uthmān! I am not such a person [as you describe]. Rather, I am one of the Companions of the Messenger of God, who had the honor of participating in the Battle of Badr and the Pledge of al-Riḍwān."[348, 349]

'Āisha chimed in at this point, "O 'Uthmān, do you make such accusations against Ibn Mas'ud, the boon companion and intimate friend of the Messenger of God?!"

In response to Umm Al-Mu'minin[350] 'Āisha, 'Uthmān shouted: "Be silent!" And then ordered Ibn Mas'ud to be thrown out of the mosque. In carrying out the order of the Caliph, Ibn Mas'ud's expulsion from the Prophet's mosque was done in a shocking and insulting manner. And Yahmūm, 'Uthmān's slave, threw himself between Ibn Mas'ud's legs and lifted him up and threw him down so hard that he broke his ribs. Ali, who had witnessed the incident, turned to "Uthmān and said, "O 'Uthmān, is this how you treat a companion of the Prophet ﷺ, solely on account of what Walid has said about him?? "He then took Ibn Mas'ud to his house and treated him until he recovered from his injury and returned to his own house.

Ibn Mas'ud settled in Medina after this incident, and 'Uthmān did not allow him to leave Medina. When he recovered from his injury and asked permission to participate in the jihad against the Byzantines, 'Uthmān turned him down again. 'Uthmān also cut off his stipend from the public treasury. Thus, Ibn Mas'ud was not able to leave Medina and

---

348 [Pledge of al-Riḍwān (literally, pledge of satisfaction) or the Pledge of the Tree was a renewed pledge of some companions of the Prophet which occurred in the year 6/628 near Mecca before the Hudaybīya Peace Treaty. The Quran refers to this event in verse 48:18. According to Sunni Muslims, the divine satisfaction with those who made this pledge is unconditional, unqualified, and eternal, and thus, all of the companions who were present in this pledge are especially venerated. However, the Shi'a hold that the satisfaction expressed in this Quranic verse is due to those people's sacrifices and their pledge on that day, but that in order for the satisfaction to be sustained, it was necessary for them to fully obey the Prophet.

349 There is a hint of sarcasm in his remark, because 'Uthmān had not participated in the Battle of Badr or in the Pledge of al-Riḍwān.

350 [The Mother of the Faithful. This is an honorific title that Allāma Askari uses for 'Āisha, based on a Quranic verse in which she is referred to as such. The Shi'a understanding of the verse is that the widows of the Prophet are referred to as such in the Quran to let the community know that marrying them after the passing of the Prophet is unlawful, just as marrying their mothers is unlawful to them. Tr.]

was kept under surveillance for the rest of his life; a period which lasted for three years. He died two years before ʿUthmān was killed.

When Ibn Mas'ud fell ill, 'ʿUthmān came to visit him and asked him what he was ailing from.

Ibn Masʿud said, "All of my sins."

ʿUthmān said, "What do you want?"

"The mercy and forgiveness of my Lord."

"Should I send for a doctor?"

"The doctor himself is the cause of my illness."

"Should I order them to pay your salary and stipend?"[351] (It had been two years since these had been cut off.)[352]

"When I was in need of it, you refused to pay it. Now that I am no longer in need of such things, you want to pay it??"

"It will remain for your children."

"God will provide for them."

"Ask God to forgive me (for what I have done to you)."

"I petition God to exact my rights from you!"

Ibn Mas'ud willed that Ammar Yasir should pray over his body, and that ʿUthmān not be allowed to attend his funeral. His will was acted upon, and his body was buried in the Baqiʿ cemetery without ʿUthmān's knowledge. When ʿUthmān became aware of Ibn Mas'ud's death and the fact that he had been buried without his knowledge, he became angry and said: "Why did you do this without informing me?" Ammar replied: "He himself had willed that you should not pray over his body." Abdullah ibn Zubayr composed this verse for the occasion:[353]

---

[351] During the time of the Prophet and of Abu Bakr, any wealth that was obtained as war booty or as *zakāt* and *jizya* tax was not kept but was distributed the same day. But Umar determined a yearly allotment. For the veterans of the Battle of Badr, the amount was five thousand dirhams; for the veterans of the Battle of Uhud and up to the Peace of Hydaybīya, it was set at four thousand dirhams, and from that point until the passing of the Prophet ﷺ, it was set at three thousand dirhams. For those who had participated [only] in battles that took place after the passing of the Prophet ﷺ, the amount varied from two thousand dirhams to two hundred. Balādhūrī, Ahmad ibn Yahyā ibn Jābir, *Futūh al-Baldān*, pp. 549, and 550-565; Ibn Abī'l-Hadīd, Abdul-Hamīd, *Sharh Nahj al-Balāgha*, 3:154; see also Tabarī, Muhammad ibn Jarīr, *Tārīkh ar-Rusul wa'l-Mulūk*, 5:33 & 2:22-23; and Ya'qūbī, Aḥmad ibn Isḥāq, *Tārīkh al-Yaʿqūbī*, 2:153.

[352] Ibn Kathīr, Abu'al-Fiḍā Ismāʿīl ibn Umar, *Tārīkh*, 7:163; Yaʿqūbī, Aḥmad ibn Isḥāq, *Tārīkh al-Yaʿqūbī*, 2:170.

[353] What we stated here concerning the story of Ibn Masʿūd was based on the following sources:

لا عرفنّك بعد الموت تندبنى   و فى حياتى ما زوّدتنى زادى

You will praise me and weep for me after I have died
While you refused to provide me with my sustenance while I was alive

This was only a portion of Ibn Mas'ud's sorrowful tale during the governorship of Walid ibn 'Aqaba. But this was not the only fruit to have been produced by Walid's government. Rather, he committed many bad deeds and seditious acts during his reign in Kufa, including the way he dealt with the Christian poet Abu Zubayd, and a Jewish magician by the name of Jundab al-Khair.

Walīd and the Christian poet Abu Zubayd

Walīd used to proclaim his imbibing of wine [publicly]. The Christian poet Abu Zubayd was his drinking buddy, with whom he used to sit and drink wine. Walid gave Abu-Zubayd Aqīl ibn Abi-Tālib's house, which was close to the mosque of Kufa, as a gift. Abu Zubayd would come out of his house and go to the governor's house and spend the night with him drinking wine. The door to Aqeel ibn Abi Talib's house opened into the mosque at the governor's house. The Christian man would pass through the mosque in his drunken state, swaying from side to side. Walid also gifted arable lands from the palaces near Kufa to the palaces in the Levant to this Christian drunkard. Abu Zubayd composed a poem in praise of Walid in response to this generosity.[354]

Writing in his *Ansāb al-Ashrāf* (Lineages of the Nobles), Balādhūrī states:

Walid had determined a stipend to be paid to Abu Zubayd from the Muslim treasury for the monthly purchase of wine and a few pigs.

Balādhūrī, Ahmad ibn Yahyā ibn Jābir, *Ansāb al-Ashrāf*, 5:36.
Dayār-Bakrī, Ḥusayn Ibn Md., *Tārīkh al-Khamīs fī Ahwāl Anfus an-Nafīs*, 2:268
Ibn Abd'al-Birr, Yusuf ibn Abdallah, *al-Istī'āb fi Ma'rifat al-Ashāb*, 1:361
Ibn Abī'l-Hadīd, Abdul-Hamīd, *Sharh Nahj al-Balāgha*, 1:236-237
Ibn Athīr, 'Alī ibn Muḥammad, *Usd al-Ghābah fī Ma'rifat al-Ṣaḥābah*, 3:384
Ibn Sa'd, Abu Abdallah Muhammad, *al-Tabaqāt al-Kubrā*, 3:150-161
Ya'qūbī, Aḥmad ibn Isḥāq, *Tārīkh al-Ya'qūbī*, 2:170

[354] Isfahānī, Abī'l-Faraj, *al-Aghānī*, 4:181.

Walid was the governor of the Muslims at that time. Umar and Abu Bakr had not done such things; thus, the discontent of the Muslims increased. Thus, Walid had no choice but to calculate the cost of the amount of wine and the pigs that he had set aside for Abu Zubayd on a monthly basis, which he determined to be a few dinars, and added this amount to Abu Zubayd's monthly stipend so that he could purchase the wine and the pigs himself, so that the Muslims would not be seen as buying him wine and pigs every month.[355]

The story of Jundab al-Khair

Walid was informed that a Jewish man named Zurarah, who was known as Natrawī and who was skilled in all kinds of magic, lived in a village near Jisr, near Babylon. Walid ordered him to be brought to Kufa so that he could see him perform his magic personally. When the magician was brought to Walid, he ordered him to perform his magic in the mosque of Kufa.

One of his magic tricks was that, in the dark of night, he would show a large elephant sitting on a horse. Another one of his magic tricks was that he himself took the form of a camel that walked on a rope. Yet another of his magic tricks was that he showed a rabbit through whose mouth he entered and came out of his anus. At the end of the show, Jundab al-Khair picked out one of the spectators and unceremoniously beheaded him with a sword, separating his head from his body; after which he stood up without a scratch on his body before the astonished spectators.

There was a man in Kufa by the name of Jundab ibn Ka'b al-Azdi who was renowned for worshipping late at night and in the early hours of the morning. When Jundab saw this, he went to the market of the swordsmiths and borrowed a sword and killed the magician with it, telling him, "Now bring yourself back to life if you are a real magician!"

Walid was very upset by this, and ordered that Jundab be executed in revenge for the blood of the Jew Zurārah. But Jundab's relatives, who were from the Azd tribe, mobilized in support of Jundab and prevented him from being executed, so Walid had no choice but to resort to a ruse and imprison Jundab so that he could kill him quietly later. When his jailer saw Jundab praying and deep in his ritual devotions from night until morning, he did not think it right to let his

[355] Balādhūrī, Ahmad ibn Yahyā ibn Jābir, *Ansāb al-Ashrāf*, 5:29 & 5:31.

hands be stained with the blood of such an ascetic man of faith and devotion. He therefore told Jundab that he would open the prison door for him to escape. Jundab replied, "If I do that, Walid will not let you live and will kill you." The jailer said, "My blood has little value in relation to obtaining God's satisfaction and saving one of His saints."

When the news of Jundab's escape was reported to Walid, he ordered the prison guard to be beheaded. Jundab escaped from Kufa covertly and managed to get to Medina, where he remained until Ali ibn Abi Talib ؑ spoke to ʿUthmān on his behalf and interceded for him. ʿUthmān accepted Ali's ؑ intercession and wrote a letter to Walid instructing him to leave Jundab be. Thus, Jundab was able to return to Kufa.[356]

The Story of Abdullah bin Saʿd bin Abi Sarh

Abdullah was the milk-brother of ʿUthmān, who had entered into Islam before the conquest of Mecca, and had emigrated to Medina. He was one of the scribes of the Prophet of God, but after a while he apostatized and returned to Mecca and said to the leaders of the Quraysh, "Muhammad obeyed my will and did whatever I desired. For example, when he said, "Write *azīzun hakīm*," I would ask, "Should I write *alīmun hakīm* [instead]?" he would say, "There's no problem with that; both are good." Thus, God ﷻ revealed the following verse about him:

$$\text{وَمَنْ أَظْلَمُ مِمَّنِ افْتَرَىٰ عَلَى اللَّهِ كَذِبًا أَوْ قَالَ أُوحِيَ إِلَيَّ وَلَمْ يُوحَ إِلَيْهِ شَيْءٌ وَمَن قَالَ سَأُنزِلُ مِثْلَ مَا أَنزَلَ اللَّهُ ۗ وَلَوْ تَرَىٰ إِذِ الظَّالِمُونَ فِي غَمَرَاتِ الْمَوْتِ وَالْمَلَائِكَةُ بَاسِطُو أَيْدِيهِمْ أَخْرِجُوا أَنفُسَكُمُ ۖ الْيَوْمَ تُجْزَوْنَ عَذَابَ الْهُونِ بِمَا كُنتُمْ تَقُولُونَ عَلَى اللَّهِ غَيْرَ الْحَقِّ وَكُنتُمْ عَنْ آيَاتِهِ تَسْتَكْبِرُونَ ۝}$$

[6:93] And who could be more wicked than he who invents a lie about God, or says, "This has been revealed unto me," the while nothing has been revealed to him? - or he who says, "I, too, can bestow from on high the like of what God has bestowed"? If thou couldst but see [how it will

---

[356] Isfahānī, Abī'l-Faraj, *al-Aghānī*, 4:183; Balādhurī, Ahmad ibn Yahyā ibn Jābir, *Ansāb al-Ashrāf*, 5:29 & 5:31.

be] when these evildoers find themselves in the agonies of death, and the angels stretch forth their hands [and call]: "Give up your souls! Today you shall be requited with the suffering of humiliation for having attributed to God something that is not true, and for having persistently scorned His messages in your arrogance!"

When Mecca was conquered by the Muslims, the Messenger of God ﷺ issued a general amnesty for the people of Mecca, but ordered that Abdullah be put to death, even though he was clinging to the covering of the Kaaba. Abdullah took refuge with 'Uthmān in fear of his life. 'Uthmān gave him quarter and kept him hidden until he brought him to the presence of the Prophet of God and asked him to spare Abdullah's life. The Messenger of God remained silent for a long time and did not raise his head until he eventually agreed to 'Uthmān's request. When 'Uthmān had left, the Messenger of God turned to those present and said, "I remained silent in order for one of you to stand up and separate his head from the body." In response, they said, "You ought to have given us an indication or a hint in this regard with a movement of your eyes." The Messenger of God replied, "It is not appropriate for a prophet to give an indication with his eyes."

When 'Uthmān succeeded to the caliphate, he appointed Abdullah to the governorship of 'Egypt' (*misr*) [357] in 25 AH on account of his ties of brotherhood with him, dismissing Amr ibn al-Ās from his post there,[358] despite everyone knowing the kind of character Abdullah was. Abdullah conquered parts of Africa, and 'Uthmān gave him the fifth share (*khums*) of the spoils of that war.[359]

---

[357] At that time, 'Egypt' or *Misr* referred to the entirety of the African continent.

[358] While it is true that the 'Amr ibn Ās whom we know was a bad person, but he was the conqueror of Egypt, and enjoyed a measure of respect among the populace; nor had he as yet committed any of the deeds that he did during the reign of Mu'āwiya at that time.

[359] Balādhūrī, Ahmad ibn Yahyā ibn Jābir, *Ansāb al-Ashrāf*, 5:49; Hākim al-Haskānī an-Neyshāpūrī, *al-Mustadrak 'Alā's-Sahīhayn*, 3:100; Ibn Abd'al-Birr, Yusuf ibn Abdallah, *al-Istī'āb fī Ma'rifat al-Ashāb*, 2:367; Ibn Athīr, 'Alī ibn Muḥammad, *Usd al-Ghābah fī Ma'rifat al-Ṣaḥābah*, 3:173-174; Ibn Hajar, Ahmad ibn Ali al-Asqalāni, *al-Iṣābah fī Tamyīz al-Ṣaḥābah*, 2:309-310; as well as in the commentary sources, such as Ibn Abī'l-Hadīd, Abdul-Hamīd, *Sharh Nahj al-Balāgha*, 1:68; Qurṭubī, Muḥammad ibn Aḥmad, *al-Jāmi' li-Aḥkām al-Qur'ān*, under verse 93 of Surah al-An'ām.

The story of Hakam bin Abi al-Ās, the Caliph's Uncle

'Uthmān had established a seat of the caliphate and allowed only four people to sit on it by his side: Abbas, the uncle of the Prophet ﷺ, Abu Sufyan, Hakam ibn Abi al-Ās, his uncle, and Walīd ibn Aqaba. Hakam ibn Abi al-Ās was a renowned hypocrite during the time of the Prophet ﷺ. In Medina, he used to walk behind the Prophet ﷺ and mocked him. He would shake his hands, shake his head, stick out his tongue, and cross his eyes. Once, the Prophet ﷺ turned back to him and said, "Stay as you are." After this, Hakam walked for the rest of his life in the same manner, shaking his arms and legs.

One day, the Prophet ﷺ was sitting with the Commander of the Faithful [Ali ibn Abī-Tālib ﵇] in one of his rooms. Hakam was eavesdropping on the conversation. The Prophet ﷺsaid to the Commander of the Faithful ﵇, "Go and bring him in." His Eminence stepped out and took Hakan by the ear as if he was a goat and took him inside the room. The Prophet ﷺ cursed him,[360] and exiled him to Taif.

Verse 60 of Surah al-Isrā' [the Verse of the Accursed Tree (*al-shajara al-mal'ūna*)] was revealed concerning the descendants of Hakam ibn Abi al-Ās ibn Umayyah,[361] or about the Banī-Umayyah generally:[362]

وَإِذْ قُلْنَا لَكَ إِنَّ رَبَّكَ أَحَاطَ بِالنَّاسِ ۚ وَمَا جَعَلْنَا الرُّؤْيَا الَّتِي أَرَيْنَاكَ إِلَّا فِتْنَةً لِّلنَّاسِ وَالشَّجَرَةَ الْمَلْعُونَةَ فِي الْقُرْآنِ ۚ وَنُخَوِّفُهُمْ فَمَا يَزِيدُهُمْ إِلَّا طُغْيَانًا كَبِيرًا ﴿٦٠﴾

[17:60] And lo! We said unto thee, [O Prophet:] "Behold, thy Sustainer encompasses all mankind [within His knowledge and might]: and so We have ordained that the vision which We have shown thee - as also the tree [of hell,] cursed in this Qur'an - shall be but a trial for men. Now [by Our mentioning hell] We convey a warning to them: but [if they are bent on denying the truth,] this [warning] only increases their gross, overweening arrogance."

---

360 Balādhūrī, Ahmad ibn Yahyā ibn Jābir, *Ansāb al-Ashrāf*, 5:27 & 5:225.

361 Hākim al-Haskānī an-Neyshāpūrī, *al-Mustadrak 'Alā's-Sahīhayn*, 4:479-481; Suyūṭī, Jalāl al-Dīn 'Abd al-Raḥmān, *al-Durr al-Manthūr fī al-Tafsīr bi-al-Ma'thūr*, 4:191.

362 Suyūṭī, Jalāl al-Dīn 'Abd al-Raḥmān, *al-Durr al-Manthūr fī al-Tafsīr bi-al-Ma'thūr*, 4:191.

During the caliphate of Abu Bakr, 'Uthmān asked Abu Bakr to allow Hakam ibn Abi al-Ās and his descendants to return to Medina, but Abu Bakr did not accede to his request. At the time of the Prophet ﷺ, 'Uthmān had asked the Prophet ﷺ, and he too had not acceded. During the caliphate of Umar, 'Uthmān came to Umar and asked him to allow Hakam ibn Abi al-Ās and his descendants to return to Medina, but Umar too did not accede to his request. When 'Uthmān himself became caliph, he returned Hakam to Medina.[363] Hakam entered Usman's house in ragged clothing, with a single goat representing the entirety of his wealth. But when he left 'Uthmān's house, he was wearing a silk coat.[364]

'Uthmān used to have Hakam sit next to him on the seat of the caliphate. One day, Hakam came to 'Uthmān, who pushed Walid aside and seated his uncle by his side. When Hakam left the room, Walid said to 'Uthmān, "Two couplets have come to me which I would like to recite to you." When 'Uthmān gave him leave to recite the verses, Walid recited the following:

لمّا رأيت لعمّ المرء زلفى قرابة دوين اخيه حادثا لم يكن قدما
تأمّلت عمرا ان يشبّ و خالدا لكى يدعوانى يوم مزحمة عمّا

When I saw that the man's uncle was close to him and enjoyed a respect that his brother did not have,
I wished that your two sons, Khalid and Amr, would grow up and call me uncle on the Day of Resurrection.

'Uthmān took pity on Walid, and said to him to make up for his brother's broken heart, "I will make you the governor of Kufa."[365] This was how Walid, who had been condemned in the Qur'an, became the governor of the Muslims of Kufa and its territories.

The Story of Sa'īd ibn Hakam ibn Abi al-Ās and Mālik Ashtar

Having removed Walid as the Governor of Kufa, 'Uthmān replaced him with Sa'īd ibn Abi al-Ās, ordering him to treat the people well. When Sa'īd came to Kufa, he washed the pulpit of the congregational mosque

---

[363] Balādhūrī, Ahmad ibn Yahyā ibn Jābir, *Ansāb al-Ashrāf*, 5:27.
[364] Ya'qūbī, Aḥmad ibn Isḥāq, *Tārīkh al-Ya'qūbī*, 2:164.
[365] Isfahānī, Abī'l-Faraj, *al-Aghānī*, 14:177.

and the government building with water.[366] Unlike Walid, who had a drunkard Christian as his drinking buddy and boon companion, and who drank openly in public, Sa'īd ibn Abi al-Ās kept the company of the Qurrā',[367] staying up late with them [in ceremonies of ritual devotion to God]. These included Malik Ashtar, Uday ibn Hatim al-Ta'i, and about fourteen other elders and sheikhs of the tribes of Kufa. In addition to being Qurrā' from Kufa, these were also tribal chieftains and sheikhs.

One day, Sa'īd's Chief of Police said to him, "I wish these rich, arable lands of Iraq belonged to the Emir so that you had better farms and orchards than you have."

In response to him, Malik Ashtar said, "If you are going to make a wish for the Emir, wish that he is able to conquer better farms and orchards, and do not wish that he becomes the owner of our properties, and leave those to ourselves."

The Chief of Police said, "What harm did this wish of mine have for you, for you to react in such a sour manner? I swear by God ﷻ, if he (Sa'īd ibn Abi al-Ās) were to will it and demand it, he could take possession of all these farms and orchards."

Malik Ashtar replied, "I swear by God ﷻ that if he intended to take them, he would not be able to do so."

Sa'īd became very angry with these words of Malik's, and turned to those who were present and said, "The rich fields and orchards of the Sawād of Iraq belong to the Quraysh. (By this, he meant the elders of the Umayyads and the clans of Taym and Udayy and the like who were in Mecca, unlike the Ansar who were originally from Yemen, which tribes Malik Ashtar and most of the people of Kufa belonged to).

Ashtar replied, "Do you intend to make the gains of our battles and what God has given us your own property and the property of your tribe? I swear by God, if anyone has harbored any ill intent with respect to these lands and farms, he will be beaten into being scared and humiliated." Following this, he rose to attack the Chief of Police, but was prevented from doing so by those present, who surrounded him.

---

366 Tabarī, Muhammad ibn Jarīr, *Tārīkh ar-Rusul wa'l-Mulūk*, 5:188 & 1:2951 of the European edition.

367 In those days, the scholars of religion who were able to explicate the meaning of the Quran were referred to as Qurrā'.

Sa'īd ibn Abi al-Ās wrote to 'Uthmān, "While Malik Ashtar and his companions, who are called Qurrā', (whereas) they are [nothing but] ruffians, are present, I am not the ruler of Kufa."

'Uthmān said: "Send them into exile!" Sa'īd sent them to the Levant and wrote a letter to Malik Ashtar in which he said, "I see that there is something in your heart which, were you to express it, [the shedding of] your blood would become lawful; go to the Levant."

Malik Ashtar went to the Levant with the other Qurrā' of Kufa, where they were honored by Mu'awiyah. After a while, there was a heated conversation between Malik Ashtar and Mu'awiyah. Mu'awiyah said, "If all human beings were the children of Abu Sufyan, they would all be wise and prudent." Malik said, "Adam was better than Abu Sufyan, yet the children of Adam were not wise and prudent." After that conversation, Mu'awiyah imprisoned Malik Ashtar. Later, the tensions arose between Mu'awiyah and Amr ibn Zarārah, as a result of which he imprisoned all the Qurrā' who had come to the Levant from Kufa. Following this, Amr apologized to Mu'awiyah, and Mu'awiyah forgave him and released everyone from prison.

The people of the Levant considered what they had seen from Mu'awiyah's way of life to be Islam. They had not seen how the companions of the Prophet ﷺ lived their lives. Thus, the conditions in which they lived their lives had not changed [under Mu'āwiya's governorship]. Mu'āwiya's governmental apparatus was similar to that of the Byzantine emperor, who ruled the Levant before Mu'awiyah. But the companions of the Prophet ﷺ, such as Abu Dharr and Ibādah ibn Sāmit and others of the generation of the 'followers'[368] and the Qurrā' who had come to the Levant from Kufa, who sat with the people and promulgated the way of life of the Prophet ﷺ.

Mu'awiyah wrote to ''Uthmān, stating that with the presence of these companions and Qurrā' in the Levant, the people of Syria would be "corrupted". He said that they teach people things they are not familiar with and corrupt them. 'Uthmān replied that he should send them to Homs, which is what Mu'awiyah did.[369]

The son of Khalid bin Walid was the governor of Homs. He would ride on horseback and make them follow him on foot, and say, "I

---

[368] [The generation who followed that of the companions and who had not been eye witnesses to the Prophet. Tr.]

[369] Balādhūrī, Ahmad ibn Yahyā ibn Jābir, *Ansāb al-Ashrāf*, 5:39-43. What we stated here was a summary.

will show you that you will not be able to do with me what you did with Sa'īd and Mu'āwiya!" After having subjected them to much harassment, the son of Khalid would tell them, "O Children of Satan! O children of Satan!" Until they eventually bowed down and expressed their repentance, after which they were returned to Kufa.[370]

Apart from these notables, the other elders of Kufa were also dissatisfied with their governors. In fact, all the tribes of Kufa were dissatisfied with the situation of 'Uthmān's government and his governors.[371]

Abdullah bin Āmir, the Governor of Basra

Abdullah bin Āmir was the son of 'Uthmān's maternal uncle. One day Shibl bin Khālid, a maternal brother of Ziad Ibn Abiyyah and the son of Sumayah Ma'rūfa, came to a gathering of the leaders of the Umayyads who were sitting around 'Uthmān, and said, "Is there not an indigent person known to you who you wish to be rich? Is it not among you one who is not renowned for whom you wish fame, such that you have given Iraq over to the tyrant Abu Mūsā al-Ash'ari (who is not of the tribe of the Quraysh, and whose tribe is one of the tribes of Yemen)?" 'Uthmān, who had been moved by Shibl's statements, appointed his sixteen-year-old cousin, Abdullah ibn Āmir ibn Kurayz to the governorship of Basra, removing Abu Mūsā al-Ash'ari therefrom!

Abdullah was a generous person. He could not deliver a single sermon at the pulpit of the congregational Friday prayers. He said, "I am bereft of two attributes: the ability to deliver sermons, and miserliness. Go to the sheep-herders market and pick up a sheep each; I will pay for them." And he paid everyone from the funds of the treasury. He then wrote to 'Uthmān, saying that the funds of the treasury were insufficient. So 'Uthmān allowed him to go and conquer new territories and spend the spoils he obtained from the conquests.[372] When 'Uthmān was killed, Abdullah took the monies of the Basra

---

[370] Ibn Abī'l-Hadīd, Abdul-Hamīd, *Sharh Nahj al-Balāgha*, 1:160 & 2:134; Tabarī, Muhammad ibn Jarīr, *Tārīkh ar-Rusul wa'l-Mulūk*, 1:2914.
[371] Ibn Abd'al-Birr, Yusuf ibn Abdallah, *al-Istī'āb fi Ma'rifat al-Ashāb*, 5:39-43; Tabarī, Muhammad ibn Jarīr, *Tārīkh ar-Rusul wa'l-Mulūk*, 5:88-90; Ibn Abī'l-Hadīd, Abdul-Hamīd, *Sharh Nahj al-Balāgha*, 1:158-160; Ibn Kathīr, Abu'al-Fiḍā Ismā'īl ibn Umar, *Tārīkh*, 3:57-60.
[372] Ibn Asākir, 'Alī, *at-Tārīkh al-Madīna[t] ad-Damishq*, 9:2nd C:231

treasury to Mecca and Medina and divided them all among the people there.[373]

Mu'āwiya during 'Uthmān's Reign

During 'Uthmān's caliphate, Ubāda ibn Sāmit, a companion of the Prophet ﷺ, was living in the Levant. One day he saw a caravan of camels loaded with skins of some liquid headed to Mu'awiyah's palace. He asked, "What are they carrying, olive oil?" (Because there are many olive trees in the Levant.) He was told, "No, they are skins of wine that they take for Mu'awiyah."

Ubāda ibn Sāmit obtained a knife from the bazaar and ripped open all of the skins of wine, spilling all the wine onto the ground. Abu Huraira, who was in the Levant at the time, said to Ubāda ibn Sāmit, "What do you care what Ubāda ibn Sāmit does? Its blame is on his own shoulders." Ubāda ibn Sāmit said, "You were not there at the time when we pledged allegiance to the Prophet ﷺ,[374] where we committed to [carrying out the Quranic ordinances having to do with the moral stewardship of the community (*ahkām-e nezāratī*) such as] *al-amr bi'l-ma'rūf wa an-nahy an al-munkar* [which is a pillar of the religion and which refers to the imperative to enjoin the doing of that which is right and to forbid the doing of that which is wrong], and not to be afraid of the reproach of others." Abu Hurayra remained silent.

Mu'awiyah wrote to 'Uthmān: "Either take Ubāda ibn Sāmit from the Levant, or I will relegate [the responsibility for the governance of] the Levant to him and come [to Medina myself]. By the order of 'Uthmān, Ubāda ibn Sāmit was returned to Medina, where he delivered a speech in which he said, "I heard the Prophet ﷺ say, 'After me, your governance and guardianship will fall to the hands of people who invert that which is right (*ma'rūf*) and that which is wrong (*munkar*). These people are not to be obeyed; anyone who sins and goes against God's law is not to be obeyed.' 'Uthmān did not say anything."[375]

---

373 Balādhūrī, Ahmad ibn Yahyā ibn Jābir, *Ansāb al-Ashrāf*, 5:30; Ibn Kathīr, Abu'al-Fiḍā Ismā'īl ibn Umar, *al-Bidāyah wa-al-Nihāyah*, 7:153-154; Ibn Athīr Jazarī, 'Alī, *al-Kāmil fī al-Tārīkh*, 3:73.

374 What Ubāda meant was the pledge of allegiance which the Ansār gave to the Prophet in Minā, which paved the way for the Prophet's migration to Yathrib.

375 Ahmad b. Hanbal, *Musnad*, 5:325; Ibn 'Asākir, 'Alī, *Tahdhīb*, 7:214; Dhahabī, Shams ad-Dīn Muḥammad ibn Aḥmad, *Siyār A'lām an-Nubalā'*, 2:10.

There was another companion by the name of Abd al-Rahmān ibn Sahl ibn Zayd al-Ansari, who took part in a jihad during 'Uthmān's caliphate. At that time, they departed from [the garrisons in] the Levant in pursuit of their conquests. Abd al-Rahmān ibn Sahl was also present in the Levant and saw the caravan of camels carrying skins of wine to Mu'awiyah's palace. Abd al-Rahmān pierced the wine skins one by one with a spear, causing the wine to be spilled onto the ground. Mu'awiyah's guards arrested him, but Mu'awiyah said, "Release him, as he is not in his right mind." When Mu'awiyah's guards told him what Mu'awiyah had said, Abd al-Rahmān replied, "I have heard the Prophet ﷺ say something about Mu'awiyah that, by God, if I were to see him, I would not sit still until I ripped open and spilled his guts."[376]

Verily, the people at the end of 'Uthmān's Caliphate had become this fearless and audacious toward his governors.

'Uthmān's treatment of Ammār

At the end of 'Uthmān's Caliphate, some of the companions came together; Miqdad, Ammār Yāsir, Talha, and Zubair and some of the other companions of the Prophet ﷺ gathered together and recorded the wrongful deeds that 'Uthmān had committed, and wrote him and told him that if he did not discontinue these deeds, they would rise up in insurrection against him.

No one dared to take the letter to 'Uthmān. Ammār took the letter. When 'Uthmān read the letter, he asked, "Is it you who has risen up in sedition against me among all of these [signatures]?" Ammār said, "I am giving you [good] counsel." 'Uthmān ordered his slaves to lay Ammār on the ground, then kicked Ammār personally in his private parts. Ammār was old and weak, and lost consciousness as a result of the intensity of the pain.[377]

'Uthman's performance with respect to the Public Treasury

'Uthmān used to say:

---

[376] Ibn Abd'al-Birr, Yusuf ibn Abdallah, *al-Istī'āb fi Ma'rifat al-Ashāb*, p. 400; Ibn Hajar, Ahmad ibn Ali al-Asqalāni, *al-Iṣābah fi Tamyīz al-Ṣaḥābah*, 2:394; Ibn Hajar, Ahmad ibn Ali al-Asqalāni, *Taqrīb al-Tahdhīb*, 6:192.

[377] Balādhūrī, Ahmad ibn Yahyā ibn Jābir, *Ansāb al-Ashrāf*, 5:49 & 5:54; Ibn 'Abd Rabbih, *al-'Iqd al-Farīd*, 2:272; Ibn Qutayba, Abd-Allāh ibn Muslim, *al-Imāma wa'l-Siyāsa*, and Ya'qūbī, Aḥmad ibn Isḥāq, *Tārīkh al-Ya'qūbī*, 2:150.

لو انّ بيدى مفاتيح الجنّة لا عطيتها بنى اميّة حتّى يدخلوا من اخرهم

If the keys of Paradise were in my possession, I would give them to the members of the Umayyad clan, so that every single one of them would be able to enter Paradise.[378]

Instead of the keys of Paradise, the keys of the treasury were in 'Uthmān's hands of, and he used to open its doors to the Umayyads freely, and made gifts of its wealth to them. Some of the gifts that 'Uthmān, the caliph of the Muslims, gave to his relatives are as follows:

1. Abu Sufyan Ibn Harb: 200,000 dirhams.[379]
2. Marwan Ibn Al-Hakam: 500,000 dinars.[380]
3. Abdullah bin Khalid: 300,000 dirhams (and 1,000 dirhams for each of his relatives).[381]
4. Sa'īd ibn al-Ās: 100,000 dirhams.[382]
5. Harith ibn Hakam ibn Abi al-Ās: 300,000 dirhams (for the men).[383] Also, the alms of the Bazaar of Madina, which was a property owned by the Prophet ﷺ which he had entrusted to the Muslims. 'Uthmān gave this Bazaar to his cousin, who charged rent from anyone who used the land that was part of the bazaar.[384]
6. Hakam Ibn Abi al-Ās: 300,000 dirhams.[385]
7. Walid ibn Aqaba: 100,000 dirhams[386]
8. Abdullah ibn Khalid ibn Usayd: 300,000 dirhams at one time, and 600,000 dirhams on two other occasions.[387]

---

378 Ahmad b. Hanbal, *Musnad*
379 Ibn Abī'l-Hadīd, Abdul-Hamīd, *Sharh Nahj al-Balāgha*,
380 Balādhūrī, Ahmad ibn Yahyā ibn Jābir, *Ansāb al-Ashrāf*, 5:25 & 5:88; Ibn ʿAbd Rabbih, *al-ʿIqd al-Farīd*, 4:283; Ibn Abī'l-Hadīd, Abdul-Hamīd, *Sharh Nahj al-Balāgha*, 1:66; Ibn Asākir, 'Alī, *at-Tārīkh al-Madīna[t] ad-Damishq*, Manuscript in the Ẓāhirīya Library, 11:1:140; Ibn Qutayba, Abd-Allāh ibn Muslim, *al-Ma'ārif*, p. 84.
381 Balādhūrī, Ahmad ibn Yahyā ibn Jābir, *Ansāb al-Ashrāf*, 5:28.
382 Balādhūrī, Ahmad ibn Yahyā ibn Jābir, *Ansāb al-Ashrāf*, 5:128.
383 Balādhūrī, Ahmad ibn Yahyā ibn Jābir, *Ansāb al-Ashrāf*, 5:28 & 5:52.
384 Halabī, Alī ibn Ibrāhīm, *Insān al-'Uyūn fī Sīra al-Amīn al-Ma'mūn* (*as-Sīra[t] al-Halabīa*), 2:87; Ibn ʿAbd Rabbih, *al-ʿIqd al-Farīd*, 2:261.
385 Balādhūrī, Ahmad ibn Yahyā ibn Jābir, *Ansāb al-Ashrāf*, 5:28.
386 Balādhūrī, Ahmad ibn Yahyā ibn Jābir, *Ansāb al-Ashrāf*, 5:30-31.

9. Zaid Ibn Thabit al-Ansari: 100,000 dirhams.[388]
10. Zubair: 59,800,000 dirhams.[389]
11. Talha: 200,000 dinars.[390]
12. Saad ibn al-Waqqās: 250,000 dirhams.[391]
13. 'Uthmān (the Caliph): 3,500,000 dirhams.[392]
14. Abdullah Ibn Sa'd ibn Abi Sarh: 100,000 dinars, which was the fifth share (*khums*) of the spoils of the African conquests.[393]
15. Zaid ibn Thabit: 100,000 dinars.[394]
16. Abdul Rahman ibn Awf: 2,560,000 dinars.[395]

During Umar's caliphate, in one of the conquests of Iran, a basket filled with royal jewels was brought and placed in the treasury by order of Umar. 'Uthmān took the basket of jewels and divided it up among his wife and daughters.[396]

---

[387] Ibn 'Abd Rabbih, *al-'Iqd al-Farīd*, 4:283; Ibn Abī'l-Hadīd, Abdul-Hamīd, *Sharh Nahj al-Balāgha*, 1:66; Ya'qūbī, Aḥmad ibn Isḥāq, *Tārīkh al-Ya'qūbī*, 2:168.

[388] Balādhūrī, Ahmad ibn Yahyā ibn Jābir, *Ansāb al-Ashrāf*, 5:54-55.

[389] Bukhārī, Muḥammad ibn Ismā'īl, *Ṣaḥīḥ al-Bukhārī*, 5:21.

[390] Balādhūrī, Ahmad ibn Yahyā ibn Jābir, *Ansāb al-Ashrāf*, 5:7. Other gifts besides these had been given to Talha, such that his worth at the time of his death has been estimated to have been in the millions of dirhams. Cf. Ibn 'Abd Rabbih, *al-'Iqd al-Farīd*, 2:279; Ibn Sa'd, Abu Abdallah Muhammad, *al-Tabaqāt al-Kubrā*, 3:158 of the Leiden edition; Mas'ūdī, Alī ibn al-Ḥusayn, *Murawwij adh*-Dhahab, 1:434; Tabarī, Muhibbiddīn, *ar-Riyāḍ an-Naḍra*, 2:258; Dhahabī, Shams ad-Dīn Muḥammad ibn Aḥmad, *Duwal al-Islām*, 1:18; Khazrajī, *al-Khulāsa*, p. 152.

[391] Ibn Sa'd, Abu Abdallah Muhammad, *al-Tabaqāt al-Kubrā*, 3:105; Mas'ūdī, Alī ibn al-Ḥusayn, *Murawwij adh-Dhahab*, 1:434.

[392] Ibn Sa'd, Abu Abdallah Muhammad, *al-Tabaqāt al-Kubrā*, 3:53; Mas'ūdī, Alī ibn al-Ḥusayn, *Murawwij adh-Dhahab*, 2:332. It is of some interest to note that according to Ibn Sa'd (*al-Tabaqāt al-Kubrā*, 3:53 of the Leiden edition), on the day of Uthma's death, he had 30.5 million dirhams in safe keeping with his treasurer. Mas'ūdī also writes in his *Murawwij adh-Dhahab* (1:433) that 'Uthmān had a huge amount of wealth at the time of his death, which included lands in the Wādī al-Qurrā and Hunayn, whose value was the equivalent of 200,000 dinars. See also, Balādhūrī, Ahmad ibn Yahyā ibn Jābir, *Ansāb al-Ashrāf*, 5:49.

[393] Ibn Abd'al-Birr, Yusuf ibn Abdallah, *al-Istī'āb fī Ma'rifat al-Ashāb*, 2:367-370; Ibn Athīr Jazarī, 'Alī, *al-Kāmil fī al-Tārīkh*, 3:38; Ibn Hajar, Ahmad ibn Ali al-Asqalāni, *al-Iṣābah fī Tamyīz al-Ṣaḥābah*, 2:309-310.

[394] Mas'ūdī, Alī ibn al-Ḥusayn, *Murawwij adh*-Dhahab, 1:434.

[395] Ibn Sa'd, Abu Abdallah Muhammad, *al-Tabaqāt al-Kubrā*, 3:158 of the Leiden edition; Ya'qūbī, Aḥmad ibn Isḥāq, *Tārīkh al-Ya'qūbī*, 2:146.

[396] Balādhūrī, Ahmad ibn Yahyā ibn Jābir, *Ansāb al-Ashrāf*, 5:85.

When Abu Musa al-Ash'ari was the governor of Basra, whatever gold and silver he brought with him as spoils of the battles he had won were taken by 'Uthmān and distributed among his wife and children.[397]

This was a brief synopsis of the ravaging of the Muslim treasury by 'Uthmān.[398]

---

[397] Halabī, Alī ibn Ibrāhīm, *Insān al-'Uyūn fī Sīra al-Amīn al-Ma'mūn* (*as-Sīra*[t] *al-Halabīa*), 2:78; Haythamī, Ahmad Ibn-Hajar, al-*Sawā'iq al-Muhriqa*, , p. 68.

[398] This was at a time when the veterans of the Battle of Badr were only paid 5,000 dirhams per annum (Balādhūrī, Ahmad ibn Yahyā ibn Jābir, *Futūh al-Baldān*, pp. 550-565; Ibn Abī'l-Hadīd, Abdul-Hamīd, *Sharh Nahj al-Balāgha*, 3:154). The difference is immense.

12 The People's Uprising against 'Uthmān and Ali's Role in it

The Revolt of the Egyptians

The Muslims were in dire straits. A group of people came from Egypt to see 'Uthmān to complain about their governor, Abdullah ibn Sa'd ibn Abi Sarh. They entered the Mosque of the Prophet ﷺ when they arrived in Medina.

'Uthmān would not allow anyone to complain about his governors. A group of the Emigrants and Ansar who were in the mosque of the Prophet ﷺ asked them why they had come to Medina from Egypt? They responded that they had come to complain about the oppression of their governor. Ali said to them, "Do not be hasty in your business, and do not rush to judgment. Present your complaint to the caliph and inform him of what is taking place, as it is possible that the governor of Egypt is acting on his own and without the order of the caliph. Go to the caliph and tell him of your problems. If 'Uthmān dismisses the governor, you will have reached your goal. And if he does not do so, then you can always come back."

The Egyptians asked him to go with them, but Ali replied, "There is no need for me to come." The Egyptians said: "While this is true, we would still like you to be present and to witness the incident." Ali replied, "He who is stronger than I am, and who is superior to all creatures, and more compassionate towards His servants, shall be your witness and observer."

The Egyptian elders went to 'Uthmān's house and asked for permission to enter. 'Uthmān said, "Why did you come here from Egypt without my permission?" They said, "We have come to complain about you and your deeds, as well as about the deeds of your Governor." The conversation between them became heated and found its way to the mosque. Ayesha and Talha involved themselves and took on the leadership of 'Uthmān's opponents from this point forward.[399]

After this, His Eminence Ali entered the story, and after having a conversation with 'Uthmān,[400] wrote a letter as follows:

In the name of God, the Most Gracious, the Most Merciful

This is a covenant that the servant of God, 'Uthmān, the Commander of the Faithful, writes for those believers and Muslims who are displeased with him. 'Uthmān vows henceforth to act in accordance with God's sacred writ (*kitāballāh*) and the paradigmatic model (*sunnah*) of the Prophet; to restore the stipends of those who have been cut off; to guarantee the safety of those who are afraid of his wrath, and to ensure their freedom; to return those who have been exiled to their families; to distribute the spoils of war among the troops [equally and equitably] without any considerations of bias and without any exception [to this rule]. On behalf of 'Uthmān, Ali ibn Abi Talib guarantees the implementation of all these obligations to the believers and the Muslims. The following witnesses also testify to the validity of these obligations:

Zubair Ibn al-Awwām, Sa'd Ibn Malik Abi Waqas, Zayd ibn Thābit, Talha ibn Ubaidullah, Abdullah ibn Umar, Sahl ibn Hanif, Abu Ayyūb Khālid ibn Zayd.

(The date of writing is Dhī Qa'da of 35 AH)

The groups that had come from Kufa and Egypt each took a copy of the treaty and departed.[401] His Eminence Ali ibn Abī-Tālib said to 'Uthmān, "It would be good for you to come out and deliver a sermon and quell the people, and bear witness before God that you have repented."

---

[399] Ibn A'tham, *Tārīkh*, pp. 46-47.
[400] The following sources are among those that provide commentary on this dialogue: Abū al-Fidā, Ismā'īl ibn Ali, *Tarikh al-Mukhtasar fi Akhbar al-Bashar*, 1:168; Balādhūrī, Ahmad ibn Yahyā ibn Jābir, *Ansāb al-Ashrāf*, 5:60; Ibn Abī'l-Hadīd, Abdul-Hamīd, *Sharh Nahj al-Balāgha*, 1:303; Ibn Athīr Jazarī, 'Alī, *al-Kāmil fī al-Tārīkh*, 3:63; Tabarī, Muhammad ibn Jarīr, *Tārīkh ar-Rusul wa'l-Mulūk*, 5:96-97.
[401] Balādhūrī, Ahmad ibn Yahyā ibn Jābir, *Ansāb al-Ashrāf*, 5:63-64.

Othman came and delivered the following sermon:

O ye people, I swear by God, I knew of all [of the issues] that you have criticized me for, and everything that I have done in the past was all done on the basis of knowledge and wisdom. But appetites of the lower parts of my soul (*an-nafs*) and my inner desires greatly deceived me, and made me see reality upside down, and ultimately misled me and turned me away from the path of truth.

I personally heard the Prophet of God say: "Whoever commits an error must repent, and whoever commits a sin must repent and refrain from adding to his waywardness. And if such a person continues in his transgressions and iniquities, he will be considered to be one of those people who have deviated completely from the path of truth."

I am the first to want to take and act on this advice. I presently ask forgiveness of God for what I have done and turn to Him. And because it is [only] those who have turned in repentance from their sin that are deserving [of forgiveness], [sinners] should repent and ask for forgiveness.

Now, when I descend from the pulpit, let your leaders and noblemen come to me and share their suggestions with me. I swear by God, if God's will be such that I should become a slave that is traded for gold and silver, I shall adopt the method of the servants of God in the best possible way, and will become abject and humble, just like them.

Othman wept at this point. The narrator says, "I saw that his beard had become wet due to the intensity of his weeping, and that people felt sorrow for and empathy towards 'Uthmān, and some of them even wept [along with him and for him], and were affected by his despondency, helplessness and repentance.

Sa'īd ibn Zayd said to 'Uthmān, "O Commander of the Faithful, no one is more sympathetic towards you than yourself; so beware! Think of yourself and [be sure to] act on that which you have promised."

Marwān's Sabotage

When 'Uthmān stepped down from the pulpit and entered his house, he saw Marwān and Sa'īd and a group of the Umayyads gathered there. When 'Uthmān sat down, Marwan turned to him and said, "Shall I speak?" When he was given permission to proceed, Marwan said, "If you had said these words when you were strong, it would have been for the good, but now that you are weak and humiliated, saying these words is tantamount to your defeat. You should not have done this, and humiliated yourself before the people."

People came to the door of 'Uthmān's house to speak to 'Uthmān about their complaints, according to what he had promised. Marwan said to 'Uthmān, "|There are mountains of people gathered!" 'Uthmān said, "I am ashamed to go [and speak with them]. You go." Marwan went and shouted at the people,

What's all this commotion? Are you here to plunder ['Uthmān]? You should be ashamed of yourselves! Everyone I see has come with his friend, everyone other than those whom I am waiting to see. What news is there that has caused all of you to sharpen your teeth? Do you intend to snatch our dominion from our grip by attacking us like this? What stupid people you are. Go back to your homes. You have made a mistake; we have never retreated in front of you, nor will we ever lose our power and dominion over you.

People Complaining to Ali and Ali's Refusal to be Involved any Further

After this incident, a group of people came and complained to Ali عليه السلام. His Eminence angrily went before 'Uthmān and said,

Have you still not quit yourself from Marwan? He will not let you be until he turns you away from Islam and from [the dictates of] your reason altogether. And you have bowed your head, and you are following him like a helpless camel on a leash that can be dragged in any direction! Marwan has no commitment to any ideology or religion, and I see that he will destroy you. I will no longer be involved in your affairs!

When Imam Ali left, 'Uthmān's wife Nā'ila came and said to him, "Ali will not come to you anymore. When you paid heed to Marwan, and he dragged you to wherever he wanted to take you." 'Uthmān said, "What should I do?" Nā'ila said, "Fear the God Who has no partner, and follow the example of your two friends who were before you. If you obey Marwan, he will lead you to your death, because Marwan has no value, esteem, awe or love among the people; and you lost [the support of] the people because of Marwan. Send someone and ask for Ali to come back and reconcile with him. Verily, there are bonds of kinship between the two of you, and he is accepted among the people, and no one will argue with what he says."

'Uthmān sent someone after Ali, but he refused to come, saying, "I told him that I would not come again."[402]

After this incident, 'Uthmān climbed the pulpit on Friday and praised God ﷻ. Before he was able to start his sermon, one of the attendees got up from the middle of the crowd and said, "O 'Uthmān, act in accordance with God's sacred writ!" 'Uthmān said, "Sit down." This exchange was repeated three times. Eventually, those present in the mosque became divided into two groups: one group was against 'Uthmān, and the other was with him. The dispute escalated and the two groups threw stones at each other, as well as at 'Uthmān, who was standing at the top of the pulpit, such that he lost consciousness and was taken home. His Eminence Imam Ali went and visited him. The Umayyads were gathered all around 'Uthmān. When Imam Ali entered, the Umayyads attacked him: "This was the result of your deeds; you did this! And by God, if you achieve what you want (i.e., governance), we will make the world miserable for you." So, the Commander of the Faithful rose up in anger.[403]

This was the situation within Medina.

Groups that Came from Different Cities

A group of 'Uthmān's opponents had gathered in Dhākhushub, outside Medina, waiting to see what would happen. Mughirah ibn Shu'bah said to 'Uthmān, "Allow me to go and send back those who are gathered outside Medina." And 'Uthmān told him to go. When Mughirah came up to them, they shouted at him, "Go back, you rake; go back, you corrupt and wicked one;[404] go back, you blind one." And so Mughira had no option but to return.

---

[402] Ibn Athīr Jazarī, 'Alī, *al-Kāmil fī al-Tārīkh*, 3:96; Tabarī, Muhammad ibn Jarīr, *Tārīkh ar-Rusul wa'l-Mulūk*, 5:112 & 1:2977-2979 of the European edition. Balādhūrī has also cited a portion of what we have stated. Cf. Balādhūrī, Ahmad ibn Yahyā ibn Jābir, *Ansāb al-Ashrāf*, 5:65.

[403] Tabarī, Muhammad ibn Jarīr, *Tārīkh ar-Rusul wa'l-Mulūk*, 5:113& 1:2979-2990 of the European edition.

[404] These taunts were levelled at Mughīra because he had been accused of fornication when he was the governor of Basra, but Umar prevented his being whipped [as required by law]. Cf. the following sources under the year 17: Abū al-Fidā, Ismā'īl ibn Ali, *Tarikh al-Mukhtasar fī Akhbar al-Bashar*, Ibn Athīr Jazarī, 'Alī, *al-Kāmil fī al-Tārīkh*

'Uthmān then called Amr ibn al-'Ās and told him, "Go to the people and invite them to [follow] God's sacred writ, and tell them that I will do that whatever they say." Amr ibn al-'Ās went and greeted them, but they said, "Go back, you enemy of God;[405] go back, you son of Nābigha.[406] Neither are you to be trusted, nor are we safe from you." Abdullah ibn Umar and the others who were in 'Uthmān's house said, "No one but Ali can silence them." 'Uthmān sent for Ali ﷺ. When Ali ﷺ appeared, 'Uthmān told him, "Call these people to [act in accordance with] God's sacred writ and to the paradigmatic example of the Prophet. Imam Ali ﷺ said, "Provided that you make a covenant and bear witness before God that you will act on whatever I tell them." 'Uthmān accepted this condition, and Imam Ali ﷺ took a covenant from 'Uthmān, who solemnly swore he would do whatever Ali ﷺ promised to the rebels on behalf of 'Uthmān. Imam Ali ﷺ left and went to Dhākhushub, the place where the rebels had gathered. When the rebels saw Imam Ali ﷺ, they told him to return, but the Imam told them that he would come forward, which the rebels accepted.

Imam Ali ﷺ recited what 'Uthmān had said, after which they asked, "Do you guarantee that he will do these things?" And Imam Ali ﷺ said that he did. And so they said that they were satisfied with this arrangement, after which the elders and nobles of the rebels entered 'Uthmān's residence along with Imam Ali ﷺ.[407] These were none other than the Egyptians who had complaints about Abdullah ibn Sa'd ibn Abi Sarh, the man whom 'Uthmān had appointed as governor of Egypt. On the previous occasion, they had sent a letter in reply to the letter of 'Uthmān, and when this reply was taken to the governor of Egypt, he had had one of them killed.[408]

Apart from Ali ﷺ, Talha, Zubair and Ayesha also intervened. They said to 'Uthmān, "Replace the governor of Egypt." He asked, "Who do you want to replace him with?" They said, "Muhammad ibn Abi Bakr." And so 'Uthmān appointed Muhammad ibn Abi Bakr to the

---

Tabarī, Muhammad ibn Jarīr, *Tārīkh ar-Rusul wa'l-Mulūk*, and Balādhūrī, Ahmad ibn Yahyā ibn Jābir, *Ansāb al-Ashrāf*, 1:423 and Ya'qūbī, Aḥmad ibn Isḥāq, *Tārīkh al-Ya'qūbī*, 2:124. See also, Ibn Abī'l-Hadīd, Abdul-Hamīd, *Sharh Nahj al-Balāgha*, 2:161; Isfahānī, Abī'l-Faraj, *al-Aghānī*, 14:139-142.

[405] , 'Amr ibn As's claim to fame was that prior to his entering into Islam, he had composed a 60-stanza ode disparaging the Prophet of God ﷺ.

[406] Nābigha, 'Amr ibn As's mother, was renowned for being corrupt.

[407] Balādhūrī, Ahmad ibn Yahyā ibn Jābir, *Ansāb al-Ashrāf*, 5:63-64.

[408] Balādhūrī, Ahmad ibn Yahyā ibn Jābir, *Ansāb al-Ashrāf*, 5:25-26.

governorship of Egypt, and Muhammad ibn Abi Bakr left for Egypt with the Egyptians, along with a letter of appointment from 'Uthmān.[409] Thus far, the story has been that of the revolt of the Egyptians.[410]

The Caliph's Ruse

There was unrest within Medina as well. Imam Ali ﷺ mediated again, and it was decided that this time, 'Uthmān would act on his promises. 'Uthmān said, "Time is needed to establish justice and restore the rights of the people." Imam Ali ﷺ said, "There is no need for a delay in Medina, and outside Medina, you have the time that it takes for your letters to arrive." 'Uthmān said, "I need some time." And so Imam Ali ﷺ said, "Let there be an interval of three days then."[411]

When Muhammad ibn Abi Bakr, whom 'Uthmān had appointed the governor of Egypt, was on the way to Egypt from Medina along with the Egyptians who had come to Medina, they suddenly saw 'Uthmān's slave riding a camel at speed. They cross-examined him, asking where he was headed. He replied that he was headed for Egypt. When they asked what he had with him, he said he had nothing. This they did not accept, and dismounted him. He was carrying an empty skin, which they opened up. The skin contained a lead tube in which there was a letter from 'Uthmān to Abdullah ibn Sa'd ibn Abi Sarh, the governor of Egypt, with 'Uthmān's seal. In this letter to the governor of Egypt, 'Uthmān had written, "When this contingent arrives, hang Muhammad ibn Abi Bakr and so-and-so, and remain in your position (and imprison all those who came to me complaining about you, and await my further orders).

After they had read the letter, they returned to Medina with Muhammad ibn Abi Bakr and went to see Imam Ali ﷺ, and showed 'Uthmān's letter to the Imam ﷺ.[412] Imam Ali ﷺ went to 'Uthmān and asked him, "What is this letter??" 'Uthmān said, "I did not write it." The people said, "Your official courier was riding your camel, and the letter is in the handwriting of your scribe, and your seal is on it!" 'Uthmān

[409] Balādhūrī, Ahmad ibn Yahyā ibn Jābir, *Ansāb al-Ashrāf*, 5:63-65.
[410] The revolt of the Egyptians started before 'Uthmān's sermon in the mosque.
[411] Ibn Abī'l-Hadīd, Abdul-Hamīd, *Sharh Nahj al-Balāgha*, 1:166; Ibn Athīr Jazarī, 'Alī, *al-Kāmil fī al-Tārīkh*, 3:71-72; Tabarī, Muhammad ibn Jarīr, *Tārīkh ar-Rusul wa'l-Mulūk*, 5:116-117.
[412] Balādhūrī, Ahmad ibn Yahyā ibn Jābir, *Ansāb al-Ashrāf*, 5:67-68.

said, "The camel has been stolen, the handwriting is similar to the handwriting of my scribe, and the seal may have been made to look like my seal." They said to him, "Resign from the caliphate, otherwise you will either be dismissed, or you will be killed." 'Uthmān did not accept. They said to him, "You have done many wrongful deeds. When you are reprimanded, you repent, but you do not keep your promises. At one time, you repented and said that you had given up your past deeds; and Muhammad ibn Muslimah acted as your guarantor. But you did wrong again. Now, you either have to step down yourself, or you will be killed." 'Uthmān said, "No, I will not resign from the caliphate. I swear by God that I will never take off the vestment that God has seen fit to invest me with!"[413]

'Āisha issues a Fatwa to kill 'Uthmān

The Mother of the Faithful (*umm al-Mu'minīn*) 'Āisha, whose heart was filled with grievances for 'Uthmān, and who entertained thoughts of having her cousin Talha accede to the caliphate, took full advantage of the people's revolt and siege of 'Uthmān, and issued her historic fatwa calling for his death. 'Āisha said:

O 'Uthmān, you have appropriated the treasury of the Muslims to yourself, and you have given the property and lives of the people to the will of the Umayyad [clan], whom you have given sovereignty and dominion, thereby placing Muhammad's nation in distress. May God withdraw the good and the blessings of the heavens and of Earth from you. If it were not for the fact that you pray five times a day like other Muslims, you would have been beheaded like a camel.[414]

When 'Uthmān heard 'Āisha speak these words, he recited the tenth verse of Surah at-Tahrīm (The Forswearal), which was revealed about 'Āisha and Hafsa:

---

[413] Tabarī, Muhammad ibn Jarīr, *Tārīkh ar-Rusul wa'l-Mulūk*, 5:120-121.

[414] It seems that these words of 'Āisha's were spoken prior to 'Uthmān's order to the Governor of Egypt being exposed, in which he had ordered that Muhammad ibn Abī Bakr be put to death. I say this because after that event, 'Āisha issued her fatwa in language that did not betray any concern about 'Uthmān being someone who prays five times a day.

ضَرَبَ اللَّهُ مَثَلًا لِّلَّذِينَ كَفَرُوا امْرَأَتَ نُوحٍ وَامْرَأَتَ لُوطٍ ۖ كَانَتَا تَحْتَ
عَبْدَيْنِ مِنْ عِبَادِنَا صَالِحَيْنِ فَخَانَتَاهُمَا فَلَمْ يُغْنِيَا عَنْهُمَا مِنَ اللَّهِ شَيْئًا
وَقِيلَ ادْخُلَا النَّارَ مَعَ الدَّاخِلِينَ ﴿١٠﴾

[66:10] For those who are bent on denying the truth God has propounded a parable in [the stories of] Noah's wife and Lot's wife: they were wedded to two of Our righteous servants, and each one betrayed her husband; and neither of the two [husbands] will be of any avail to these two women when they are told [on Judgment Day], "Enter the fire with all those [other sinners] who enter it!"

'Āisha had a fierce and rebellious temperament, and had learned of the letter that her brother Muhammad had discovered on his way to Egypt, in which 'Uthmān had ordered the murder of her brother and those who were with him, and which was written in the handwriting of 'Uthmān's scribe and had 'Uthmān's seal. 'Uthmān's reciting of this verse to the Mother of the Faithful (*umm ul-Mu'minīn*) 'Āisha, who was willing to give her life for her relatives, angered her so much that she unrestrainedly and explicitly ordered the assassination of the caliph and issued a fatwa stating that he was an unbeliever (*fatwā bi kufrash dād*). 'Āisha cried out, "Kill Na'thal, for he has become an unbeliever!" (*uqtilū na'thal, fa qad kafar*).[415]

'Āisha referred to 'Uthmān as *na'thal.*[416] By doing so, she violated the sanctity of the caliphate. Needless to say, all of the evil committed by the leaders of the Umayyads and their governors and people in position of authority [that were appointed by the caliph, such as] Marwan and Hakam ibn Abi al-'Ās, Walid and Sa'īd and Abdullah ibn Sa'd ibn Abi Sarh, all have their share of blame. All of the inequities

[415] Tabarī, Muhammad ibn Jarīr, *Tārīkh ar-Rusul wa'l-Mulūk*, 4:474; Ibn Abī'l-Hadīd, Abdul-Hamīd, *Sharh Nahj al-Balāgha*, 2:77; Ibn Athīr Jazarī, 'Alī, *al-Kāmil fī al-Tārīkh*, 3:87; Ibn Athīr al-Jazrī, Mubārak ibn Muhammad, *al-Nahāya fī Gharīb al-Hadīth wa'l-Āthār*, 4:156; Ibn A'tham, *Tārīkh*, p. 155.

[416] What is meant here by the word *na'thal* is 'that Jew'. The word *na'thal* has other meanings too, of course. It also means 'stupid old man' and 'male hyena'. It is also said that *na'thal* was the name of an Egyptian man who had a long beard. (Cf. Ibn Athīr al-Jazrī, Mubārak ibn Muhammad, *al-Nahāya fī Gharīb al-Hadīth wa'l-Āthār*, Fīrūzābādī, Abū al-Tāhir Majīd al-Dīn Muhammad ibn Ya'qūb, *al-Qāmūs al-Mūhīt*, Zubaydī's *Tāj al-'Arūs*, and Ibn Manżūr al-Ansārī, Muhammad ibn Mukarram, *Lisān al-'Arab* under the heading, *na'thal*).

that were wrought against the Muslim, and the plundering of the treasury, all have significant effects in [engendering and fostering] these acts of insurrection.

The Words of Jahjāh al-Ghaffārī

While 'Uthmān recited his sermons, he leaned on the cane on which Abu Bakr and Umar leaned. Jahjāh al-Ghaffārī, who was one of the Ansar ("Helpers' from Medina), stood up and said, "Get up, o *na'thal*, and come down from this pulpit!"[417] Another hadith report has him state the following, "Come [down from the pulpit] and let me have you mount a camel and take you to a volcano and throw you in it!" None of the people said anything in response to what he had said. The Umayyads brought 'Uthmān down from the pulpit and took him home.[418]

The Siege of Uthmān's House

Most of the people surrounding Uthmān's house were Egyptians. The Ansar also helped. The Egyptians, who had come with the intention of performing the major pilgrimage (*al-Hajj*), had arranged to go to Mecca with the people of Kufa and the people of Basra. They came in from the outskirts of Madina, and the people of Madina also helped, and besieged 'Uthmān's house. In the meantime, 'Āisha's letters had reached the cities and had a significant effect on the revolt of the people against "'Uthmān,[419] who besieged the caliph and shut off his water supply on Talha's order.[420]

'Āisha, who saw 'Uthmān's murder as a *fait accompli*, did not want to be in Medina while this happened. She thus made arrangements for performing the major pilgrimage (*al-Hajj*). As she prepared for the pilgrimage, 'Uthmān said to Marwan and Abd al-Rahman ibn Attāb, "Go and ask 'Āisha to stay; maybe she will stop the

---

[417] Balādhūrī, Ahmad ibn Yahyā ibn Jābir, *Ansāb al-Ashrāf*, 5:47-48; Dayār-Bakrī, Ḥusayn Ibn Md., *Tārīkh al-Khamīs fī Ahwāl Anfus an-Nafīs*, 2:260; Ibn Abī'l-Hadīd, Abdul-Hamīd, *Sharh Nahj al-Balāgha*, 1:165; Ibn Athīr Jazarī, 'Alī, *al-Kāmil fī al-Tārīkh*, 3:70; Ibn Hajar, Ahmad ibn Ali al-Asqalāni, *al-Iṣābah fī Tamyīz al-Ṣaḥābah*, 1:253; Ibn Kathīr, Abu'al-Fidā Ismā'īl ibn Umar, *Tārīkh*, 7:175; Tabarī, Muhammad ibn Jarīr, *Tārīkh ar-Rusul wa'l-Mulūk*, 5:114; Tabarī, Muhibbiddīn, *ar-Riyāḍ an-Naḍra*, 2:123.

[418] Ibid.

[419] Balādhūrī, Ahmad ibn Yahyā ibn Jābir, *Ansāb al-Ashrāf*, 5:103.

[420] Balādhūrī, Ahmad ibn Yahyā ibn Jābir, *Ansāb al-Ashrāf*, 5:90.

people and prevent them from killing me." They went to 'Āisha and said to her, "Do not go on the major pilgrimage, but stay; perhaps God ﷻ will repel this rebellion against this man ('Uthmān) through you."[421] 'Āisha replied, "No, I have packed my luggage and made the *hajj* pilgrimage obligatory on myself; I cannot change my plans now." They said to her, "Whatever you have already spent, we will give you double that amount." But 'Āisha still did not accept their offer,[422] after which Marwan recited this couplet:

و حرّق قيس عليّ البلاد　　　　فلمّا اضطرمت أحجما

Qais set the city on fire against me; And when its flames rose up and engulfed me, he washed his hands of me.[423]

In response to Marwan, 'Āisha said, "O Marwan, do you think that I am in any doubt about your master?[424] I swear to God that I wished I could put him in one of my bundles and was able to carry him and throw him into the sea."[425] After this, 'Āisha started towards Mecca.

In that year, by the order of 'Uthmān, Abdullah ibn Abbas was in charge of the major pilgrimage (*Amir al-Hajj*). He reached 'Āisha in the region of Sulsul,[426] and 'Āisha said to him:

I swear you to [your covenant with] God not to scatter the people who are angry with this man ('Uthmān) with this captivating and penetrating tongue that you have, and not to cast doubts in them about this selfish and defiant man. The people have become conscious of the work that is before them, and have recognized the right path that they must take, and they have gathered in groups from the cities concerning

---

[421] Balādhūrī, Ahmad ibn Yahyā ibn Jābir, *Ansāb al-Ashrāf*, 5:81.
[422] Ya'qūbī, Aḥmad ibn Isḥāq, *Tārīkh al-Ya'qūbī*, 2:142.
[423] The verse appears as follows in Balādhūrī, Ahmad ibn Yahyā ibn Jābir, *Ansāb al-Ashrāf*, 5:75. و حرّق قيس عليّ البلا　د فلمّا حتّى اذا اضطرمت اجذما
[424] Ya'qūbī, Aḥmad ibn Isḥāq, *Tārīkh al-Ya'qūbī*, 2:124.
[425] Balādhūrī, Ahmad ibn Yahyā ibn Jābir, *Ansāb al-Ashrāf*, 5:75; Ibn Sa'd, Abu Abdallah Muhammad, *al-Tabaqāt al-Kubrā*, 5:25 of the Leiden edition; Ibn A'tham, *al-Tārīkh*, p. 155.
[426] Sulsul is the name of a place that is located within a few *mīl*s of Medina. The correct pronounciation of the name is Ḍulsul, but historians have written it as Sulsul everywhere.

the matter that has been raised. I personally saw Talha having gained access to the keys of the treasury. If he takes over, he will undoubtedly follow the same path of his cousin Abu Bakr.

In response to 'Āisha, Ibn Abbas said, "Mother,[427] if something should befall this man and he is killed, the people will not bow down to anyone but our leader, Ali." 'Āisha quickly retorted, "I do not want to argue with you."[428]

The Keys of the Treasury in Talha's Hands

Talha had obtained the keys to the treasury, and people had gathered in his house because of this, so his house was packed full of people. As the siege on 'Uthmān became more constricted, he sent someone to fetch the Commander of the Faithful [Ali ibn Abī-Tālib ﷺ].

Prior to this, Imam Ali ﷺ had told 'Uthmān that he would no longer come to him if called upon to do so; but he came despite this. 'Uthmān told him, "I have rights over you in several ways: the right of Islamic brotherhood and kinship,[429] and being the groom of the Messenger of God ﷺ. If you chose to discount all of this and assume that we are in the era of pre-Islamic ignorance, it would still be a disgrace for the family of Abd al-Manāf to lose power and the leadership of governance to one of the sons of the Taym tribe (i.e. to Talha).

In response, Imam Ali ﷺ said, "Information [about this matter] will reach you."

He then left 'Uthmān's house and went to the Prophet's mosque. There he saw Usama (the son of Zayd, the freedman of the Prophet), put his hand on his shoulder, and together they went to Talha's house. When they reached Talha, Ali ﷺ said to him, "Talha, what is this commotion that you have started?!" Talha replied, "O Abu al-Hasan, you have arrived too late; you have come at a time when things are beyond the point of no return (*kār az kār gozashte*)."[430]

---

427 The wives of the Prophet were referred to as 'Mother' (*umm*).

428 Balādhūrī, Ahmad ibn Yahyā ibn Jābir, *Ansāb al-Ashrāf*, 5:75; Tabarī, Muhammad ibn Jarīr, *Tārīkh ar-Rusul wa'l-Mulūk*, 5:140; Ibn A'tham, *al-Tārīkh*, p. 156.

429 The Banī-Umayya and Banī-Hāshim clans [of the Quraysh] were paternal nephews to each other.

430 What he was saying to Imam Ali was for him not to interfere, as his, Talha's accession to the caliphate had now become certain.

When Imam Ali saw that talking to Talha was useless, he did not say anything and left his house and went to the treasury. He ordered, "Open the door of the treasury!" When he was told that they did not have the key, which was with Talha, he ordered the treasury door to be broken, and he personally began distributing gold and silver coins, as well as the gold and silver that was piled up in the treasury. Those who had gathered around Talha, one by one came out of his house and went to Ali ﷺ and became beneficiaries of the wealth of the treasury.

Talha was left on his own. He went to Uthmān and said, "O Commander of the Faithful, I ask God for forgiveness for what I have done. I entertained a thought in my mind, but God did not want it and put a barrier between me and my desire." 'Uthmān replied, "I swear by God that you did not come to repent, but that you came because you found yourself to be defeated in the midst of this affair! I will leave it to God to carry out the vengeance for this act of yours!"[431]

Talha shuts off 'Uthmān's Water Supply, and Ali delivers Water to him

Tabari writes that 'Uthmān was under siege for forty days, and that during this time, Talha prayed with the people.[432] None of the companions of the Messenger of God were equal to Talha in terms of their opposition to 'Uthmān. Talha and Zubair had taken charge. Talha ensured that the water would remain cut off from 'Uthmān's house, and would not allow drinking water to be taken in. Imam Ali said to Talha, "What kind of thing is this that you are doing?? Let the man draw his water from the well." Talha said, "No," and refused to agree to this.[433]

Tabari writes that because the besiegers intensified their actions by preventing water from reaching 'Uthmān's house, 'Uthmān sent someone to Imam Ali ﷺ asking him to help, and to think of a way to bring some water to his house. Ali ﷺ talked to Talha, and when he saw that Talha would not accept such a request, he became very angry,

---

[431] Balādhūrī, Ahmad ibn Yahyā ibn Jābir, *Ansāb al-Ashrāf*, 5:78; Ibn Athīr Jazarī, 'Alī, *al-Kāmil fī al-Tārīkh*, 3:64; Muttaqī al-Hindī, *Kanz al-U'mmāl*, 6:389, hadith #5965; Tabarī, Muhammad ibn Jarīr, *Tārīkh ar-Rusul wa'l-Mulūk*, 5:154. See also, Mubarrad, *al-Kāmil*, p. 11 (Leiden); *Zuhr al-AAdāb*, 1:75, Ibn A'tham, *al-Tārīkh*, pp. 156-157; Tabarī, 5:3071 of the European edition.

[432] [I think what is meant by this is that Talha lead the performance of the public acts of ritual devotion or 'prayers'.]

[433] Balādhūrī, Ahmad ibn Yahyā ibn Jābir, *Ansāb al-Ashrāf*, 5:90.

so much so that Talha had no choice but to agree to Imam Ali's ﷺ demand, and finally allowed some water to be taken to 'Uthmān.[434] However, they continued to disallow water to be taken into the house. 'Uthmān went up onto the roof of the house and asked if Ali ﷺ was among them. When they said no, he asked if Sa'īd was among them. When he was told no again, he remained silent for a while, then lowered his head and asked, "Is there anyone who will ask Ali ﷺ to bring water for us?" When this news reached Imam Ali ﷺ, he had three large skins of water taken into the house. The slaves of the Banī-Hāshim and the Banī-Umayya wrapped their arms around the skins in order to protect them from the rebels, and by the time the water reached 'Uthmān's house, some of them were wounded.

In this situation, Mujammi' ibn Jāriah al-Ansari passed by Talha. Talha asked him, "Mujammi', what is your master 'Uthmān doing?" He replied, "I swear by God, I think that he will eventually be killed." Talha scoffed, "If he is killed, neither would a [divinely] commissioned prophet have been killed, nor would [we lose] an archangel [from our midst]."[435]

Abdullah ibn Ayyash ibn Abi Rubī'a says, "When 'Uthmān was under siege, I went to him one day and talked with him for about an hour. While we were talking, he took my hand and had me listen to the words of those who were gathered behind his house. At that time, I heard someone say, 'What are you waiting for?' And another replied, 'Wait, maybe he will repent and turn away from his ways.' While "Uthmān and I were listening, Talha ibn Ubaydullah passed by, and then stopped and asked, 'Where is Ibn 'Udays?'[436] They said that he was present, and Ibn 'Udays came up to Talha, who whispered something in his ear. Then Ibn 'Udays returned and ordered his men not to let anyone in or out of 'Uthmān's house from now on. 'Uthmān said, 'O God, rid me of the evil of Talha, for he incited the people against me... he tore the veil of my respect, even though he had no such right!'"

Abdullah continues, "When I wanted to leave the house of the Caliph, I was prevented from doing so in accordance with the order of Ibn 'Udays, they prevented me from leaving, until Muhammad ibn Abu Bakr, who was passing by, told them to let me pass, and so they released me."

---

[434] Tabarī, Muhammad ibn Jarīr, *Tārīkh ar-Rusul wa'l-Mulūk*, 5:113.
[435] Balādhūrī, Ahmad ibn Yahyā ibn Jābir, *Ansāb al-Ashrāf*, 5:74.
[436] Ibn 'Udays was the leader of the Egyptian insurrectionists.

The Murder of 'Uthmān and Imam Ali's Reaction

Imam Ali ﷺ was informed that they had decided to kill 'Uthmān. He ordered his sons, Hasan ﷺ and Husain ﷺ to take their swords and to stand at the door to 'Uthmān's house and not to allow anyone to reach the caliph. Imam Ali's ﷺ sons obeyed their father's order and went to stand guard at 'Uthmān's house. There was a strange situation around the Caliph's palace at that point, where the people insisted on finishing 'Uthmān off. Eventually, fighting broke out, and Their Eminences Hasan ﷺ and Husain ﷺ were wounded while trying to defend 'Uthmān. Hasan's ﷺ face turned red with his blood, and Qanbar, Imam Ali's ﷺ slave, took a serious injury to his head.

Muhammad ibn Abu Bakr feared that the Banī Hāshim would become angry at seeing what had happened to Imam Ali's sons, and start some new problem. So he brought two of the attackers to the fore and said to them, "If the Banī Hāshim see what has happened, especially that Hasan's blood has been shed on his face, I am afraid that they will drive the people away from 'Uthmān's house with their swords, and prevent out plans from coming to fruition. It is more expedient for us to reach 'Uthmān by climbing the wall and to kill him quietly."[437]

Ibn Abī al-Hadīd writes, "Talha, who had covered his face with a cloth to keep from being seen in the public, was shooting arrows at 'Uthmān's house.[438] It was decided that Muhammad ibn Abi Bakr and two other people would climb the walls of the house adjacent to 'Uthmān's house, and reach 'Uthmān in that way. Muhammad ibn Abi Bakr said, 'I will hold 'Uthmān and you two come and kill him.' The three left, and when they reached 'Uthmān, Muhammad ibn Abi Bakr sat on his chest. 'Uthmān said to him, 'Your father Abu Bakr would be upset if he saw you sitting on my chest.' Muhammad ibn Abi Bakr's resolve was weakened, and the other two men came and killed him."[439]

When 'Uthmān was killed, they gave glad tidings to Talha. However, when Imam Ali ﷺ heard the news, he became angry, and when Talha saw him, he said, "What has happened, O Abu al-Hassan, that has made you so angry?" Imam Ali said to Talha, "May God curse

---

[437] Balādhūrī, Ahmad ibn Yahyā ibn Jābir, *Ansāb al-Ashrāf*, 5:69; Tabarī, Muhammad ibn Jarīr, *Tārīkh ar-Rusul wa'l-Mulūk*, 5:118; Ibn Athīr Jazarī, 'Alī, *al-Kāmil fī al-Tārīkh*, 3:68-70.
[438] Ibn Abī'l-Hadīd, Abdul-Hamīd, *Sharh Nahj al-Balāgha*, 2:404.
[439] Ibid, in the footnote.

you! Is a companion of the Messenger of God supposed to be killed?!" Talha replied, "If he had kept his distance from Marwan, he would not have been killed."[440] In another hadith report, it is stated that Talha said, "He was neither a [divinely] commissioned Prophet, nor was he an archangel."[441]

The People's Pledge of Allegiance to Imam Ali, and 'Uthmān's Burial

'Uthmān's body had been left on the ground for three days, and no one had been allowed to bury him, [and this situation continued] until the people pledged their allegiance to Imam Ali ﷺ, after which the Umayyads asked Imam Ali ﷺ to allow 'Uthmān's family to bury his body. Imam Ali ﷺ gave his permission and ordered that 'Uthmān be buried. After the Maghrib prayer, five people came and picked up the body and took it: Marwan and his fifth daughter and three of his slaves.

When the people heard about this, they filled the skirts of their shirts with stones and sat in wait on the path that 'Uthmān's body was to take. When "Uthmān's body reached them, they rained stones on his coffin and attacked it with the intention of overthrowing it. This incident was reported to Imam Ali ﷺ, who tasked some guards to repel the disturbance that was being caused around 'Uthmān's body, and to protect it from harm. These guards took possession of the body, as they had been ordered to do, and kept it secure until it reached its destination. Thus, 'Uthmān's body was buried in the Hash Kawkab Cemetery, which is adjacent to the al-Baqī' Cemetery, and is where the Jews buried their dead.

At the funeral of her father, 'Uthmān's daughter wailed and mourned loudly, while at the same time, the people rained stones on them and shouted, *na'thal! na'thal!*[442]

After Mu'awiyah ascended to the caliphate, he ordered that the wall of the Hash Kawkab Cemetery be demolished and for the part [that 'Uthmān was buried in] to be joined to the al-Baqī' Cemetery. Mu'awiyah also ordered the Muslims to bury their dead around the tomb of 'Uthmān, so that the tomb of 'Uthmān would thereby be joined

---

440 Balādhūrī, Ahmad ibn Yahyā ibn Jābir, *Ansāb al-Ashrāf*, 5:69-70.
441 Balādhūrī, Ahmad ibn Yahyā ibn Jābir, *Ansāb al-Ashrāf*, 5:74.
442 Ibn A'tham, *al-Tārīkh*, p. 159; Ibn Athīr Jazarī, 'Alī, *al-Kāmil fī al-Tārīkh*, 3:76; Tabarī, Muhammad ibn Jarīr, *Tārīkh ar-Rusul wa'l-Mulūk*, 5:143-144; Tabarī, Muhibbiddīn, *ar-Riyāḍ an-Naḍra*, 2:131-132.

to the graves of Muslims. Even today, the tomb of 'Uthmān lies at the end of the al-Baqī' Cemetery.

The End of the Saqīfa

The story of the Saqīfa, which was planned by several people during the time of the Prophet ﷺ, came to an end after 'Uthmān was killed. The Saqīfa was planned in such a way that the co-conspirators would accede to the caliphate one after the other. If 'Uthmān had not been killed, he would have appointed someone, and Imam Ali ﵇ would not have become caliph. However, the arrangement they had made in the Saqīfa was broken by the insurrection of the people against 'Uthmān and his assassination, and the people were liberated. When the Muslims were liberated from the bonds of the Saqīfa [arrangement], the Emigrants and the Ansar and the Companions of the Prophet ﷺ rushed to the door of Imam Ali's ﵇ house, and Imam Ali ﵇ came to the Mosque of the Prophet ﷺ where the people pledged allegiance to him.[443]

[443] Ibn A'tham, *al-Tārīkh*, pp. 160-161; Ibn Athīr Jazarī, 'Alī, *al-Kāmil fī al-Tārīkh*, 3:76; Tabarī, Muhammad ibn Jarīr, *Tārīkh ar-Rusul wa'l-Mulūk*, 5:142-143; Muttaqī al-Hindī, *Kanz al-U'mmāl*, 3:161, hadith #2471; Balādhūrī, Ahmad ibn Yahyā ibn Jābir, *Ansāb al-Ashrāf*, 5:70; Hākim al-Haskānī an-Neyshāpūrī, *al-Mustadrak 'Alā's-Sahīhayn*, 3:114.

13 The *Shaqshaqīya* Sermon of Imām Ali[444]

On one of the last days of his caliphate, Imam Ali ﷺ delivered a sermon that came to be known as the Shaqshaqīya Sermon,[445] in which he briefly touches on key events from the time when Abu Bakr came to power to the time the of the people pledged their allegiance to himself, and the events that followed. We thought that it would be appropriate to include this sermon at the end of the book.

"Nay, by God, the son of Abū Quhāfa [Abū Bakr] had exacted the caliphate for himself while he knew full well that my position in it was like that of the pivot in a mill; the flood waters flow down beneath me, and the birds do not soar high up to me, yet I hung up a curtain before it and turned aside from it [the caliphate]. I then started thinking whether I should attack with a severing hand or should watch patiently the blind darkness in which the old man becomes decrepit and the young man old, in which the believer tries his utmost till he meets his Lord, and I came to the conclusion that patience in a situation like this was wiser.

So I adopted patience, although there was a mote rankling in my eye and a bone sticking in my throat on seeing my heritage being plundered, till the first one [Abū Bakr] died and handed over the reins of the caliphate to another person ['Umar] after him. [Here, Ali ﷺ quotes a verse from the poet Asha, which reads] "How vast is the difference between this day of mine when I am on the back of the camel

---

[444] The translation (with some modifications) is due to Syed Husain M. Jafri, where it appears at the beginning of the second chapter of his excellent pioneering work *The Origins and Early Development of Shī'a Islam*, (Oxford University Press, 1976).
[445] The third sermon of the *Nahj al-Balāgha.*

[i.e. suffering from the hardship of a rough journey] and the day of Hayyān, brother of Jāber [i.e. when he was comfortably placed under the power and prestige of Hayyān]." How hard did they [Abū Bakr and 'Umar] squeeze its udders and how they made it [the caliphate] travel on a rugged path, which inflicts deep wounds and is rough to the touch, in which one stumbles frequently and has to offer excuses, so that its rider is like the rider of a difficult mount: if he draws its reins tight, its nose is pierced, and if he relaxes it, he plunges into destruction. And so the people were afflicted, by God, with stumbling, refractoriness, capriciousness, and cross-purposes. But I kept patience in spite of the length of time and the severity of the ordeal, until he ['Umar] went his way."

"In the end, the third of them [Uthmān] stood up shrugging his shoulders arrogantly. And there stood with him the sons of his father, eating up the property of God as the camels eat up the springtide verdure, until what he had twisted became untwisted. His destruction was complete, and his greediness made him fall to the ground. Then all of a sudden I was frightened to see a crowd of people around me, thick as the hyena's mane, thronging towards me from every direction until [my sons] al-Hasan and al-Husain were mobbed, and my two sides were split, gathering around me like a herd of goats. But when I took up the [reins of] government, one group broke its pledge, another rebelled, and some others transgressed, as if they had not heard the words of God, who says: [28:83] *As for that [happy] life in the hereafter, We grant it [only] to those who do not seek to exalt themselves on earth or to spread corruption in it: for the future belongs to those who are [ever] wary [lest their actions provoke] God's [wrath].* Nay, by God, they have heard these words and comprehend them, but the world is sweet in their eyes, and they are pleased by its gaudiness. Nay, by Him who has split the seed and created the soul, were it not for the presence of those who are [yet] present and the establishment of the arguments [against my withdrawing from the burden of governance] by the existence of the helpers, as also [for] the fact that it is not pleasing to God for those who know better [to stand] idly by and to watch the fullness [of the oppression] of the oppressor and the hunger of the oppressed, I would have thrown back its [the caliphate's] rope on its shoulder and made its last [incumbent] drink from the cup of the first one, and you would have found that your world is as distasteful to me as the dripping from the nose of a goat."

Bibliography

Translator's note: The purpose of this bibliography is not to enable those who are interested in following up on a given subject to be able to refer to the exact book that was used by the author (including the book's edition, publication date, publisher, etc.). For that information, researchers are referred to the original work in Persian. The purpose of this concise bibliography is to provide the reader with an at-a-glance look at most of the sources used by the great Allāma Askari in his research for this valuable opus. As can be seen, most of the work is drawn from Sunni sources, which is an innovation in Shī'a scholarship and historiography of which Allāma Askari was the outstanding pioneer within Shī'a circles.

Abū al-Fidā, Ismā'īl ibn Ali, *Tarikh al-Mukhtasar fi Akhbar al-Bashar*,
Abū-Nasr ibn Mutahhar ibn Tāhir, *al-Baladu wa'l-Tārīkh*,
Ahmad b. Hanbal, *Musnad* (241 AH);
Amīn, Ahmad, *Ḍuhay al-Islām*
Aminī, Allāma, *al-Ghadīr*,
Askari, Allāma Murtaḍā, *Abdullāh ibn Sabā*,
Askari, Allāma Murtaḍā, *Aqā'id al-Islam min Qur'ān al-Karīm*,
Askari, Allāma Murtaḍā, *Ahādith Umm al-Mu'minīn 'Āisha'*,
Askari, Allāma Murtaḍā, *al-Qurān al-Karīm wa Riwāyāt al-Madrisatayn*,
Askari, Allāma Murtaḍā, *Hadīth al-Kisā fī Kutub Madrisat al-Khulafā' wa Madrisat Ahl al-Bayt*,
Askari, Allāma Murtaḍā, *Mu'ālim al-Madrisatayn*
Askari, Allāma Murtaḍā, *Naqsh-e A'imma dar ihyā'-e dīn*,
'Ayni, Badr'ad-dīn, *'Umdat al-Qārī*,
Balādhūrī, Ahmad ibn Yahyā ibn Jābir, *Ansāb al-Ashrāf* (279 AH);
Balādhūrī, Ahmad ibn Yahyā ibn Jābir, *Futūh al-Baldān*,
Bayhaqī, Ahmad ibn Husayn, *Sunan al-Kubrā*,
Bukhārī, Muḥammad ibn Ismā'īl, *Ṣaḥīḥ al-Bukhārī*, (256 AH);
Dāramī, Abu Muhammad, *Musnad al-Dāramī* (255 AH);
Dayār-Bakrī, Ḥusayn Ibn Md., *Tārīkh al-Khamīs fī Ahwāl Anfus an-Nafīs* (966 AH);
Dhahabī, Shams al-Dīn Muhammad ibn Ahmad, *Ma'rifa al-Qurrā' al-Kubar*,
Dhahabī, Shams ad-Dīn Muḥammad ibn Aḥmad, *Siyār A'lām al-nubalā'*
Dhahabī, Shams al-Dīn Muhammad ibn Ahmad, *Tārīkh al-Islam* (748 AH);
Dīnwarī, Abū Ḥanīfah Aḥmad ibn Dāwūd, *Kitāb al-Akhbār al-Tiwāl* (282 AH);
Diyār-Bakri, Husain ibn Muhammad, *Tārīkh al-Khamīs fi Ahwāl an-Nafs an-Nafīs*,
Fīrūzābādī, Abū al-Tāhir Majīd al-Dīn Muhammad ibn Ya'qūb, *al-Qāmūs al-Mūhīt*
Hākim al-Haskānī an-Neyshāpūrī, *al-Mustadrak 'Alā's-Sahīhayn*,
Halabī, Alī ibn Ibrāhīm, *Insān al-'Uyūn fī Sīra al-Amīn al-Ma'mūn* (*as-Sīra[t] al-Halabīa*),
Haythamī, Ahmad Ibn-Hajar, *Majma' az-Zawāid wa Manba' al-Fawā'id*,
Haythamī, Ahmad Ibn-Hajar, al-*Sawā'iq al-Muhriqa*,
Ibn Abd'al-Birr, Yusuf ibn Abdallah, *al-Istī'āb fi Ma'rifat al-Ashāb* (463 AH);
Ibn 'Abd Rabbih, *al-'Iqd al-Farīd*,
Ibn Abī'l-Hadīd, Abdul-Hamīd, *Sharh Nahj al-Balāgha*,
Ibn Abī'l-Hadīd, quoting Jawharī's *Saqīfa* in his *Sharh Nahj al-Balāgha*,

Ibn 'Asākir, 'Alī, *Tahdhīb*,
Ibn Asākir, 'Alī, *at-Tārīkh al-Madīna*[t] *ad-Damishq*,
Ibn A'tham, *al-Tārīkh*,
Ibn Athīr Jazarī, 'Alī, *al-Kāmil fī al-Tārīkh* (630 AH);
Ibn Athīr al-Jazrī, Mubārak ibn Muhammad, *al-Nahāya fī Gharīb al-Hadīth wa'l-Āthār*,
Ibn Athīr, 'Alī ibn Muḥammad, *Usd al-Ghābah fī Ma'rifat al-Ṣaḥābah* (630 AH);
Ibn Hajar, Ahmad ibn Ali al-Asqalāni, *al-Iṣābah fī Tamyīz al-Ṣaḥābah*,
Ibn Hajar, Ahmad ibn Ali al-Asqalāni, *Fath al-Bārī fī Sharh Sahīh al-Bukhārī*,
Ibn Hajar, Ahmad ibn Ali al-Asqalāni, *Taqrīb al-Tahdhīb*,
Ibn Hishām, 'Abd al-Malik, *al-Sīrah al-Nabawīyah*, (213 AH);
Ibn Jawzī, Abd al-Rahmān b. Ali, *Siffa*[t] *as-Safwa* (597 AH);
Ibn Kathīr, Abu'al-Fiḍā Ismā'īl ibn Umar, *al-Bidāyah wa-al-Nihāyah*,
Ibn Kathīr, Abu'al-Fiḍā Ismā'īl ibn Umar, *Tārīkh* (774 AH);
Ibn Khallakān, Aḥmad, *Wafyāt al-'Ayān*,
Ibn Māja, Muhammad ibn Yazīd, *Sunan* (273 AH);
Ibn Manżūr al-Ansārī, Muhammad ibn Mukarram, *Lisān al-'Arab*
Ibn Qutayba, Abd-Allāh ibn Muslim, *al-Imāma wa'l-Siyāsa* (270 or 276 AH);
Ibn Qutayba, Abd-Allāh ibn Muslim, *al-Ma'ārif*,
Ibn Sa'd, Abu Abdallah Muhammad, *al-Tabaqāt al-Kubrā*,
Ibn Sayyid an-Nās, Muhammad ibn Muhammad, *'Uyūn al-Athar*
Ibn Shahna, Md ibn Md, *al-Kāmil*,
Ibn Shahrāshūb, Muhammad ibn Ali, *Manāqib Āl Abi-Tālib*,
Ibn Shubba al-Numayrī, Umar, *Tārīkh al-Madīnat al-Munawwara*,
Irbilī, *Kashf al-Ghamma*,
Abū Naīm Isfahānī, *Hilyat al-Awliā*,
Isfahānī, Abī'l-Faraj, *al-Aghānī* (356 AH);
Koleynī, Shaykh Muhammad b. Ya'qūb, *'Usūl al-Kāfī*,
Khatīb al-Baghdādī, Ahmad ibn Ali, *Tarīkh al-Baghdād*,
Majlisī, Allāma Muhammad Bāqir, *Bihār al-Anwār*
Mālik ibn Anas, *al-Muwatta*,
Mas'ūdī, Alī ibn al-Ḥusayn, *al-Tanbīh wa'l-Ishrāf* (346 AH);
Mas'ūdī, Alī ibn al-Ḥusayn, *Murawwij adh-Dhahab* (413 AH);
Mufīd, Shaykh Muhammad ibn Nu'mān, *al-Irshād fī Ma'rifat Hujaj Allāh 'al'al-'Ibād*, (413 AH);
Mufīd, Shaykh Muhammad ibn Nu'mān, *Al-Amali* (413 AH);
Mufīd, Shaykh Muhammad ibn Nu'mān, *al-Jamal*,
Muslim ibn al-Ḥajjāj, *Ṣaḥīḥ Muslim* (261 AH);
Muttaqī al-Hindī, *Kanz al-U'mmāl* (975 AH).
Nasā'ī, Aḥmad ibn Shu'ayb, *al-Sunan*,
Nasr ibn Muzāhim, *Waq'at Siffīn*,
Neyshāpūrī, Nizām'ad-dīn Hasan, *Gharā'ib al-Qur'ān wa Raghā'ib al-Furqān* (*Tafsīr al- Neyshāpūrī*)
Qomī, 'Alī ibn Ibrāhīm *Tafsīr al-Qomī*,
Qurṭubī, Muḥammad ibn Aḥmad, *al-Jāmi' li-Aḥkām al-Qur'ān*
Saddūq, Shaykh Abu-Ja'far Muhammad ibn Ali ibn Bābawayh, *al-Khisāl*,
Saddūq, Shaykh Abu-Ja'far Muhammad ibn Ali ibn Bābawayh, *Ilal ash-Sharā'i*,
Saddūq, Shaykh Abu-Ja'far Muhammad ibn Ali ibn Bābawayh, *Man lā Yahdharahū al-Faqīh*,
Saddūq, Shaykh Abu-Ja'far Muhammad ibn Ali ibn Bābawayh, *Ma'ānī al-Akhbār*,

Shahrastānī, Muhammad ibn Abdul-Karīm, *Mafātīh al-Asrār wa Masābīh al-Abrār fī Tafsīr al-Qur'ān,*
Shawkānī, Muḥammad, *Fatḥ al-Qadīr*
Suyūṭī, Jalāl al-Dīn 'Abd al-Raḥmān, *al-Durr al-Manthūr fī al-Tafsīr bi-al-Ma'thūr*
Suyūṭī, Jalāl al-Dīn 'Abd al-Raḥmān, *al-Itqān fī 'Ulūm al-Qur'ān*
Suyūtī, Jalāladdīn, *Tarikh al-Khulafā* (911 AH);
Tirmidhī, Muḥammad ibn 'Īsá, *Sunan al-Tirmidhī,*
Ṭabarī, Muḥammad ibn Jarīr, *Jāmi' al-Bayān fī Tafsīr al-Qur'ān,*
Tabarī, Muhammad ibn Jarīr, *Tārīkh ar-Rusul wa'l-Mulūk,*
Tabarī, Muhibbiddīn, *ar-Riyāḍ an-Naḍra*
Tabresī, Abu-Ali Faḍl ibn Hasan, *al-Ihtijāj,*
Tabresī, Abu-Ali Faḍl ibn Hasan, *I'lām al-Warī bi I'lām al-Hudā,*
Tayālasī, Sulaymān ibn Dāwūd, *Musnad,*
Wāḥidī, 'Alī ibn Aḥmad, *Asbāb al-Nuzūl,*
Ya'qūbī, Aḥmad ibn Isḥāq, *Tārīkh al-Ya'qūbī,*
Zamakhshari, Ab'al-Qāsim Mahmūd ibn Umar, *al-Kashshāf*
Zubayr ibn Bakkār, *al-Muwaffaqiāt* (256 AH);
Wāqidī, *al-Mughāzī.*

www.ingramcontent.com/pod-product-compliance
Lightning Source LLC
Chambersburg PA
CBHW030300100526
44590CB00012B/459